AESTHETICS IN GRIEF AND MOURNING

Aesthetics in Grief and Mourning

Philosophical Reflections on Coping with Loss

Kathleen Marie Higgins

THE UNIVERSITY OF CHICAGO PRESS
CHICAGO AND LONDON

The University of Chicago Press, Chicago 60637
The University of Chicago Press, Ltd., London

Published 2024
Printed in the United States of America

33 32 31 30 29 28 27 26 25 24 1 2 3 4 5

ISBN-13: 978-0-226-83104-6 (cloth)
ISBN-13: 978-0-226-83105-3 (e-book)
DOI: https://doi.org/10.7208/chicago/9780226831053.001.0001

Library of Congress Cataloging-in-Publication Data

Names: Higgins, Kathleen Marie, author.
Title: Aesthetics in grief and mourning : philosophical reflections on coping with loss / Kathleen Marie Higgins.
Description: Chicago ; London : The University of Chicago Press, 2024. | Includes bibliographical references and index.
Identifiers: LCCN 2023025155 | ISBN 9780226831046 (cloth) | ISBN 9780226831053 (ebook)
Subjects: LCSH: Grief. | Aesthetics.
Classification: LCC BF575.G7 H54 2024 | DDC 155.9/37—dc23/eng/20230624
LC record available at https://lccn.loc.gov/2023025155

⊗ This paper meets the requirements of ANSI/NISO Z39.48-1992 (Permanence of Paper).

For Bob, with continuing love

Contents

1
Aesthetics in Contexts of Loss—A Few Preliminaries

> The aim of art, as I see it, must always be the ultimate liberation from and transcendence of sorrow.
>
> —GUSTAV MAHLER[1]

MOVED TO POETRY

India's ancient epic poem the *Rāmāyaṇa* includes an account of how it came to be written. The text tells the story of a day when the sage Vālmīki (to whom the poem is traditionally attributed) has gone bathing in a river. Appreciating the beauty of the scene, he catches sight of a pair of singing curlews, furthering his delight. But his deep pleasure is suddenly cut short—an arrow pierces the breast of the male bird and kills it, and its disconsolate mate begins to wail. Vālmīki is so moved by the bird's lament that he curses the hunter whose arrow had caused its grief.

But to Vālmīki's own astonishment, his words come out in verse. His reaction has been spontaneous, so how could this have happened? Noting the metrical pattern of the stanzas he has uttered, he decides to call this type of verse a *śloka*, for it arose in connection with sorrow (*śoka*). After he returns home, Vālmīki is still ruminating on his experience when he is visited by Brahma, the Lord of Creation. Brahma announces that he had directed Vālmīki's poetic utterance through his own divine intention. He then tells the sage to write the *Rāmāyaṇa*, the story of the hero Rama, and to write it in *ślokas*, which Vālmīki proceeds to do.

Vālmīki is often characterized as the father of Indian poetry, and the *Rāmāyaṇa* is a founding work within the Indian literary tradition. Strikingly, it self-referentially describes its starting point as the poet's response to another creature's grief. Brahma does not explain why he chose to give artistic form to Vālmīki's utterance in the *Rāmāyaṇa*, but the form selected is seemingly so apposite that the god calls for its use throughout the work. In this book, I will argue that the aptness of *ślokas* for expressing Vālmīki's empathic grief is a particular case of a more general phenomenon. I will contend that aesthetic means are well-suited for responding to grief and for reasons hinted at in Vālmīki's story. As for him, so for us, aesthetic practices can facilitate a shift from stunned reaction and impasse to reengagement with life.[2]

The idea that loss bears an intimate connection with aesthetics was suggested some time ago by Arthur Danto. In his book *The Abuse of Beauty*, he reflects:

> I feel we understand too little about the psychology of loss to understand why the creation of beauty is so fitting as a way of marking it—why we bring flowers to the graveside, or to the funeral, or why music of a certain sort defines the mood of mourners. It is as though beauty works as a catalyst, transforming raw grief into a tranquil sadness, helping the tears to flow and, at the same time, one might say, putting the loss into a certain philosophical perspective. Recourse to beauty seems to emerge spontaneously on occasions where sorrow is felt.[3]

Catherine Wilson similarly draws attention to literary works and other artistic and art-like practices that respond to the loss of loved ones. In her article "Grief and the Poet," she suggests that literary works are "monuments to attachment, carefully crafted and embellished, that dignify commonplace losses." Her primary aims in the article are to explain why readers and audiences enjoy distressing fictions and to justify the claim that their responses are genuine emotions, but she draws attention to the centrality of grief as a literary theme. It is, she tells us, a "poetic emotion par excellence."[4] This seems to be the perspective of many of the contributors to a "community crowdsourced epistolary poem" compiled by *Morning Edition*'s poet-in-residence Kwame Alexander from poems written as letters on postcards. Alexander reported that "most people wrote letters to children or people who passed on."[5]

Aesthetic activities are also a staple of grief counseling. Many grief therapists encourage artistic activities as starting points to help clients gain insight into their emotions and to provide vehicles for emotional expression. Psychotherapists Barbara E. Thompson and Robert A. Neimeyer contend that in the "process of exploration, articulation, validation, and transformation" involved in responding to a person's death, "the bereaved and those who walk with them naturally reach beyond the constraints of public language, and into the figurative, musical, performative, and visual vocabularies of the arts, even in the context of psychotherapy."[6] Philosophers may find the idea that such methods are "natural" problematic, but the commonplace that "no words" are adequate after someone has died suggests a widespread sense that communicative resources beyond ordinary language are needed.[7]

My aim is to consider the significance of aesthetic activities that can be beneficially undertaken in response to great loss. I share with Danto the belief that aesthetic means help us heal in these circumstances, and in this book, I will attempt to explain some of the reasons they are so useful. I will also follow Danto and Wilson in focusing on loss that involves death, taking the experience of bereavement as my paradigm case. Aesthetic practices are beneficial for dealing with other kinds of losses as well, but I will nevertheless restrict my focus here. A reason for doing so is that the extreme disorientation involved in bereavement and the salient role of aesthetics in socially prescribed mourning practices make the interface of aesthetics and grief especially visible in cases of this sort.

In addition to their role in funerary rituals, aesthetic practices serve a variety of other purposes in contexts of bereavement—stabilizing the grieving person's impressions, expressing strong emotions, facilitating reflection, providing resources for orienting oneself and guidance for moving forward, affording means for offering gestures of sympathy, reconstructing interpersonal connections, and renewing relationships with the dead. As I will suggest in the following chapter, the points of connection between aesthetics and grief are multifarious, so much so that the rarity with which they are discussed in tandem is rather remarkable.

Why is the relationship between aesthetics and grief largely overlooked? One possible explanation is that the term *aesthetic* bundles too much together for claims about the connection to be anything but vague. On this view, we might do better to restrict our consideration to some subcategory of the aesthetic and the role it plays in grief. One obvious candidate for limiting the scope of discussion would be to focus on beauty in relation to loss, as Danto does.

The strategy of confining our attention to beauty, however, would restrict the topic unduly. Focusing on beauty would likely skew discussion in the direction of judgments about aesthetic value apart from practical usefulness, for beauty has often been conceptually dissociated from utility in Western aesthetics. This would preempt attention to the functional roles that aesthetic phenomena can play in connection with grief, a topic I plan to emphasize (and indeed one that Danto brings up with his grief-related aesthetic examples). We might follow some recent authors in equating beauty with aesthetic value broadly, but that would make attention to beauty no more restrictive than attention to the aesthetic in general.[8] In any case, in the context of his comment, Danto is taking *beauty* to name one among many possible aesthetic values.

One reason for extending our consideration to other values is that the practices Danto mentions as illustrations of beauty in contexts of loss—the use of flowers and beautiful music in funerary contexts—are not typical in every culture. While funerary activities in societies around the globe are aesthetic in having quasi-theatrical aspects, a concern with beauty is not necessarily evident. In many societies, for example, musical lamentations that incorporate stylized sobbing are the norm, not the somber but soothing organ music that many Westerners associate with funerals. One might listen to the funerary sung-weeping tracks on *Bosavi: Rainforest Music from Papua New Guinea*, a three-disc Smithsonian Folkways compilation of Steven Feld's recordings of music from the Kaluli tribe in Papua New Guinea.[9] The recordings are moving in the extreme and shaped in accordance with culturally specific aesthetic values, but is this lamentation "beautiful"? Arguably not.

Feld has also recorded instances of Por Por music, a type of music developed by members of the Truckers' Union of the La section of Accra, Ghana, for performance in members' funeral processions. Por Por music employs squeeze-bulb honk horns of the sort formerly used on trucks, as well as percussion designed to resemble the sounds of air pumps inflating blown-out tires.[10] *Beautiful* does not seem the most pertinent term of aesthetic praise for this music. Nor, for that matter, does the music of the New Orleans jazz funeral seem to be aimed at provoking the "tranquil sadness" that Danto mentions.[11]

Granted, sometimes we use the term *beautiful* without precision when we are deeply moved, and in this secondary sense it might be applied to Kaluli sung-weeping or Por Por funerals. But even this sense may not encompass every culture's mourning rituals. Funeral rituals that are obligatory in some societies challenge the aesthetic sensibilities of others. Janet McCracken, for example, describes the Sag-deed funerary ritual of the ancient Zoroastrians, which involves "leaving a corpse to be eaten, digested, and scattered on the ground by dogs and birds."

> The faithful are instructed to purify *the places* through which the dead have been carried by "caus[ing] a yellow dog with four eyes [a dog with two spots above the eyes], or a white dog with yellow ears, to go three times through

> that way" (Fargard 8/III:16). This Sag-deed, or "look of the dog" upon a dead body, causes the evil spirits to fly away out of it—"to the regions of the North," i.e., *not* the ground. . . . For Zoroastrians, however, because they practiced exposure of the dead instead of burial or cremation, the dog had the additional purifying power of being able to devour corpses with impunity and *go on*.[12]

Sky burial, the exposure of the corpse to birds of prey, continues to be practiced in some cultures. Sky burial and the ancient Sag-deed both involve ritual, marked by presentation before witnesses, and I would consider them to fall within the range of the aesthetic on this basis. But it would be odd to call these rituals beautiful in any ordinary sense of the term.

Another reason to focus on the aesthetic broadly, as opposed to a more restrictive aesthetic category, is that recognizing the aesthetic character of the many practices commonly utilized in connection with grief and mourning helps us to recognize the significance of the aesthetic in human life. Cultural traditions for mourning the dead have prominent aesthetic dimensions, and personal engagement in aesthetic practices can help one address many challenges that come with grief. Aesthetic phenomena have important roles to play in helping us weather one of the most distressing types of events in human experience, the death of a loved one. This tells us something about the aesthetic: It does not merely make life more pleasant; it is a lifeline that we depend upon.

THE TERM *AESTHETIC*

Having explained why I plan to consider aesthetic phenomena in a broad sense, I should say more about how I understand the aesthetic. As a name for a specific area of philosophy, the significance of the term *aesthetics* has changed at various points since it was first coined by Alexander Gottlieb Baumgarten (1714–1762). As used in the eighteenth century, *aesthetics* referred to the science (that is, *Wissenschaft*, or systematic scholarly study) of what is known through the senses.[13] This is somewhat broader than the contemporary connotations of the term as many understand it. However, this usage is evident in social scientist Stephen K. Levine's discussion of art therapy when he observes that "sensing . . . can be considered to be an aesthetic activity, a mode of human existence that grasps the world as embodied form."[14] In what follows, I will occasionally consider as "aesthetic" a phenomenological orientation we have toward sensory objects within the physical world, and to that extent, I also will be concerned with something approximating the eighteenth-century understanding of *aesthetics*, though this will only be one of the senses of the term that I will make use of.[15] As I proceed, I will be considering phenomena related to the various connotations that have had currency at some point or another in the history of the field.

Baumgarten delineated aesthetics as a field for the study of "sensitive knowing," which he took to contrast with the "clear and distinct perception" that Descartes had championed as the criterion for truth. In this, he follows Leibniz, who had observed that not all knowledge involves clear and distinct perception. "Clear and confused perception" also yields knowledge. While conceptual knowledge can be clear and distinct, everything that is apprehended through the senses involves clear and confused perception, for one does not have complete and adequate ideas in relation to all the features of the perceived object, as clear and distinct perception requires. Baumgarten, building on this observation about sensory perception, contends that the kind of clarity involved in our knowledge of a particular object as a whole is "extensive clarity," in contrast with the "intensive clarity" of specific features that are abstractly grasped. This consideration points to another aspect of aesthetics that will figure in my discussion, concern with attending to the individual particularity of specific objects.

Aesthetics since Baumgarten has directed considerable attention to art (as Baumgarten himself did and as I will sometimes do). This association has had strong enough persistence that Berys Gaut, among others, takes *aesthetics* to be approximately equivalent to "philosophy of art."[16] However, as is increasingly acknowledged in the field, the range of aesthetics is much broader than this, including among its topics natural phenomena, non-artistic sensory objects, non-sensory objects, and a wide variety of everyday phenomena.

Are there any constraints on what makes a phenomenon "aesthetic"? James Shelley suggests that two claims that were central to the concept of the aesthetic in the eighteenth century have retained centrality in subsequent discussion within the field. He formulates these claims in terms of aesthetic judgment, meaning the aesthetic evaluation of some object. The claims are (1) the "immediacy thesis," which holds that aesthetic judgments are not reached through reasoning, but have "all the immediacy of straightforwardly sensory judgments"; and (2) the "distinterest thesis," which holds that serving one's interests is not the basis for an aesthetic judgment. Shelley plausibly analyzes many more recent theories of the aesthetic as building on these two theses, though interpreting them sometimes in ways that differ from how they were considered in the eighteenth century. For example, he notes that many contemporary aestheticians would consider aesthetic value immediate and non-inferential, but would not insist that our perception of this value is grounded in sensory properties.[17]

The theses that Shelley indicates can be understood quite minimally, with *perception* being understood to include the gamut of more or less immediate judgments of value within experience, and lack of self-interest being sufficiently established if one refrains from pursuing immediate gratification and maintains some degree of reflective distance.[18] The way that I will use the term *aesthetic* generally conforms with the criteria suggested by Shelley's theses if they are so minimally interpreted. I will not be focusing on aesthetic *judgment* per se, as Shelley's formulations do, since that term suggests explicit evaluation. Nonetheless, the various matters that will concern me are matters of aesthetic judgment in the traditional sense, according to which *judgment* refers to apprehension of aesthetic value that may or may not involve critical evaluation or comparison.

My broad use of the term *aesthetic* conforms to current trends in scholarship. I follow the field in taking the scope of aesthetics to include consideration of beauty, appreciation and/or evaluative judgment of both sensory and imagined objects, the cultivation of taste, non-instrumentally valued experiences, human preference patterns, contemplative perception, artworks, the experiential affordances of natural and built environments, and many "everyday" phenomena. I will not devote attention to cultivation of taste, evaluative judgments, or preference patterns in what follows, but over the course of my discussion, I will consider points of connection between the rest of these areas and possible ways of dealing with grief.

The scope of the term *aesthetics* as currently understood in the field may strike some readers as excessively permissive. I will not defend this scope here, and it should be clear that I am not especially interested in policing conceptual boundaries. I think most of my examples are well within the range of what would commonly be considered aesthetic both in the philosophical subfield and outside it. Nevertheless, I recognize that my characterization of certain phenomena I describe as "aesthetic" may strike certain readers as tendentious. To provide some rationale for what I include within the category, I propose that several marks are prima facie indicators of a phenomenon's aesthetic status.

The first such mark is that the phenomenon is presented to an audience, with the manner of presentation being subject to evaluative responses. Ritual, for example, is usually aesthetic on this criterion. It is typically performed before witnesses (who may also be participants) and thus it is theatrical to some extent. It is subject to judgments as to whether or not it is appropriate to the circumstances, and evaluative judgments take account of whether it is performed in an attentive and affectively fitting manner.

The following are additional marks that serve as prima facie grounds for categorizing a phenomenon as aesthetic:

- The phenomenon gives symbolic expression to emotional content by means of some material medium.[19]
- The phenomenon exhibits properties commonly regarded as aesthetic (such as beauty, sublimity, elegance, and the like).[20]
- The phenomenon involves some object that is clearly bounded so as to have an internal structure, and the elements within it are integrated to achieve a unified effect and stand in a coherent relationship with one another.[21]
- The phenomenon admits of variations in style, which often reflects authorship (which may be individual or collective).
- The phenomenon can be judged on the basis of taste and subjective impressions of tastefulness, matters on which there can be differences of opinion.
- The phenomenon is widely recognized as a work of art or handicraft or utilizes a medium that is widely regarded as artistic.

The presence of these marks gives us prima facie reason to consider an object to be aesthetic or to have aesthetic dimensions. Each of them, often in combination, figures in practices commonly undertaken in connection with grief and mourning.

Having given some positive characterizations of ways in which phenomena can be aesthetic, let me now indicate some associations with the term that I wish to dispel. Sometimes aesthetic concerns are distinguished from moral ones. While the terms *aesthetic* and *moral* do have distinct purviews, I am not convinced that a sharp distinction can be maintained, particularly in the context of interpersonal behavior. Etiquette involves behavior that I would take to be morally desirable, perhaps sometimes even obligatory; that does not prevent it from involving aesthetics. Many breaches of etiquette are aesthetically objectionable, if morally unacceptable as well. To shake hands with each person in a group except a particular individual, whom one pointedly excludes, conveys an insult in a manner that is quasi-theatrical, and it can be a gesture of extreme disrespect. Chewing with one's mouth open is aesthetically offensive, but it can also be a pointed gesture of disregard for those present and thus also morally offensive.

As I use the term, therefore, *aesthetic* is not to be understood in contrast with the moral.[22] Some moral obligations (often those concerned with showing respect for others) are best fulfilled through aesthetic means. Philosopher Robert Audi notes that certain moral obligations require that certain actions be performed in a certain manner. He terms these "adverbial duties" or "duties of manner," and he notes that performing a morally required action in an inappropriate manner can render the action morally wrong. "One reason we have duties of manner is that the *way* we do things is often morally important and broadly under voluntary control. We are properly judged morally, as in other ways, by *how* we do what we do, as well as by what acts we perform."[23] Such duties are matters of performance and properly considered aesthetic.

Doing one's moral duty is often accomplished by means of aesthetic gestures, and this is often true in connection with grief. "Paying one's respects" when a death has occurred, for example, is accomplished through socially scripted behavior that must be performed in an appropriate manner. In certain close relationships, some have claimed, paying one's respects in some fashion is morally mandated.[24] Those who are closely related to the deceased may feel so strongly motivated to do this that they do not think of it either as an obligation or as aesthetic. But to the extent that paying respects is a matter of making certain socially scripted, public gestures conveying love and sorrow, it has an aesthetic character.

My sense of *aesthetic* also does not exclude actions and objects serving practical functions, as I have already indicated. Although many Western thinkers (for example, Kant) have considered aesthetic appreciation as requiring the bracketing of any practical concern, the compatibility of aesthetic and practical value is taken for granted in many cultures and increasingly acknowledged by Western aestheticians.[25] Moreover, even if one takes the bracketing of practical aims to be intrinsic to aesthetic experience, engaging in practices that afford aesthetic experiences may have practical benefits. Taking a dance lesson or seeing a movie can relieve stress, even though immersion in either may preclude focusing on that fact. Aesthetic practices often serve practical ends. In circumstances of loss, they can be healing and help to connect the bereaved with the social world, a matter we will be exploring.

I should add that my construal of *aesthetic* does not imply exclusive or primary attention to the perceiving subject's position, although Western thought over the past several centuries has tended to have this emphasis.[26] The topic of aesthetic agency has become increasingly prominent within aesthetics in recent years, and I consider this a sanguine development.[27] I see one of the values of aesthetic practices in connection with loss to be its enabling bereaved individuals to experience themselves as agents, not merely passive victims of circumstances. This experience is available in connection with aesthetic contemplation, which involves active deployment of one's attention, but it is also available in many creative and expressive practices. The distinction between activity and passivity in aesthetic engagement is typically not sharp. For example, even as a member of the audience for certain artworks (many popular songs, for example), one can have a sense of vicarious emotional expression. My use of the term *aesthetic practices* is meant to refer to the full range of ways that we can engage with aesthetic phenomena, including those in which the active aspect may not be evident from a third-person perspective.[28]

THE RELATION OF GRIEF AND MOURNING

Another matter of usage that I should explain is how I understand the other two major terms in my title, *grief* and *mourning*. I use these terms conjunctively, for I see them as unavoidably interconnected. Indeed, the terms are not always differentiated by theorists who study bereavement. Matthew Ratcliffe points out that *Trauer*, in the title of Sigmund Freud's influential essay "Trauer und Melancholie" ("Mourning and Melancholia"), does not distinguish between the two.[29]

The English terms *grief* and *mourning* can be used almost interchangeably, and those who differentiate do not concur on the basis for doing so. According to Thomas Attig, both terms refer to "processes of accommodating to loss," with overlap between some aspects of grief and certain senses of *mourning*. *Mourning* can refer either to the involuntary effects of bereavement ("the grief reaction"), which include "the full range of our experiences of emotional, psychological, physical, behavioral, social, cognitive, and spiritual impacts of bereavement," or to the more active "grieving response," which involves engagement with bereavement and its impacts.[30] Attig also sees *mourning* as ambiguously referring to both "what we do within ourselves to transform our relationship to the one who has died" and "the ways our societies and cultures tell us to behave in response to loss through death."[31] *Grief* is also ambiguous, as I will consider further in chapter 3. The term is used in reference to short-term emotions but also to the extended process of responding to the death of a loved one.

One way to differentiate is to define *grief* as one's "internal" response to a loved one's death and *mourning* as one's "external" behavior, particularly behavior that is socially scripted within a culture. Michael Cholbi distinguishes the terms along these lines. He characterizes *grief* as "private at its core," defining it as "the specific and personal emotional reaction individuals have to other individuals' death." He defines *mourning*, by contrast, as "the public or behavioral face of grieving," which is "often ritualistic."[32]

Using the private/public distinction as a basis for differentiating is conceptually straightforward, but in practice these domains are not easily kept separate. Emotional reactions are rarely if ever purely private. They are often evident in external behavior, particularly when they are as overwhelming as they typically are in grief. How one grieves is also influenced by internalized societal norms, which bereaved persons use to assess whether their behavior and feelings are contextually appropriate. Other people react to a bereaved person's behavior or their failure to act as anticipated, and the bereaved may feel pressured to conform to expectations.[33] While one can restrict *mourning* to culturally scripted funerary practices, this stipulation would result in a very narrow definition, with limited application to practices in many contemporary industrialized societies, where clear expectations for rituals are minimal. It would probably also be more restrictive than common usage, which has no trouble with the application of *mourning* to "inner" phenomena, as in sentences such as "He was still mourning his wife."

While specifying the distinction between *grief* and *mourning* in terms of inner responses and external behavior works for certain purposes, my topic makes drawing a sharp line especially difficult. I will be arguing that aesthetic practices, many of which involve behavior and action in the external world, are well-suited to helping people deal with many psychological aspects of grief, suggesting that even relatively invisible psychological responses to loss are interconnected with external behavior. Moreover, many aesthetic undertakings within grief involve appeals to the social world for validation, and social uptake can mitigate the feelings of isolation that grieving people often experience.

Psychotherapist Juliet Rosenfeld takes yet another approach to distinguishing grief and mourning, characterizing them as different phases of responding to loss. Grief, as she understands it, is "an acutely painful obsessive enmeshment with the person who has died and yet is fiendishly alive in your mind."[34] It may persist for several years, but when it starts to lift, mourning begins. Mourning is a more hopeful and more temporally extended emotion than grief, characterized by greater agency and potential for expression. Rosenfeld's definitions in terms of temporal sequence and agency promise clarity in distinguishing grief and mourning. However, her distinction reverses the temporal relationship implied by defining *mourning* as a matter of socially defined ritual behaviors, many of which follow fairly directly on the death. The open-endedness of mourning by comparison with grief in her account also seems the reverse of what is assumed by most who distinguish the terms on the basis of the inner/outer distinction. While external, socially scripted behaviors (wearing mourning clothes, for example) can persist over an extended period of time, their temporal course is typically specified, sometimes very precisely. Grief, on most understandings, does not unfold on a clear schedule and may never decisively resolve.

Partly because the terms are used so variously, I use *grief* and *mourning* conjunctively. I will be considering phenomena that correspond to common construals of each of these terms. Most often, I will refer to *grief*, taking the term to cover the entire range of subjectively experienced impacts of bereavement and various responses to these impacts. I will thus use *grief* as an umbrella term for the entire process of reacting and responding to a loved one's death. On occasion I will use *mourning* in reference to culturally scripted behavior and to other formal and informal ritual practices (which may be individually devised). But I will sometimes use the terms interchangeably.

My usage should not obscure the fact that my use of *grief* sometimes overlaps others' use of *mourning*. In particular, I note philosopher Jonathan Lear's account of mourning as "a living on in the hearts and minds of others in the characteristic ways we humans miss others."[35] In my usage, the continued presence of the deceased person in survivors' hearts and minds is an aspect of their grief, an ongoing process that evolves over time, though I find *mourning* completely appropriate for what Lear is describing. His work is informed by psychoanalysis, and I take his use of the term to be akin to Freud's, in which the distinction between *grief* and *mourning* is not at stake.

So that the ambiguity of the terms *mourning* and *grief* does not interfere with clarity in what follows, I will attempt be clear about which aspects of grieving and mourning are in focus as I proceed. I should add, however, that I will not be so cautious when it comes to *bereavement* and *grief*. While strictly *bereavement* refers to the fact of having lost a loved one and *grief* refers to responses to that fact, I will not always maintain this verbal distinction. I will take "while grieving" and "in bereavement" to be more or less equivalent. I realize that in reality, bereaved people do not necessarily experience grief or even feel pain in response to a loved one's death, though commonly they do. I will be describing the psychological impacts of bereavement and grief in generalized terms, treating the typical case as though it were essential. To avoid unwieldy expressions and qualifications of my claims at every point, I will treat bereavement as though it implies the experience of grief. In the typical case, this is so, but we should recognize that this is an abstraction, not an accurate characterization of all cases.

THE PROBLEM OF CULTURAL DIFFERENCE

A methodological problem affecting my use of all the major terms in my title is that these notions are not obviously generalizable across time and across cultures. I certainly do not assume that there are standard conceptions of the aesthetic or grief or mourning that can be appropriately applied irrespective of context. Historical and cultural contexts are always important determinants of how human beings experience the world. Generalizations that apply in many cases may not hold across the board, and factors that shape the experience of the aesthetic and/or grief in one situation may differ from those that shape such experiences in others.

Nevertheless, I think it is justifiable to generalize to some extent in light of common aspects of the human condition, such as mortality, our social nature, and capacities that typify members of our species. Human beings everywhere have experiences of loss and have some common capabilities and tendencies that they may draw upon in contending with it. They also have a need for interpersonal connection that may be unmet when events have damaged the integrity of their social worlds. These are among my assumptions when I speak generally of aesthetic responses to loss, where the "aesthetic" includes many modes of symbolic communication differentially employed around the globe.

That said, I am obviously more familiar with practices extant in my own cultural context than in any other, though many of them resemble those employed by members of other industrialized societies or of certain social classes within them.[36] The cases I take as paradigmatic emerge from this context, though I try to remain alert to ways in which they are not representative of "human" experience. In particular, my discussion presupposes the present juncture within my own historical context, in which psychological theory no longer takes mental health to require that one sever attachments to the dead. The aesthetic ways of sustaining relationships with deceased loved ones that I encourage may be out of keeping with taboos in other societies and thus may be inappropriate for them.

Recognizing the challenge posed by cultural difference, philosopher and psychiatrist Thomas Fuchs acknowledges that his phenomenological approach, which attempts to describe "typical basic structures" of grief, is a product of the European intellectual tradition and may reflect European typologies that are not necessarily apt for characterizing grief in other cultures. He notes the importance of not construing his account as normative, yet he concludes, "Notwithstanding these reservations, a phenomenological investigation still assumes that there is a core structure to the experience of grief which despite all variations may be addressed and carved out to a certain extent."[37]

I consider myself to occupy a position quite similar to that of Fuchs. That my perspective is limited and derives from a specific cultural and historical position is inevitable, and this calls for intellectual humility. Still, the deaths of loved ones and the use of practices that can be considered "aesthetic" (in terms of the features I have described) are ubiquitous. Associations between bereavement and aesthetic practices are evident in diverse cultures, and scholarly investigation into why strikes me as appropriate. I will attempt to gesture toward patterns that link bereavement and aesthetic practices, while acknowledging that the way that these patterns play out will depend on the specific individuals involved and on many situating factors.

AESTHETICS IN GRIEF AND EVERYDAY AESTHETICS

I will be discussing the use and creation of artworks, but also examining the aesthetic character of many practices that are neither art in any conventional sense nor objects traditionally considered "aesthetic." My interest in such practices is in keeping with the growing scholarly trend toward consideration of aesthetics in ordinary life. I take my project here to be a contribution to everyday aesthetics. Even when I mention artworks, I will often be concerned with their value for helping us deal with our ordinary lives.

The scope of what counts as everyday aesthetics is debated. Some complain that the category excludes almost nothing aside, perhaps, from artworks and natural objects traditionally seen as suited to disinterested contemplation. Many have placed emphasis on "ordinary" life and its routines in their accounts of everyday aesthetics, while some would include the occasional experience of relatively rare events, among which Yuriko Saito lists "parties, sporting events, holidays, weddings, and travelling."[38] Some debate has focused on whether everyday aesthetic experience typically requires recognition of an ordinary object's extraordinary features or the defamiliarization of something familiar.[39] However these issues are resolved, everyday aesthetic phenomena are usually envisioned against a backdrop of circumstances that are stable enough for the familiar and habitual to play a central role. Even when aesthetic analysis focuses on such relatively rare events as parties, the presumption is that instances of the phenomenon in question exhibit a sufficiently standard structure to allow for the identification of a type with a character worth delineating.[40]

Saito submits, however, that everyday aesthetics should "explore whether and how rapid changes to the familiar everyday affects the nature of everyday aesthetics as a discourse."[41] I take it that she means that the very nature of the "everyday" is unstable, and acknowledgment of this recognition might lead to a revision of how the purview of everyday aesthetics is understood. Saito is surely right that disruptions of familiar patterns are increasingly part of everyday experience. These disruptions can have distinctive aesthetic effects, causing us to experience the environment as uncanny or foreboding, for example. They can also motivate pursuit of aesthetic antidotes, as when someone seeks out a "feel-good" film in response to the sense that personal life is not on an even keel.

Following Saito's lead, I propose that the *unfamiliar* everyday should be recognized as part of the remit of everyday aesthetics. The acceleration of changes in the cultural landscape is causing an exponential expansion of the number of everyday experiences in which unfamiliarity is a significant aspect. In this book I will not attempt to analyze the aesthetic features of encounters with the unfamiliar every day in general terms. But I will focus on aesthetics in relation to a particular kind of everyday encounter with unfamiliarity, that experienced in grief.

Grief may seem so radically personal that one would need an oxymoronically private language to express it, yet it has some common features that allow us to say something about what it is like. Grief is an everyday phenomenon in that large numbers of people are always in its thrall. It is also an everyday experience of becoming defamiliarized with the world. Although we may usually recognize theoretically that our framework of expectations is fragile, in grief this fragility becomes an experienced fact, for the frameworks have been disrupted. Grief undercuts our ability to feel synchronized with our social world, revealing how remarkable it is that we have done this with ease in other circumstances. Grief makes us aware of aspects of our environment that we earlier ignored or experienced differently. We also grapple with the sense of being disoriented and "on our own" in a radical way. All this amounts to an encounter with radical unfamiliarity in everyday life.

Where is the aesthetic in all this? All over the place. Grief makes our sensory experience conspicuous, often rendering it sufficiently strange to prompt some degree of reflection. Our words, which rely on a stable framework of reference, are poorly designed for indicating the ways in which the framework itself has come apart, so we may be drawn to figurative and other symbolic modes of communication that may take artistic form. Or we may find ourselves using broad gestures to signal our meanings to other people and realize that they are doing the same. The etiquette of paying respects and conveying sympathy is shot through with aesthetic gestures, as noted previously. We engage in actions that are designed to be witnessed, and we undertake them with concern that they are properly performed.

Human beings have often gravitated toward aesthetic modes to express emotions and reflections in relation to the death of a loved one, and I aim to show some of the reasons why this is apt. While I will mention in passing some of the techniques that grief counselors employ to help their clients, these will not be my primary focus. Instead, I will consider the potential benefits that incorporation of aesthetic activity into everyday life might offer the bereaved. While some of these activities (such as participation in funerals) are culturally scripted, many are more "everyday" and improvisatory, such as attending to sensory objects, telling stories, reflecting on previous experiences with artworks, experiencing music, and engaging in creative projects. Such practices can help grieving people to cope with their experiences and to "relearn the world," in Attig's resonant phrase.[42] Examining some of these possibilities, I will suggest, can help us recognize the value of aesthetic engagement for living a good life and treating ourselves and each other with respect and appreciation.

WHY CONSIDER AESTHETICS IN RELATION TO GRIEF

Given my interpretation of *aesthetic*, one might wonder about the point of my project. If so many activities and objects count as aesthetic, it may seem trivial to note that aesthetic phenomena are pervasively involved in contexts of grief and mourning.[43] However, I think the point is important. The aesthetic character of various activities has too often been shortchanged because attention to other aspects have obscured it, and this means that noting their aesthetic aspects is at least informative.

The trivialization of aesthetic matters is common in both scholarly and popular imagination. Aesthetic considerations are commonly considered to be unimportant, even frivolous, by comparison with other, more serious concerns. This is a reason, I suspect, that aesthetics does not seem obviously relevant to the circumstances of bereaved people. Death is serious, if anything is, so one might perceive a tonal mismatch between confronting the reality of death and attending to aesthetic matters.

Some may also consider attention to aesthetics in the wake of a death a problematic, potentially unhealthy way of evading confrontation with death's reality. They may accept that gestures of condolence such as sending flowers and cosmetic efforts to dignify the appearance of the corpse are designed to alleviate the discomfort of the bereaved. Yet they may harbor the suspicion that such practices are aimed at hiding the ugliness of death, a veneer that may delay the mourner's coming to grips with the reality of the situation. This might lead them to conclude that aesthetic activity in this context is both superficial and potentially harmful.[44]

The fear that aesthetic activities will interfere with bereaved individuals' assimilation of the death may be compounded by reservations about the common tendency to imagine the deceased person as a witness to one's ritual and commemorative actions. Many post-loss activities that involve a performance dimension encourage envisioning the deceased as a witness.

Those who are squeamish about ideas of posthumous survival and communication with the dead may be uneasy about the performative aspect of many post-loss activities. Again, they may worry that such activities can harm the bereaved by helping them to resist acknowledging the death.

The presentational character of certain loss-related activities may trigger another trivializing reaction toward the aesthetic, the sense that the primary aim is display. Doing things "for show" seems to be the wrong sort of motive in funerary contexts, as Donald Keefer suggests in reference to eulogies. However important aesthetic qualities are for a eulogy to serve its function, "focusing on those, as such, would distract our attention from the dead and our loss. . . . The excellence of its form should no more be our focus during a eulogy than the reassuring midwestern tones of Tom Brokaw should be as he reports on some tragic event."[45] Viewing a funeral as an opportunity to show off one's talent as a speaker or to parade one's sartorial elegance would be unseemly, deflecting attention away from the deceased toward oneself.

One may find further reason for caution about attending to aesthetics in connection with someone's death if one accepts the idea that aesthetic and moral considerations can be sharply distinguished. Those who endorse this idea are likely to consider aesthetic considerations secondary to moral ones, since part of the idea of a moral requirement is that it is not defeasible, but aesthetic preferences are unproblematically open to revision. In the wake of a person's death, there is also a tendency to moralize. Certain ways of behaving (including the performance of many culturally specified rituals) are considered morally required in such circumstances, while some behaviors are deemed moral offenses or indications of character flaws.[46] The grieving themselves also tend to judge their own informal behaviors in moral terms. Judith M. Simpson points out that this tendency applies even to decisions regarding the disposal of clothing that belonged to the deceased:

> Clothing is disposed of according to a strict moral code, perhaps because the bereaved do not feel that the rights of ownership have fully passed to them. . . . Generally speaking, it is deemed wrong to sell it for profit even when an expensive or "designer" item is concerned. In the mourner's view, commodity value is eclipsed by the item's role as a relic of the dead. . . .[47]

The ideas that aesthetic matters are superficial, escapist, "for show," and unimportant by comparison to moral concerns feed into a widespread tendency to trivialize aesthetics. This tendency has obscured the many roles aesthetic objects and activities can and do play in relation to loss. One reason to investigate the connection between aesthetics and grief is to counteract this trivialization of aesthetics by showing how valuable aesthetic activity can be in the context of confronting a life crisis.

I see two other reasons for considering the many ways that aesthetics is or can be involved in experiences of grief and mourning. First, aesthetic practices serve therapeutic ends. They help people who have experienced loss cope with their situations and realign with the larger world. I think it is worthwhile to draw attention to this role for aesthetic practices, particularly in light of the tendency of traditional Western aesthetics to deny or ignore the practical value of aesthetic phenomena. Second, aesthetic practices have ethical functions, helping us to live good lives. They can help us handle such extreme emotional and existential crises as the loss of a loved one, and this sheds light on the centrality and importance of the aesthetic for both individual and community flourishing. In what follows, I will primarily direct attention to the therapeutic value of aesthetic practices for those who are grieving, suggesting toward the end of the book how the many beneficial roles aesthetic phenomena can play in bereavement help illuminate the role of aesthetics in our emotional and interpersonal lives more generally.[48]

WHAT LIES AHEAD

The range of ways that grief and aesthetics can interact is exceedingly large. Indeed, once I started to look for connections, the territory began to seem vast. But some may doubt this. To give some sense of the pervasiveness of aesthetic practices that can be valuably utilized in bereavement, I will proceed to itemize some of them in chapter 2.

I will go on to discuss the beneficial functions that aesthetic phenomena might serve in relation to grief. In order to do so, I will need to say a bit about grief and what the experience of bereavement is like. This will be the burden of chapter 3. I will describe some of the disorienting and distressing features of grief (particularly in the early stage of bereavement), the needs these give rise to, and aspects of the process that ensues. I will address the question of whether the relinquishment of attachment to the deceased person should be seen as a goal in grief. My answer to this question will be a resounding "No."

The chapters that follow consider roles that aesthetic practices of different sorts can play in addressing the needs of the grieving and helping them set their lives on a new course. Chapter 4 will discuss ways that certain aesthetic practices can offer reassurance and facilitate reorientation after the shock of the death of a loved one. I will argue that early on, when a bereaved person feels only shakily connected to the surrounding world, the mere tangibility of sensory objects can be experienced as grounding. Aesthetically appreciating their features can cast the world in a more positive light than is otherwise likely. Material objects associated with the deceased can also offer the reassurance that this world still offers points of connection with the person, mitigating the sense that the person is entirely gone.

This early phase of bereavement commonly results in alterations in perception that diverge from what one understands as normal. These can be disorienting, and they may prompt doubts about one's ability to manage. I will suggest that one may find resources for dealing with disorientation and self-doubt through drawing on one's aesthetic background, that is, one's history of engaging in practices of aesthetic contemplation of artworks and other phenomena. Many artworks require one to envision and orient oneself within scenarios unlike those one has previously encountered. Artworks that unfold temporally, moreover, often require their audience to track developments, attending to contrasting tendencies, and being patient with emergent tensions while longing for their resolution. A background of aesthetic experiences in which one has successfully oriented oneself in imagined situations and imaginatively navigated tension-filled trajectories can help one to recognize that one has developed skills that may be useful in the current situation.

In chapter 4, I will also consider the role that some artworks can play in suggesting ways to think about features of one's current circumstances. Even early after the loss, a grieving person might find some artworks serviceable as maps or templates that can guide them through the strange terrain of grief, though this guidance may continue far beyond the early days of bereavement.

For reasons we will later consider, grieving people often feel isolated, especially soon after the loss. Chapter 5 will discuss some of the roles aesthetic practices can play in helping a bereaved person to overcome this sense of isolation. I will suggest that music is especially beneficial for enabling grieving individuals to feel connected with and supported by other people. It enables the bereaved to express their emotions in a way that is intelligible to others, and it makes social connections evident, particularly in rituals in which people are brought together. In such contexts, it can also help create a shared space for private reflection, allowing the bereaved to feel the supportive presence of others even while engaging in inwardly directed thought. And although grieving people commonly feel out of step with the flow of time that others experience, music provides a short-term reconnection with an intersubjective temporal flow, alleviating the feeling of alienation from the social world.

Chapter 5 will also draw attention to the many practices in which small gestures made by many people create a powerful cumulative aesthetic impact. Such participatory actions in response to a death allow the bereaved to witness other people joining their efforts to honor the deceased and to recognize that the felt need to respond to the loss is to some extent socially shared. Certain practices associated with funerary rituals make use of the aesthetic strategy of amassing small gestures. Cumulative aesthetic effects can also serve to honor the deceased and convey the support of the social world far beyond the immediate aftermath of the loss.

Storytelling is another aesthetic activity that testifies to the fact that others share the sense of loss with the grieving person and seek to process it interpersonally. Spontaneous storytelling among those who gather for rituals helps the bereaved to recognize that others also feel the loss and care about the deceased. The stories that are shared confirm that the very person the bereaved is mourning was known and valued by others. They also revive impressions of that individual's lively presence by causing listeners to envision the person acting within the world, sometimes in ways that were previously unknown to the hearer. While sharing stories is especially common soon after the loss, this practice can continue to enrich the bereaved person's sense of the deceased far into the future.

Chapter 6 builds on the earlier suggestion that certain artworks can model aspects of the experience of grief by emphasizing their usefulness in efforts to communicate. Those who have not had similar experiences may not easily comprehend bereaved people's efforts to describe how they are thinking and feeling. Artworks, with their capacity to expand the horizons of their audience, can be useful for bridging such communication gaps. When particular artworks are commonly known, grieving people can use them as resources for forming comparisons with their present experience. They can also assist empathetic listeners by giving them some impression of what is being described. Some artists have also used artistic devices (such as negative space) and images (such as the figure of the ghost) to convey aspects of the experience of grief. Referring to such devices and images can expand bereaved individuals' resources for making themselves understood.

Chapter 7 further considers the roles that aesthetic means can play in facilitating interpersonal connection, focusing on those between the bereaved and the deceased. Aesthetic practices can help bereaved people to maintain and transform relationships to deceased loved ones by providing channels for directing communications toward the dead, constructing representations that stand in for them, honoring them through memorial projects, and enabling them to perform their reciprocal relational roles. Such activities, which may continue far beyond the loved one's death, can also help to assuage the guilt that survivors often feel in relation to the departed, removing that obstacle to renewing the relationship.

The value of aesthetic activities for sustaining relationships with the deceased helps illuminate the importance of the aesthetic in human life more generally. For the bereaved, aesthetic practices of the sort described in chapter 7 help to integrate continued attachment to the deceased with ongoing participation in the world of the living. This helps the grieving person to overcome the feeling of being incapable of going forward after the death of a loved one. Aesthetic practices also benefit human communities in general. Aesthetic practices building on traditions that developed in the past help communities to feel connection with those who have died while also gesturing toward those who occupy the different parts of the timeline, past, present, and future. Aesthetic practices sustain our awareness of our intergenerational relationships and our role in carrying forward the contributions the dead have made to our personal and societal worlds.

Aesthetic practices are not the only cultural phenomena that cause us to recognize the continuity of relationships across generations. As Lear points out, religion and the humanities in general do this, too.[49] Aesthetic practices, religion, and the humanities all involve investing what happens with meaning, and, significantly for my topic here, they all involve mourning in Lear's broad sense of the phenomenon. They are all a part of the intergenerational enterprise of keeping alive ideas and achievements that contribute to human flourishing despite the deaths of their originators. This is a distinctive way that we miss the dead, and a way that we transfigure loss into something meaningful.

I agree with Lear about the transformative power of mourning and about the essential connection between the entire human cultural enterprise and our confrontation with and transfiguration of loss. Aesthetic phenomena are among the most powerful and pervasive means we have for contending with grief and renewing engagement with life. Their ubiquity, however, may be obscured by the extent of their formal variety. The gamut of loss-related phenomena with notable aesthetic character is immense. I will devote the following chapter to a brief survey of the range, attempting to order it into certain broad subcategories.

2
Aesthetic Proliferation

AESTHETIC GESTURES IN BEREAVEMENT

If you have ever lost a loved one, aesthetics was probably not uppermost in your mind. If you gave a candid description of how the situation felt, your account would probably be, in Arthur Frank's terminology, a "chaos narrative," an incoherent and fragmented story in which sequences of events seem entirely random.[1] The disorientation and demands imposed by the circumstances are typically so relentless that little energy is left for explicit aesthetic reflection.

Yet even at such junctures, aesthetic choices and activities abound. "As far back as people have thought about the subject," historian Thomas Laqueur tells us, "care of the dead is regarded as foundational—of religion, of community, of civilization itself."[2] This care of the dead involves many practices that are straightforwardly aesthetic in nature. Ritual prescriptions for treatment of remains and funerary protocols set norms, violation of which offends taste and custom. These ritual requirements and efforts to assimilate loss ubiquitously exhibit aesthetic features, calling attention to the way remains are dealt with, the details of ritual performance, and the demeanor to be maintained. Societies vary greatly in prescribing specific behavior from those touched by a death, but such practices as preparing the corpse, engaging in funeral processions, participating in funerary events, wearing appropriate attire, signaling others through stylized expressions of mourning, and so forth involve aesthetic concern with manner of performance or presentation.

Aesthetic objects and activities connected with grief and mourning are so diverse that some may think the category hopelessly unwieldy and urge us to refrain from lumping them all together. Certainly, I think we should attend to specific subcategories, and I will frequently do so in this book.

However, attending to the range of aesthetic phenomena related to bereavement can bring important matters into focus. It can help us to recognize the fundamentally aesthetic character of many of our ways of showing respect and communicating emotion. It can also reveal the functionality of aesthetics in dealing with some of the major crises in life.

This chapter provides a tour, in effect, of aesthetic practices that commonly figure in the contexts of bereavement and mourning. The variety of types considered provides a preliminary indication of the complexity of the aesthetic terrain associated with loss. Our survey will also reveal some of the issues of taste that can arise in connection with the phenomena considered. Lest what follows become completely unfocused, I will organize it into several categories: (1) mourning-related rituals, (2) disposal of remains, (3) communication and etiquette connected with mourning, (4) memorials and memorabilia, and (5) artworks honoring the dead and exploring loss.

MOURNING-RELATED RITUALS

Laqueur's expression "care of the dead" sums up a variety of ritual activities through which the living fulfill perceived obligations to attend to the dead. Initially, even before funerary rites occur, the death of another human being mandates certain ways of treating the cadaver. Most societies require handling it in prescribed ways, often assigning closest kin the role of cleaning it and preparing it for cremation or burial. Even at this early stage of reckoning with a loss, survivors behave in accordance with social specifications that amount to performing aesthetic gestures. Many of these are quasi-theatrical in being performed before witnesses, and often the deceased is envisioned as a witness to these practices.[3]

Besides the aesthetic features of socially prescribed behaviors, personal aesthetic responses may also characterize this stage of mourning. Sociologist Jacque Lynn Foltyn describes the body of her beloved ex-husband shortly after his death, "With his gray-blue skin, hollow cheeks, and emaciated body, Matt's cadaver reminded me of an El Greco Christ, beautiful and horrible at the same time." She also comments that she "had been unprepared for the sight and feel of Matt's corpse body" and "was moved by its vulnerability."[4]

Adornment of the cadaver is not a universal practice, but it is relatively common.[5] Whole suits made of jade, designed to protect the corpses of prominent individuals, have been discovered in ancient Chinese graves. Stephen Davies draws attention to the antiquity of such practices, noting the extensive adornment of the cadaver of a man buried in a 28,000-year-old grave in Sungir, north of Moscow: "About 3,000, mostly cylindrical, mammoth-ivory beads decorated the man's clothing and Arctic fox canine teeth adorned his headdress." The cadaver was also wearing twenty-five painted mammoth-ivory bracelets and a colored pendant.[6] In current times in many traditions, cadavers are dressed in shrouds or in clothing worn during life, with great care taken as to how this is done. The HBO film *Taking Chance* emphasizes the attention paid to aesthetic detail in connection with American military funerals. In the film, Kevin Bacon plays a military officer who volunteers to accompany the body of a deceased marine home from the field of action.[7] The officer comments approvingly about everything having been done to make the military uniform in which the deceased would be buried perfect, with every button polished, even though no one would see it at the man's closed-casket funeral.

Ubiquitously, societies prescribe funerary rituals, and the sense of obligation to perform them in the wake of a loved one's death is extremely strong. Even the ancient Chinese philosopher Mozi (470–391 BCE), noteworthy for his objections to elaborate funerals, considers simple funerals to be a necessity.[8] Too perfunctory a funeral or the absence of one implies that no one considers the deceased to be someone who matters.[9] Laqueur describes Victorian funerals as marking the status of the deceased, with degrading pauper funerals indicating a societal mindset in which the poor were seen as superfluous. The horror of such funerals, he argues, was so great that very poor people organized and contributed funds to burial societies to insure themselves against the disgrace of being subjected to one.[10]

The sense that the death of a human being calls for rituals is so strong that members of one society sometimes feel the obligation to mark the passing of someone from an out-group, even one with whom one has a hostile relationship. A case in point is Martha Mullen, who succeeded in securing a burial location for Tamerlan Tsarnaev, a suspect in the Boston Marathon bombing, whom she did not know personally. She said she felt it her Christian responsibility to find a cemetery that would accept his remains, and she worked with the Islamic Funeral Services of Virginia to arrange for the burial.[11] The US sea burial of Osama bin Laden may in part reflect a similar sentiment, though perhaps it was merely a precaution against providing his supporters with a pilgrimage site or further inflaming their wrath. Even this last motivation demonstrates the presumption that failure to handle the corpse respectfully and perform some funeral ritual amounts to a gesture of contempt. One need only consider the outrage provoked when the bodies of fallen soldiers are desecrated by an enemy.[12] Achilles' dragging the body of Hector behind his chariot in the *Iliad* is taken to be reprehensible because it so brazenly defiles the corpse and obstructs the performance of the proper rituals by Hector's family and fellow soldiers.

The social specifications for funerary rituals differ considerably across cultures. They are typically undertaken with an audience in view (whether it is conceived as being God or gods, the spirit of the deceased, and/or the social world), and they are often judged on the basis of aesthetic criteria, particularly when they are deemed to be in some way deficient. Rituals admit of stylistic variety that reflect the aesthetic choices, at least, of those who organize them, and these choices are often made with reference to the status or the tastes of the deceased.

Funeral rituals may be generic within a society or societal subgroup (for example, an ethnic or religious tradition within a larger social group), or they may vary in relation to the deceased person's social roles within life (or perhaps those of the person's next of kin). The ancient Confucians defended differential funeral practices to reflect differences in social rank. They were particularly offended if a funeral or coffin was too grand to be proportionate to the role the deceased individual had played in life.[13]

In many cases, religious traditions mandate how funerals are to be conducted and the degree and nature of aesthetic embellishment that is acceptable or prescribed. Nevertheless, within these constraints survivors may still specify details, or the deceased may have done so on a "pre-need" basis (to use the funeral industry's expression). In many contemporary industrialized nations—or more aptly, certain classes or subgroups within them—mourners are given considerable freedom of choice in the format and specifics of funerals.

Sites for funerals and associated practices have their own aesthetic character. In the United States, funeral homes are often involved in funerary practices even when the funeral itself is conducted elsewhere (in a temple, synagogue, or church, for example). Funeral homes can be sites for visitation, and they typically have a distinctive atmosphere. Traditionally they are characterized by a tone of dignity and understatement, with soothing music playing and with flowers incorporated into an otherwise visually calm display of the urn or coffin (open or closed). In the case of a religious institution, the site is usually designed to accommodate various kinds of services, but temporary arrangements and decorations (such as flowers) and background music (if any) may similarly signal the character of the occasion.

Funeral homes may themselves be sites for funerals, and many are more flexible with respect to the aesthetics of funeral services than are religious institutions. In recent years, for example, some have played up funerals' theatrical character by offering options for themed events. Motorcycle-, military-, and sports-themed funerals are fairly common. Websites advertising themed funerals usually also include green funerals in the category.

Although such funerals may represent a political commitment more than a thematic interest, the regulating idea of greenness may provoke an aesthetic response, either positive or negative. J. K. Rowling's character Gavin in *The Casual Vacancy* objects to the wicker casket used at a friend's green funeral, seeing it as a veritable "picnic basket."[14]

Themed funerals allow for emphasis on the special interests of the deceased, while perhaps also offending the tastes of those who find such whimsy undignified. According to the *UK News*, "Recent unusual funerals included a funeral director dressed as Darth Vader in a Halloween-themed event, mourners dressed as Superman, Batman and Robin, everyone wearing a leopard print item of clothing and a funeral based on the TV series *Only Fools and Horses*."[15] For those interested in planning ahead, the internet provides access to a variety of blogs offering suggestions for funerals with a *Star Wars* theme.[16]

The United States has led the way in exotic funeral themes. Television network TLC's short-lived reality show *Best Funeral Ever* documented funerals with uncommon themes, including Christmas (featuring snow, Christmas décor, and the coffin in a sleigh), and State Fair (in which mourners could take fair rides with the urn).[17] A barbecue-oriented funeral was held for the singer of the "Baby-Backed Ribs" theme song for the Chili's restaurant chain, and Clinton Yates describes it as follows: "The funeral features a BBQ-sauce fountain, a casket that looks like a smoking pit and a Flintstones-sized prop of a side of ribs. There is a ceremonial dipping of a rib into the barbecue sauce as some sort of commemoration."[18] Yates, among others, questions the tastefulness of these more outré funerals and the very existence of the TLC series.[19] The fact that the show only lasted for a few episodes may reflect similar judgments on the part of the viewing public.

Even in the case of more conventional funerals, aesthetic criteria are commonly used to assess whether they have been performed in a satisfactory manner. Typically, in contemporary American society, the aim is for a funeral to be "beautiful" (in the sense of being moving) and suited to the person it honors. Efforts are often made to tailor the funeral to the particularity of the deceased individual, and funerals are often praised when they do this well. Themed funerals can reflect this motivation, but so do less idiosyncratic rituals.

To give some examples from funerals in which I have participated, the tastes of the deceased have sometimes been reflected through selection of music and readings and by making sure that requests that the deceased had made known are honored. Distributed memorial cards and programs may be customized to bring to mind characteristics or particular interests of the person, and the suggestion of a charity for contributions "in lieu of flowers" may reveal special concerns of the deceased. If a reception is held in connection with the ritual, choices made regarding the refreshments offered, the decoration, (possibly) the display of pictures, and the use of music (or lack thereof) can all be made with deference to the person's tastes and sensibility. I have certainly heard remarks to the effect that the arrangements were what the deceased "would have liked," suggesting that this aim is kept in view by at least some of those participating.

DISPOSAL OF REMAINS

Cultural traditions usually have requirements regarding the disposal of remains as well as specifications for funerals. Sky burial, as we noted earlier, is prescribed in certain traditions. A common practice in many parts of the world is a double burial, the removal of the corpse to a temporary location where it is kept for some time before a final burial later on.[20] Anthropologist Robert Hertz, in a 1907 essay, notes that the second burial usually occurs only after the bones of the corpse have been laid bare, but that cremation, smoking the corpse, and endocannibalism expedite this process in some societies. Hertz contends that endocannibalism, the ritual eating of the deceased person's flesh by close relatives, is motivated in part by efforts to spare "the deceased the horror of a slow and vile decomposition" and to allow "his bones to reach their final state almost immediately. Furthermore, it secures for the flesh the most honourable of sepultures."[21] This summary of possibilities may be enough to demonstrate to some readers that normative practices in certain contexts may be seen as aesthetically objectionable in others.

In the contemporary industrialized world, embalming of the corpse is a common procedure. In the United States, embalming is not a legal requirement in every case. According to the Federal Trade Commission:

> No state law requires routine embalming for every death. Some states require embalming or refrigeration if the body is not buried or cremated within a certain time; some states don't require it at all. In most cases, refrigeration is an acceptable alternative. In addition, you may choose services like direct cremation and immediate burial, which don't require any form of preservation. Many funeral homes have a policy requiring embalming if the body is to be publicly viewed, but this is not required by law in most states.[22]

Obviously, the decision as to whether to display the corpse for public viewing is an aesthetic matter, even if this is regulated by religion or custom. In any case, embalming is often extolled for making the corpse appear lifelike.

Making a cadaver appear to be alive is an aesthetic desideratum that has shaped Western expectations regarding the treatment of the lifeless body in recent centuries, according to John Troyer.[23] He points out that mechanical embalming techniques developed in the latter half of the nineteenth century enabled not only preservation of the corpse, but also control of its appearance to a hitherto unprecedented degree. These techniques, along with the postmortem photography that had become prevalent somewhat earlier, produced in the public what Troyer calls "embalmed vision," in which the dead appear alive and the fact that the corpse is inanimate "is impossible to recognize or decipher without the assistance of" captions.[24] Photographers could control how the dead body appeared, and thus they could present it in accordance with aesthetic preferences.[25] Embalmers, Troyer reports, "simply copied the photographic image's aesthetic (to produce the effect of 'deep sleep') for the dead body."[26] Aesthetic fine-tuning of the appearance of the corpse was also possible. Citing James Farrell, Troyer points out that one early twentieth-century advertisement for embalming services included a differential price list for alternative emotional expressions that could be produced, with the highest price charged for "giving the features the appearance of Christian hope and contentment."[27]

Beyond the question of embalming, another aesthetically burdened decision in contemporary industrialized society is whether to cremate or to bury. Again, taste is not the only basis for deciding among the options. Religious traditions frequently restrict or specify modes of disposing of cadavers. But many people have strong aesthetic views about whether incineration or decomposition is preferable.[28] Historically, aesthetic appeals were made by both sides of the debate over the appropriateness of cremation. Laqueur points to French Revolutionary playwright and science-fiction writer Louis-Sébastien Mercier, who insisted that "the private sepulchers made possible by having one's dead grandfather and uncle in urns that could be put in the cupboard were 'an affront to the calm and repose of society.'" On the other side, he cites the remarks of spiritualist Jon Page Hopps presiding at the cremation of Alice Dunn: "What is more beautiful than that the poor dead body, purified, should be dismissed into the sunshine?"[29]

Cremation has become increasingly popular in the contemporary Western world, and this has had an impact on the funeral industry, which makes far less profit on cremations than on burials. A consequence has been that the industry has developed innovative products and services (including themed funerals), and this provides an arena for considerable aesthetic diversity in an era in which many funerary details are left to the discretion of families. The marketing for both innovative and traditional offerings typically targets the tastes and sensibilities of the bereaved and those planning for their own funerals. The "death care" industry's services are virtually all geared to display and often are promoted with reference to this fact.

Mourners can reflect both aesthetic tastes and social-economic standing by choosing from among the array of receptacles for human remains. Pierre Bourdieu has argued that aesthetic tastes are often signals of social class, and certainly caskets and other receptacles for remains can be vehicles for conspicuous consumption.[30] In the case of coffins, for example, American funeral homes usually offer a variety of styles with some high-end models, differentiated from others by their materials, color, décor, and degree of protection from the elements. Funeral director Robert Webster describes the "eye appeal" and "sophisticated finish" of the pricier caskets, as well as "interior upgrades such as velvets, tailoring, and head-cap panels, custom designed with any theme imaginable." Coffins in sturdy materials such as copper and bronze defend against decomposition of the loved one's body and assert the social status of the deceased. Webster reports that bronze caskets used to be referred to as "gangster caskets" because of the impression that for the Mafia, "a great sendoff seemed to be part of their public image."[31]

In addition to displaying economic status, decoration of caskets can be used to indicate the role the deceased person occupied in life. This is the case with the *abebu adekai* (proverb boxes), or "fantasy coffins," of south Ghana, painted wooden coffins that are made in the shape of some object associated with the deceased, often related to the person's profession. Such coffins are carried in funeral processions, and according to a joint report in *Slate* magazine and *Roads & Kingdoms*, they are viewed as a "fashionable way to celebrate a death." They are being commissioned by non-Ghanaians, too, presumably with the intention of making an aesthetic statement.[32]

A coffin is not essential for burial, however. The growing interest in green burials has prompted the development of other lines of products. Kinkaraco Green Funeral Products offers a "Mort Couture" collection of 100% biodegradable "shrouds for those who appreciate the finer things in Life and in Death," including herbal-lined shrouds, silk shrouds, shrouds appealing to minimalist sensibilities, pet shrouds, and shrouds for cremation. The company has introduced some practical innovations in shrouds, such as rigid backboards, handles, pockets for mementos, and lowering straps.[33] (Kinkaraco also appealed to aesthetic tastes through product placement on HBO's television series *Six Feet Under*, which had an episode that featured its products.[34])

Cremation and interment are not mutually exclusive options, and urns are often buried or in other ways interred. If cremation is chosen, decisions regarding selection of an urn resemble those involved in selecting a coffin, such as choices about what material should be used and how it should be decorated, if at all. The aesthetic features of urns, like those of coffins, can make a statement about the status and concerns of the deceased (often as interpreted by close kin). The stylistic range of available urns is remarkable. One can choose artistic pottery urns, urns incorporating figurines or small sculptures, "his-and-her" urns (sometimes in the form of intertwining swans or two halves of a heart), urns using trademark images (from one's alma mater or *Star Trek*, for example), and urns that are replicas of the head of the deceased (or anyone else, for that matter).[35]

Urns are not the only possible terminus for cremains, however. Ashes can be transformed into artificial reefs and gemstones. They can be used to make a pencil or mixed with oil paints for making a portrait of the deceased.[36] They can be converted into soil for a memorial plant.[37] Ashes can be converted into glassworks, incorporated into pottery, or deposited inside objects that are meaningful to the deceased (such as a fishing pole or musical instrument).[38] Some may consider some of these aesthetically appealing ways to remain "close" to their loved ones, though others are likely to find them aesthetically repellent.

What of cases in which the cremains are scattered? Those who intend to scatter ashes may confront an unanticipated practical challenge with aesthetic aspects. Ambient conditions can cause problems, both because a lack of breeze interferes with the effort to spread the ashes and because wind can blow the ashes back onto the person(s) doing the scattering. Having the ashes of one's loved one blowing onto one's face is more than disagreeable. The funeral industry has come up with a solution to this problem. The "release urn" relegates the scattering to a mechanical device that blows the ashes in a particular direction regardless of weather conditions. Websites featuring these devices praise the elegance and smoothness of the procedure.[39] Alternatively, those of means can have ashes scattered from an airplane by professionals (with or without relatives accompanying them), hire a service that enables scattering at sea, have the remains scattered by sending them up in a large helium-filled balloon, or have them shot into space.[40] One is tempted to say, "Sky's the limit."

COMMUNICATION AND ETIQUETTE AFTER A DEATH

A third broad category of aesthetic activities in response to loss encompasses various communicative means in which news about a death is conveyed and responses communicated. Modes of communicating news of a death range from the highly stylized to the informal. Among them are obituaries (in print and online), messages conveyed through mail and email, announcements on social media platforms, newsletter notices, and (in some places) physically posted signs. Such communications are probably not typically judged in aesthetic terms except when they offend sensibilities.[41] Nevertheless, collectively they reflect changes of societal tastes over time. The newspaper announcement of my infant aunt's death in the 1930s was bluntly titled "Dead." A newspaper's having a regular obituary section obviates the need to convey this basic point through a headline. Tim Bullamore claims that obituary writing has undergone a relatively recent stylistic change, and he praises the "postmodern" obituary, which is more candid than earlier obituaries about the failures and foibles of the deceased.[42] I suspect that the move away from whitewashing details in the life of the deceased has other, less enthusiastic critics as well. The ethical status of composing more critical obituaries may be complicated by the fact that for individuals who have public notoriety, obituaries are often largely written before their actual deaths.

The internet, email, and social media have had an impact on the way that news of a death is spread, as well as on the way that news is processed.[43] Funeral homes routinely facilitate the online posting of obituaries on such websites as Legacy.com. These sites usually give visitors the opportunity to post eulogizing comments and memories, enabling those who knew the person to share stories and reflections both before and after any ritual event.

Online stylistic conventions can differ in certain ways from those assumed normative in other circumstances, as Tony Walter observes with respect to the employment of direct address.

> Many online messages are addressed directly to the dead. . . . Online, addressing the dead is done in the knowledge that there is a living audience which, by accepting such direct address and even actively joining in, legitimates a practice about which hitherto some people may have felt somewhat embarrassed, and it informalises traditions of addressing the dead via the newspaper; so much so that addressing the dead informally has on many sites become a new norm.[44]

Online obituaries also tend to have a feel of greater immediacy than do obituaries in printed media, which often take the tone of atemporal objective reporting. Brief notices of a death, prior to the construction of an obituary, might be posted very quickly on social media platforms such as Facebook and Twitter. This does not, of course, preclude the later addition of more lengthy descriptions of the person or links to obituaries. The open-endedness of what is presented on websites and social media also makes them suitable for presenting ongoing responses to a death through tribute sites.

A eulogy is another loss-related form that communicates to the public. Its purpose is not primarily to communicate the fact of a person's death, but instead to honor the person and convey the significance of the person's life. Eulogies are most often delivered at funerals and other commemorative gatherings. Keefer contends that eulogies succeed in their goal—to give eloquent expression to the impossibility of doing justice to the deceased—by means of their aesthetic characteristics. Most of the best ones have a structure that develops, with a beginning, a middle, and an end. And yet, Keefer observes, eulogies can also be aesthetically off-putting.

> Part of the agony of writing a eulogy arises from aesthetic anxieties. Often, we listen with rapt attention to a eulogy, marveling at the speaker's eloquence and experiencing the range of transcending aesthetic feelings associated with our engagement with tragic literature. On the other side, there are so many ways a eulogy can trigger an adverse aesthetic response: a résumé, meta-eulogy, self-absorption to name just a few. Engagement with a eulogy can be completely derailed when the author is perceived to be more interested in creating an artwork than praise for the dead.[45]

The aesthetic burden of the eulogy, Keefer observes, is that it should be beautiful and moving, but not be an object of aesthetic contemplation and admiration itself. Good eulogies, which achieve this aim, occasion epiphanies that can provoke awe and a related sense of gratitude—accomplishments akin to those sometimes achieved by art.

Jacques Derrida similarly finds eulogies paradoxical, and for reasons that initially sound quite different from Keefer's but are, I think, rather similar. His concern is that in speaking for his departed friend, who is no longer able to speak directly, he would be indulging in narcissism and conjuring up his imaginary picture of the friend, not really directing attention to the deceased. Try as he might to avoid this, his presentation might occlude attention to the actual person, whose absence makes the problem hard to avoid.[46]

The types of communication so far considered are ostensibly modes of describing and praising the person who has died, usually constructed with a fair amount of forethought. They often serve as vehicles for emotional expression as well, but this seems to be a secondary aim. On the other end of the spectrum would be communicative modes in which expression of immediately experienced emotion is foregrounded. Although descriptions of the deceased might be incorporated into them, informing auditors about the person or the death is not their ostensible purpose. Indeed, this aim would interfere with the directness of emotional display.

Probably the most obvious case of an emotionally expressive communicative mode is lamentation, or ritual wailing, employed by mourners in many cultures. Lamentation typically involves a fair amount of improvisation, and it often appears to express raw emotion. But Greg Urban notes that lamentation exhibits several characteristic stylistic features, drawing attention to the ways that it is shaped by aesthetic structures.[47] He cites the following generic characteristics:

> (1) the existence of a musical line, marked by a characteristic intonational contour and rhythmical structure; (2) the use of various icons of crying; and (3) the absence of an actual addressee, which renders the ritual wailing an overtly monological or expressive device, despite the importance that may accrue to its status as public, with the desired presence of someone to "overhear" it.[48]

Although cultures have distinctive styles of lamentation, the sonic resemblances with crying are easily identified, and it is cross-culturally recognized as expressing grief.

On the other end of the spectrum of means for personal expression is "CARL." Patrick Stokes reports that this mobile robot mourner is "equipped with a screen, microphone and speaker" and "can attend funerals on your behalf, allowing 'you' to move around the room and talk to your fellow mourners via Skype."[49] Proxy funeral attendance was not the original problem CARL was developed to solve. Steve Gray, its originator, reports that he was initially thinking of how he might communicate with his distant father, who had senile dementia, and asking himself, "Why don't I rig up the computer with a webcam so that I can log on to it from my home here in Oregon, allowing me to launch the Skype call myself?" Then he decided that if he put wheels on the computer, it could follow his father around the house. But if it could follow Gray's father, it can also mingle with those who gathered for a ritual. The practice of hiring professional wailers suggests that mourning by proxy is nothing new. But perhaps *proxy* is the wrong description, and we might better say that CARL extends the possibilities for participating in mourning rituals oneself while at great distance.[50]

Storytelling is another communicative aesthetic practice in which grieving people participate. Social psychologist Paul Rosenblatt points out that in many societies, those who grieve find it valuable to "develop a narrative about the person who died, how the death came about, what the death means, what the bereaved person's relationship is with the deceased, and what has happened as a result of the death."[51] Tony Walter agrees, arguing that such collective storytelling practices help stabilize the way participants view the deceased, and he sees this as valuable for negotiating the challenges of bereavement.[52]

As in the case of the eulogy, focus on aesthetic success while sharing stories about the bereaved would be foreign to the activity. Nevertheless, telling others what happened is an aesthetic practice in that it involves selection and organization of the elements of the story, as is the case in any narration. Although much of the selection may be unconsciously guided, this may also be true in the construction of more "artistic" narratives. Moreover, even if only to explain what happened, efforts are made to organize the elements of story into a coherent form.

These days, many stories are told online. In principle, these need not be different in content from those narrated in person, but the more distanced relationship of the narrator to the audience may have an impact on the aesthetic characteristics of the story. Comparing blogs about loss with conventional grief narratives, Bärbel Höttges points out that blogs are essentially open-ended in form and that they typically manifest "unfiltered grief." By contrast, conventional grief narratives are much more likely to exhibit a definite narrative shape.[53] Perhaps, though, it would be more apt to say that blogs "stage" unfiltered grief, given that we cannot tell from a blog posting any more than we can from a musical recording whether it testifies to occurrent emotion or utilizes conventional techniques to suggest that it does.

Thus far I have only touched on the specialized etiquette demands set into motion by a person's death, but etiquette norms are applied both to communication and other behaviors on the part of mourners and those who interact with them.[54] They should thus be included in an account of aesthetics in bereavement, for they are bases for evaluating particular ways of acting in terms of aesthetic categories such as fitness and proportion.

In some times, places, and societal niches, mourning attire has been culturally mandated, and it might be considered a matter of etiquette. Mourning clothes signal that the wearer is in mourning. In certain social contexts, fine aesthetic details have been scripted to convey more specific information about the mourner's situation, as was the case among the British upper class during the Victorian era. Regulations for dress stipulated what was to be worn at different points in the mourning process. Black crape was subject to measurement, with the requisite amount being gradually lessened. After some time, trim of a different color (such as gray or mauve) could be worn, though the item of clothing to which the trim was added remained black. At a certain stage, gray or other dark but non-black attire replaced black clothing. Mourning did not rule out jewelry, but if worn, it had to be black for a certain period.[55]

Although the Victorians were unusually precise regarding the distinct stages of mourning and the appropriate attire and degree of social involvement suited to each, the custom of mourning attire was a widespread practice in much of Western society only a century ago. Even now in American society, a vestige of the practice remains in the sense among many that wearing somber colors is de rigueur at funerals.

Etiquette also regulates behavior in interacting with those who have lost a loved one. In my own social setting, those within the social circle of the bereaved and/or the deceased are expected to get in touch with the bereaved to convey condolences, for example.[56] The aesthetic contrivances of sending flowers or sympathy cards to close members of the family of the deceased are widely utilized, though the custom of using sympathy cards to convey condolences has become common only relatively recently. Western societies apparently differ in their expectations of the cards' appropriate emotional tone. Birgit Koopmann-Holm and J. L. Tsai have found stylistic differences between German and American sympathy cards, with the former tending to be direct in expressing sympathy with the recipient's sorrow and the latter tending to emphasize ways of seeing the loss in some positive light (suggesting that the deceased is in a better place or that the person will live on in our memories).[57] The relatively positive contents in American sympathy cards are often reinforced by means of an aesthetic shorthand of stock images, such as blooming plants to evoke the idea of continuing life or a lighted background to suggest passage to the afterlife.[58]

The development of social media, having created a new assortment of communication possibilities, has also resulted in a new set of issues regarding etiquette and appropriate comportment after someone's death. Stokes considers the question of how we should regard "digital remains" of a person who has died, referring to the person's social media posts and other aspects of the person's online presence. He thinks they are "more like what's in the coffin than the condolence book at the front of the funeral parlour."[59] They should therefore be treated with respect, and we need norms to establish what amounts to respectful behavior.

Online sites offer opportunities for people in virtual communities to mourn together and share stories, but they also create incentives for questionable conduct. The growing but often disparaged practice of posting selfies taken at funerals falls into this category. This seems another practice of the sort Keefer criticizes, that of using funerals as occasions for self-promotion and diverting attention from the person who has died. Another practice that is widely seen as a violation of etiquette and moral propriety is making posts that insult the deceased or the person's mourners for the commenter's own amusement.[60]

Stokes draws attention to another problematic online phenomenon that arises when a person's Facebook site is converted into a de facto tribute site by those who post commemorative messages. Even when those who post might be assumed to be sincere in their desire to honor the dead or to "address" the person in public space, ironically the person's own digital presence becomes fainter and fainter as the posts accumulate. This is because the new posts go to the top of the page, with the result that the deceased person's own posts are pushed further and further to the bottom. Stokes considers this a form of "overwriting" the dead.[61] He sees this as both morally problematic and inconsistent with the commenters' own goals of preserving the memories of the person. Formatting changes to online platforms may be needed if this problem is to be resolved. Insofar as the posts are aimed at memorializing, they share the purpose of many other aesthetic practices related to loss, as will become evident in the following section.

MEMORIALS AND MEMORABILIA

Catherine Wilson, as previously noted, focuses on literary works as means of memorializing, but she also itemizes many other kinds of memorials and mementos that keep memories of the deceased alive for those who mourn them. She includes, for example, "practices aimed at keeping alive a sense of the presence of ancestors, such as the preservation of letters, heirlooms, and keepsakes, and the construction of tombs and monuments." She adds, "Ceremonial columns, bronze equestrian statues, decorated, inscribed walls and plaques, pyramids, and sepulchres all have this mnemonic function."[62] Stokes makes a similar point about portraiture, observing that it "has preserved the appearance of the dead for as long as humans have been able to draw; the increasing sophistication of art is in some ways a technology of embalming."[63] Photographs and videos have expanded the means through which we can preserve the way our deceased loved ones appeared in life. Although they are very high end, we might add chatbots to this list. Controversy surrounds the use of chatbots as ways of remembering the dead because they extrapolate from what the deceased said in life and put new words in the virtual person's mouth. But they are means of preserving the appearances of the dead (and for some who object to them, that is part of the problem, as we will consider further in chapter 7).[64]

One broad category of memorials consists of those marking sites of interment or sites where deaths have occurred. The idea that interment sites should be marked is now taken for granted in many societies. In contemporary Western society, this extends to a conviction that the dead should be specifically named, to such an extent that Laqueur says of the names of the deceased that there is "a moral imperative to hold on to them in public settings."[65]

The means of marking the location where someone is buried admit of much aesthetic variety. Simple crosses have been utilized in much of the West for many centuries, but many such sites are marked with more or less elaborate artistic monuments that may be aesthetically evaluated (as being dignified or kitschy, for example). Tombstones have been a common contemporary means of marking graves, and though often standardized, the degree and kind of ornament on a tombstone is a matter of aesthetic choice.[66] Even US military cemeteries, despite their rows of uniform headstones, offer the option of an inscribed "emblem of belief" to personalize the gravestone of a particular individual.[67] The list of available options was expanded in February 2023 to include seventy-nine possibilities, with a process for proposing more. The options include emblems for atheists and druids as well as more traditional religious symbols and an image of a dancing sandhill crane.[68] On the other extreme of the continuum from uniformity to aesthetic diversity is Vyšehrad Cemetery in Prague, where many artists of significance are buried. Many of the tombstones are full-fledged artworks, in some cases sculptures made by those interred.

Although crafting one's own tombstone is unusual, it is a relatively common practice to erect artistic works on the grave sites of the more prominent members of society (those whom Laqueur calls the "special dead").[69] In the case of the most preeminent, the tombs themselves may be remarkable artistic achievements. The Passage Tomb in Newgrange, Ireland, and the Pyramids are examples. Karsten Harries observes, "When we look to prehistory, the history of architecture almost reduces to a history of tombs."[70] Mausoleums, buildings for holding the remains of the dead, trace back to 350 BCE, when the Mausoleum at Halicarnassus (now Bodrum, Turkey) was erected. It is adorned with sculptural reliefs, and it was completed to hold the tomb of Mausolus, who had been the governor of a province within the Persian Empire, and his sister/wife.[71] The term *mausoleum* is itself a memorial to Mausolus, from whose name it derives.

One might question whether such ancient tombs should be considered aesthetic gestures in response to loss, for the craftspeople who constructed them were presumably not grieving and quite probably working under duress.[72] There is also the possibility that even those who ordered their construction (such as China's first emperor, Qin Shi Huang) were acting in accordance with self-interest, either directing the building of their own tombs to magnify their stature and prepare a majestic afterlife or assembling tombs of grandeur for others in an attempt to appease potentially angry ghosts. I think even these tombs should be categorized as aesthetic responses to loss, for they are certainly memorials, and they express emotion occasioned by loss (or envisioned loss), including fear (or its anticipation) and respect for the deceased. In some cases, too, architectural wonders have been produced as manifestations of grief more restrictively considered. The Taj Mahal, a mausoleum, was commissioned by Shah Jahan to commemorate his favorite wife. (He had plans for a matching black mausoleum for his own remains, but it was never constructed.)

Even in the case of less ostentatious tombs, display value is often evident. One need only go to certain churches to see tombs that are designed to draw attention to their memorial purpose. Harries takes as an example the Augustinian priory church at Diessen.

> Of death . . . speaks a stone in the pavement under our feet that calls attention to the vault beneath the choir in which the founders of the church lie buried. We are not allowed to forget that this church is a grave of saints. . . . We see in glass shrines the bones of two of the founders, whose names and relics speak of the triumph of time, but also of a saintliness that triumphs over time. Although dead, they live in this church.[73]

Other churches monumentalize the remains of important personages in ornate tombs, which are sometimes artworks of a quite opulent character. Those of Charles the Bold and his daughter Mary in the Church of Our Lady in Bruges fall into this category. Each tomb has a gilded bronze image of the person buried, impressively attired (Charles with full armor) and wearing a crown, atop black polished stone.

Such special tombs, even if one only considers those in European churches, reveal a wide variety of artistic styles, some bordering on the macabre. A far from unique example is provided by tombs in the Cathedral of the Assumption of Our Lady and Saint John the Baptist in Kutná Hora in the Czech Republic, which houses the remains of two saints. Positioned on the two sides of the sanctuary are shrines incorporating glass coffins in which the saints' skeletons (with fabricated faces attached) are cushioned on sumptuous pillows and clothed in finery. These shrines are even more striking for being in an otherwise quietly decorated church in High Gothic style that is associated with the Cistercian order, which was founded with the aim of returning monastic life to simplicity.

With the development of the modern cemetery, as Laqueur has extensively documented, ordinary people of means and even of the middle class had vastly expanded opportunities for the aesthetic enhancement of the site of a loved one's interment. The aesthetics of the location were also exploited in efforts to add to the grandeur of a tomb. "Tombs, great numbers of them, represented the dead of the cemetery, and they were situated to take advantage of its best features, natural and manmade."[74] The cemeteries themselves were also designed with aesthetics in mind. Laqueur describes them as "parks, the progeny of eighteenth-century gardens—Elysium or Arcadia," some of them "really arboretums in which the gardens enveloped the dead and their tombs to such an extent that it was not clear who served whom."[75]

A very different aesthetic sensibility guides another site-sensitive strategy for memorializing deceased loved ones. This is the construction of shrines along roadsides and at other locations considered significant, often because they are sites where deaths have occurred. These shrines direct the public's awareness to particular losses. They often have a homemade character, implying an intimate connection between those who assembled them and the deceased, though frequently they are constructed anonymously. These "spontaneous shrines," to use the terminology of Jack Santino, demand the public's attention to the deceased person who is being memorialized, often in a very personal manner.[76]

Responses to such shrines vary. Some find them moving, even heartbreaking. Robert Bednar describes his reaction to a shrine he encountered, which included photographs of the deceased: "This person *has been,* this person *was in the process of being alive* when he arrived at this particular spot, but here is where their drive was traumatically interrupted. Now, they *are* dead, and this is the particular place where they were transformed from someone who is to someone who *was.*" The shrine had "its own performative agency" by staging the trauma of the young man's death "in front of me, and in front of everyone else driving by."[77] Others, however, find roadside shrines invasive, obtruding into the public sphere with what should remain private.[78] This negative reaction, however, seems to corroborate Bednar's point about the performative power of the shrines. They are not merely publicly visible; they commandeer one's emotions.

Sometimes spontaneous shrines are located at some distance from a significant site, often for practical reasons (as for instance, a situation in which the site is too dangerous or damaged to be accessed safely).[79] Many makeshift shrines in New York after September 11, 2001, would fall into this category. Those shrines had at least tacit approval of landlords and public officials, who made no effort to dismantle them.[80] This is not always the case, and some shrines are secretly constructed because they are not legally sanctioned.[81] Sometimes, too, a site only symbolically connected with a death becomes a temporary shrine. In the wake of the death of Princess Diana, some people in Kansas City laid flowers alongside a very visible statue of Winston Churchill and his wife called *Tribute to Married Love*, presumably interpreting it as the most obvious local symbol for the British. The temporary character of such shrines makes them less effective than more enduring memorials for keeping the deceased alive in memory, but the gestures that rendered them shrines seem more immediate as a consequence.

Personal effects of the deceased are frequently displayed at roadside shrines, home altars, grave sites, and other memorial settings, and the reactions of those who see them may resemble the response Bednar describes, though perhaps such objects are less evocative than photographs for those who did not know the deceased. One might be emotionally affected by a teddy bear on any child's grave, but the intensity of the response may depend on how vividly one envisions a child enjoying the toy, which is largely projection in the case of a stranger. For someone who has known the person, however, displayed possessions of the deceased can contribute to a sense of loss being staged in one's presence. This can also be the effect of being given an item that belonged to the deceased, for so understood, such objects remind one of the person making use of them while underscoring the person's permanent absence. The dissemination of personal effects also enables those who receive these objects to incorporate them into their own memorializing practices. When these objects are used by recipients, this can extend a memorializing dimension to everyday activities. This may be particularly salient when these objects are wearable, as is true of watches, jewelry, and items of clothing.

Another category of wearable items used in memorializing are those produced specifically for this role. Memorial tattoos fall into this category (though tattoos are sufficiently permanent that they should perhaps not be described as "worn"). So do commemorative T-shirts, and certain businesses specialize in their design and production.[82] These wearable memorials give creative control over the memorial design to anyone who wants to assert it and at a price that is widely affordable. Jasmine Sanders, reporting for the *New York Times*, offers a brief history of commemorative T-shirts, pointing out that they seem to be a successor to the graffiti art and murals that memorialized deceased hip-hop artists. T-shirts offer "a miniature, and more personal, canvas" that is particularly welcome when civic authorities restrict public graffiti. Sanders also sees their proliferation as a consequence of "a variety of kitschy '90s nostalgia" that had been picked up by high fashion.[83]

Commemorative T-shirts are much more transient than many types of constructed memorials, which are often designed to be lasting to signify the endurance of the bond between the living and the dead. The T-shirts express continuation of bonds with the deceased in a different way, infiltrating everyday life in a manner that is communicative. Sanders opens her article by describing a Chicago man who has lost a brother to gunfire and has a new T-shirt made each year for an annual commemorative event. The man describes the T-shirts as a way to making younger relatives aware of his slain brother.

The memorial T-shirt phenomenon sometimes has a political undercurrent. Sanders notes that they often commemorate victims of gun violence, and she notes the shirts' role within African American communities, which so often experience the sudden death of one of their young members: "Despite their own lifespans, the shirts . . . function as a refutation of the supposed anonymity of gun violence. . . . They are a memorial to both the deceased and to the ways they died. And . . . [they] function as an indictment, where the law has provided none."[84] This political function is facilitated by T-shirts being vehicles of public display, visible to the world at large.

Although I have separately considered funerals, perhaps other commemorative rituals should be included in the general category of memorials. In some societies or communities, a formal ritual of commemoration is traditionally some considerable time after the death. Among these would be the Jewish ceremony called "the unveiling," in which the headstone is placed on the deceased person's tomb, and the Te Hura Kōhatu ritual practiced by Anglican Māori, in which a memorial stone is placed at the burial site around the first death anniversary.[85] Other commemorations may be unique to the specific loss. For example, collective memorial events are sometimes held in connection with events in which many have died. Examples would be the Dutch "Remembrance Day" on May 4th honoring those who died in World War II and the many memorials held in New York City, Washington, DC, and Stoystown, Pennsylvania, on September 11th to honor those killed in the terrorist attacks on that date in 2001. Being performed considerably later than funerals, such ceremonies highlight the intention of keeping the dead alive in memory. They share this temporal distance from the deaths with most of the projects that fall into the next category I will consider, that of artworks honoring the dead and/or exploring dimensions of loss.

HONORING THE DEAD AND EXPLORING LOSS THROUGH ARTWORKS

The most obviously aesthetic vehicles for emotional expression are artworks, but many artworks require considerable time for their production. Consequently, they tend not to be direct expressions of occurrent emotions, as lamentation and spontaneous storytelling often are. They tend toward “emotion recollected in tranquillity,” in William Wordsworth’s phrase.[86] For this reason I consider artworks that express grief as a distinct category of loss-related aesthetic phenomena.

The boundary between this category and the previous one is not sharp, as is obvious from the fact that certain types of formal artworks have already been mentioned in the preceding section. I add this section to consider those artworks created after a lapse of time allows for a degree of reflective distance from a death and those that explore loss without necessarily being directly associated with a particular event. Whether or not an artist is responding to a particular loss may not be evident to the audience. Wilson observes, for example, that one may not know when reading certain poetic works whether they respond to an actual loss or an imagined one, and this leads her to conclude that whether or not a loss is fictional is not decisive for our emotional response.[87] While memorializing someone and exploring loss are quite different goals, either (or both) may motivate a particular work of art, and it may be difficult or impossible to determine which is operative in any given case.

High art traditions are replete with artworks that commemorate or played a role in funerary contexts. In addition to architectural works, which have already been considered, some of the oldest and best-preserved artworks in other media were funerary in their intent. Some of these straightforwardly manifest the aim of caring for the dead. A touching instance of the previously mentioned jade suits is that of Princess Dou Wan, wife of Liu Sheng, from a tomb of the late second century BCE discovered in Mancheng district, Hebei province. Because it is so well preserved, it reveals the extent of the effort to treat the body of the deceased with meticulous care. Many art museums that display Chinese antiquities include in their collections *mingqi*, sculptural representations of attendants and models of practical items (such as homes, granaries, and farm animals) produced with the intention of burying them with the deceased for the person’s use in the afterlife.[88]

Noël Carroll points out that literature, paintings, sculptures, musical works, and films are art forms that all have instances with commemorative aims. He also observes that some artistic genres are specific to the expression of loss, including “the epitaph, the elegy, and, to some extent, the eulogy.”[89] Wilson also emphasizes the elegiac work.[90] Death masks and reliquaries might be added to this list, although neither of these forms is particularly favored in the Western world at present.[91]

In fact, the full range of traditional artistic media have been utilized in connection with loss, and some of the great works of art history fall into this category. To mention only a few Western examples, Plato’s dialogues (works of literature as well as philosophy) and Josquin des Prez's "Déploration sur la Mort de Johannes Ockeghem" can be seen as efforts to memorialize beloved teachers. Allen Ginsberg's poem "Kaddish" is dedicated to his deceased mother, Naomi Ginsberg. Kurt Vonnegut Jr. claimed that he produced all his fiction with his late sister Alice in mind, considering whether what he was writing would have struck her as funny.[92] Innumerable books are dedicated to a particular person in memoriam.

Edvard Munch, who experienced numerous deaths in the family in early life, produced many paintings on the topic of death and grief. He claimed that *The Sick Child*, for example, referred to his sister's death. He revised that image many times, as he did other works related to death, including *The Dead Mother and Her Child* and *Death in the Sick Room*. A more recent work of this sort in a different medium is Terrence Malick's *Tree of Life*, dedicated to his deceased brother. Film dedications to actors who appear in a film but died before it premiered are not at all uncommon.[93]

As for works depicting grief, one need only consider painted crucifixion scenes, pietàs and other sorrowful mother depictions, and numerous paintings and sculptures that present the death of the Buddha to realize how prevalent this theme is.[94] Mothers grieving for their lost children is a thematic staple in European art, evident in works by Käthe Kollwitz, Georg Minne, Albert Edelfelt, and others.[95] Arthur Danto points to Robert Motherwell's *Elegies to the Spanish Republic* series and Picasso's *Guernica* as profound expressions of grief in the face of political loss.[96] Numerous literary works of fiction, including Lionel Shriver's *We Need to Talk about Kevin*, tell stories in which grief is a central theme.[97] A good number of films also take loss and grief as subject matter.[98]

Music plays many roles in connection with grief and loss (some of which I will discuss further in chapter 5). I have already cited examples of music composed or (in the case of lamentation) improvised to mourn the deaths of particular individuals. The poetry that Gustav Mahler set in his *Kindertotenlieder*, by Friedrich Rückert, was written in response to the death of two of his children from scarlet fever.[99] But music can also express grief and loss without a direct connection to specific deaths. Musical compositions for funerals, designed to be performable on repeated occasions, are in most instances typically not anchored to the loss of a particular person. And composed Requiem Masses and Kaddishes set to music may be performed entirely apart from funeral rituals.

Music that was not originally intended for commemorative purposes can also develop associations with grief. Samuel Barber's *Adagio for Strings*, the second movement of his String Quartet, Op. 11, for example, developed such associations because Oliver Stone used it recurrently in the soundtrack for battle scenes in *Platoon* (1986), a film about the Vietnam War. Some music that originally had no association with loss has become de rigueur in certain rituals of mourning, the playing of "Taps" (originally devised to signal lights-out) at the funerals of veterans, for example, or "Danny Boy" at certain Irish American funerals.[100]

Although they have been previously mentioned, tomb monuments and headstones fall into the general category of artworks to honor the dead, and they are typically added to grave sites quite some time after funerals have taken place. Some monuments and headstones arguably fall into the category of kitsch, but this does not diminish their status as artworks. Headstones and monuments function as they do because they are positioned to mark graves. Commonly they are not "site-specific" artworks in the contemporary use of this term, which suggests designing the work for placement in a precise location because of the site's characteristic and rather stable features, but their aesthetic impact is often affected by aspects of the site. Within modern cemeteries they are usually surrounded by growing populations of other monuments that compete with them for visual attention.

Many public memorials are artworks made to honor the dead.[101] They bear the imprint of the collective decision-making that determines their construction, and they are often sites of aesthetic controversy. The dispute over the Vietnam Veterans Memorial in Washington, DC, designed by Maya Lin, is a case in point. Some veterans argued that the memorial, consisting of two extended black granite walls that bore the names of the American casualties of the war, was too abstract and insufficiently heroic. The response to their complaints took the form of the inclusion of a flagpole as part of the memorial, the addition of words at the beginning and the end of the wall, and the erection of Frederick Hart's sculpture *The Three Servicemen*.[102] The last is a realistic sculpture of a rather traditional sort, though it exceeds the realism of most in that it presents servicemen as young, ethnically and racially diverse, wearied, and rather stunned. The placement of the sculpture puts the memorial designed by Maya Lin within the line of sight of the servicemen, and one might interpret the soldiers' dispirited expressions as responses to the immensity of the loss documented by the wall of names. Although I think the arrangement of the sculpture in relation to the wall is both aesthetically compelling and in keeping with the spirit of Lin's original work, the erection of the sculpture did not end controversy about the memorial. Kirk Savage points out that the changes "satisfied neither Lin nor her critics."[103]

Having mentioned Kutná Hora, I should perhaps mention that city's famous ossuary, which is a short walk from Sedlec cathedral and constitutes a striking example of memorializing art. Ossuaries are in general aesthetically fascinating. In many the bones are no longer identifiable as having belonged to particular individuals, and in these cases, they do not serve to carry on the memory of a person or to serve as "monuments to attachment," in Wilson's words. If anything, as memento mori, they are the opposite, standing as reminders that all is transient.[104]

What is distinctive, but not unique, about the Sedlec Ossuary is that the bones are used as materials for artistic decoration.[105] The bones have been arranged to form four large pyramids (or bells, depending on one's interpretation), a chalice, a monstrance, a wreath, numerous garlands of skulls, four pillars, a huge coat of arms of the Schwarzenberg family (which had commissioned it), and a hanging chandelier. Bones are also used to form words on the walls, including the signature of the artist responsible for the elaborate constructions and the date.

The Sedlec Ossuary prompts varied responses, not all of them favorable. Denise Inge, who undertook a tour of ossuaries after her vicar husband was assigned to a parish that had one, describes complex reactions. "Are these bones artist's materials or human remains?" she asks. "And the 'what are they?' has triggered an as yet undescried 'what am I?'"[106] She is less disturbed by the pyramids than by the more figurative and functional employments of the bones. She reports being

> disquieted by the bone plaques and chalices, the dismembering they reiterate, the frippery of skull garlands, the jocular tilt of the chandelier. There is something subversive in these that offends the sense of decency in me; perhaps one of the points of art is to subvert and disturb 'normal,' but I find them contrived and off-putting.[107]

While Inge eventually reconciles herself to the initially shocking display, the inner struggle she reports reveals the possibility of mixed aesthetic reactions and divergent views about the tastefulness of certain creative projects undertaken in response to loss.

In response to this chapter's examination of many ways in which aesthetics can be involved in grief and mourning, one might think that there is little point in drawing attention to the aesthetics/grief connection. After all, it appears that grieving people already find their way to aesthetic reflection and activity, so little more needs to be said. I think more should be said, however.

First, while grief and mourning typically involve practices that have aesthetic aspects, many of the ways in which these aspects can be functional, helping those who are grieving to cope and reorganize their lives, are probably not widely appreciated. Grief therapists and counselors may recommend artistic therapies as beneficial to their clients, but grieving people who do not seek out professional help (and even some who do) may be unaware of the extent to which aesthetic activity might help their adjustment and more generally benefit them. Second, although aestheticians are devoting increasing attention to aesthetic practices within everyday life, the long-term emphasis in the Western tradition on artworks (particularly those from high art traditions) has resulted in an underemphasis on the aesthetic dimension of many valuable means for dealing with personal loss.

Third, grief is not well understood. Philosophical and psychological theories of emotion have difficulty accounting for it, and the breakdown of one's framework of standing assumptions within grief has such wide-ranging impacts over extended periods of time that it can be hard to recognize that they are connected.[108] Aesthetic interventions that assuage some of grief's painful aspects and facilitate what Thomas Attig describes as "re-learning the world" are themselves diversely focused. I think it is worthwhile to make the interconnections between them and facets of grief more evident.

Fourth, the Western tradition's theoretical divorce between aesthetics and the practical details of life has encouraged the impression that aesthetics is something we turn to when we want to take a break from life. If, as I am convinced, aesthetics is central to our interaction as social beings and to our understanding of how to live well, this impression is misguided. Noticing ways in which aesthetics can help in one of the most challenging situations that most of us face in life, the loss of a loved one, can put us in a position to recognize its importance in our lives more broadly.

Despite the diverse ways in which aesthetic phenomena are utilized in loss, the connections of aesthetics and bereavement remain underappreciated. One consequence is that while organized grief therapy and support groups often employ them, bereaved people are often unaware of the extent to which aesthetic activity might help them in their circumstances. In later chapters, I will consider specific ways that aesthetic practices can be beneficial, but before doing so, I should offer some account of grief. I will do so in the following chapter.

3

Grief and the Phenomenology of Bereavement

GRIEF AS AN ANOMALOUS EMOTION

One might expect that given the unavoidability of death in human experience, grief would be well understood. One might also assume that grief would be a major focus in philosophical theorizing. Neither of these expectations would be warranted. Michael Cholbi describes the historical record as revealing a long-standing philosophical "antipathy toward grief."[1] Although he is among a number of contemporary philosophers who are resisting that tendency, it is striking how rarely philosophers in the Western tradition have directed much attention to grief (or loss). Cholbi considers the philosophical neglect of grief a consequence of the traditional view that grief is a shameful manifestation of human vulnerability and dependence.[2] I would add that the contemporary marginalization of applied philosophy within the field makes it plausible that grief has been further ostracized from discussion because the topic is hard to detach from the therapeutic needs of those who are grieving, a concern far removed from the realm of "pure" philosophy.

To the extent that the needs of the bereaved are acknowledged, grief might seem to call for regulation (to use the psychological term) just as other emotions do, and this might in turn suggest a clear role for aesthetic activities. We can regulate anger, for example, by listening to calming music. We can regulate frustration (at least according to John Dewey) by tidying a room.[3] And so forth. With grief, however, regulation is not so straightforward. We earlier noted that *grief* is not consistently defined. Even when taken as the name of an emotion, the term is ambiguous between an episode of a certain character and a long-term process. Regulation is more easily directed at the former than the latter, but episodes of grief themselves are embedded in an extended emotional process.[4] Cholbi sees this as reason to describe grief as "less an emotion than an emotional pattern or *process*."[5]

Because grief is necessarily temporally extended, it does not fit the dominant paradigm in philosophy and psychology of emotions as short-term episodic occurrences.[6] As a consequence, most general theoretical accounts of emotion do not devote much attention to grief.[7] Grief is not easily modeled on physicalist accounts, which take the essence of an emotion to be the physiological changes that occur in response to some stimulus. Probably the most popular physicalist account currently on offer is the theory that "basic" emotions are essentially "affect programs," which combine a variety of physiological responses including facial and vocal expression, arousal of the autonomic and central nervous systems (ANS and CNS, respectively), and biochemical changes.[8] According to this theory, an emotion terminates when the arousal and biochemical effects subside. That grief is not among the putative basic emotions associated with affect programs is unsurprising given the rather abbreviated time frames that emotions, on these views, involve.

"Cognitivist" theories, which hold that ideas about objects or situations play a role in constituting emotions, might seem better suited for analyzing grief than physicalist accounts, for grief seems to require some awareness of a loss. But cognitivism is also compatible with taking short-term episodes as paradigmatic. Even if a cognitive appraisal is taken to be a precondition, cause, or constituent of an emotion, emotions might in many cases still be short-lived, particularly if they motivate action that alters the situation enough that the appraisal no longer applies.[9]

Some cognitivist accounts abstract from time entirely, foreclosing consideration of emotions as processes from the start. A case in point is Donald Gustafson's account, which analyzes the concept of grief instead of the grief experience. He uses a belief-desire model to characterize grief, contending that grief is irrational because it involves a desire (for the deceased to return to life) that is incompatible with belief (that the person has died).[10] So interpreted, grief seems static as well as incoherent. Similarly static, though emerging from a different philosophical tradition, is Max Scheler's account of shared grief:

> Two parents stand beside the dead body of a beloved child. They feel in common the "same" sorrow, the "same" anguish. It is not that A feels this sorrow and B feels it also, and moreover that they both know that they are feeling it. No, it is a feeling-in-common. A's sorrow is in no way an "external" matter for B here, as it is e.g. for their friend, C, who joins them and commiserates "with them" or "upon their sorrow." On the contrary, they

> feel it together, in the sense that they feel and experience in common, not only the same value-situation, but also the same keenness of emotion in regard to it. The sorrow, as value content, and the grief, as characterizing the functional relation thereto, are here one and identical.[11]

Scheler seems not to think that *grief* and *sorrow* require further analysis, at least given his purposes in the context in which this passage appears (a book about sympathy).[12] And although the experience of grief he describes seems to be temporal in the sense that two people undergo it at the same time, he does not characterize grief as having any trajectory.[13]

Whatever its merits for purposes of neurological research on emotion, the episodic paradigm does not fit grief.[14] Wittgenstein implies as much when he asks, "Why does it sound queer to say: 'For a second he felt deep grief'?"[15] His implication is that it is part of the very nature of grief that it is a temporally extended process.

If grief is recognized as a process, as I think it should be, understanding it requires attention to its temporal structure.[16] Efforts to track that structure, however, may lead to further difficulties situating grief on the theoretical map. Philosophical and psychological accounts of emotion commonly aim at individuating and categorizing emotion types. Grief, when understood as temporally extended, is hard to individuate, for it involves what Sonja Rinofner-Kreidl describes as the "interlacement of different emotions" and "a typical range or cluster of sub-emotions."[17]

Nina Jakoby itemizes various emotions that may be involved in the grieving process, including "guilt, aggression, yearning, anxiety, or fear," along with anger and "feelings of hopelessness."[18] I would add others, including regret, loneliness, a sense of abandonment, frustration, feelings of impotence, protective urges, melancholy, and despondency. Besides emotions considered painful and distressing, the process often involves emotions usually taken to have more positive valence, such as love, affection, admiration, humor, gratitude, and, in certain cases, relief.[19] While the term *grief* is sometimes used narrowly to refer to pangs of distress in response to a loss (as when one refers to "bouts of grief"), usually the scope of the term is taken to be broader. These considerations raise questions about grief's status as an emotion. Is it a single distinct emotion, an encompassing emotion that includes others, a loosely connected collection, or not an emotion at all?[20]

Another reason that some theorists have found grief to be theoretically perplexing is that its relation to motivation seems aberrant. Most theories of emotion associate it with motivation to action, such as the "fight-or-flight" response associated with fear.[21] William Lyons is among the philosophers who classify grief as atypical, arguing that unlike most emotions, grief "seems to be mainly a reactive emotion rather than an active motivating one." He describes it as a "nonactive, still" emotion that is "in extreme cases, even catatonic." Grief does not seem to provoke efforts to seek help from others, either. "One might be more likely to want to be left alone," he observes. "Assistance would only be an intrusion."[22] Catherine Wilson similarly argues that "grief . . . is a kind of paralytic emotion; there is no parallel to the adaptive fight-or-flight response elicited by fear, or to the approach-and-charm response elicited by desire."[23] Robert Solomon characterized grief (until late in his career) as being "cut off entirely from effective action and open only to 'adventitious' (though more or less appropriate) expression."[24]

In psychology, the issue has often been framed in terms of whether grief has inherent "action tendencies."[25] This is a particular concern for psychologists such as Nico Frijda, who contends that different types of emotions set up distinctive action tendencies that are typically functional for the person who has them. It is far from evident what grief's distinctive action tendency would be, for it does not seem to incite behavior that is particularly adaptive, if it can be said to prompt behavior at all. Perhaps we can say that it motivates withdrawal behavior, but seeking to be left alone does not have obvious adaptive benefit. Considering grief's theoretically anomalous character, Frijda concludes that emotions are functional only "most of the time." Of grief, he claims that it "is not useful; the capacity that enables grief is." And characteristic grief behavior strikes him as dysfunctional: "Longing for something definitely lost is meaningless; so is vomiting after hearing morally disgusting information."[26]

James Averill agrees with Lyons that grief tends to provoke withdrawal and lethargy, though he argues that this is consistent with an action tendency that he thinks does characterize grief. Grief, he claims, moves us to bolster relationships. It motivates us to do what is required to prevent such painful losses. Grief has a function, one that is preventative. It drives us to repair relationships with living people when rifts occur, preventing them from becoming permanent losses that themselves trigger grief.[27] The function of grief is to motivate the preservation of long-term attachments, and this motivation is provoked even in cases in which the object of attachment has died. Averill's account may seem odd in that it implies that grief is purposive with regard to relationships with the living, but not with regard to the relationship on which a grieving person is particularly focused, that with the deceased loved one.

Solomon, despite his early endorsement of the view that grief is aberrant, later recanted that position and offered another theory of grief's action tendencies:

> I once thought that grief might be viewed as a kind of degenerate emotion, a *breakdown* of emotion rather than an emotion itself. I have come to see that this underestimates the value and significance of grief and provides an inadequate and unimaginative analysis of both the emotion and the process of grieving.[28]

The later Solomon sees grief as functional, its function being the continuation of love.[29] Although grief may prompt withdrawal, this facilitates reflection on the person and the relationship. Action tendencies are also evident in grief's promotion of a "strong desire to commemorate and honor the deceased" and the life of the person as a whole.[30] Thomas Attig similarly sees grief as motivating reflection on one's relationship with the deceased. He describes grief as demanding a relearning of this relationship as well as a relearning of the world; he maintains:

> Nothing is more important, more difficult, or potentially more rewarding than this labor of love. The rethinking here is about the nature, possibility, and desirability of love in separation from the deceased, hope that motivates the search for such love, and memory that grounds the possibility.[31]

If the action-tendency model is disconnected from the episodic paradigm, we can recognize motivational tendencies in grief, that is, in grief understood as a long-term process. When we recognize that temporal prolongation is a characteristic of grief, we also can more easily make sense of the multiplicity of emotional episodes that may be involved. Noticing the temporal extension of grief primes us to attend to its various possible trajectories and the varying challenges that emerge depending on the relative recency of the loss.

Philosophers and social scientists who direct attention to grief, specifically, generally acknowledge that it takes time. But despite broad agreement that grief is a process, no consensus has been reached on how to characterize that process. Questions arise concerning whether there are normative benchmarks for the progress of grief, whether the process has an end point, and whether ties with the dead should be relinquished, matters to which we shall presently turn.

STAGE THEORY AND THE QUESTION OF AN END POINT

One influential theory of grief as a process is that it unfolds in a series of stages. Probably the most popular version of this view is that of Elisabeth Kübler-Ross. She identified stages that she claims are commonly undergone by terminally ill patients as they come to grips with the fact that they are dying. The stages she specifies are denial, anger, bargaining, depression, and acceptance, which she thinks frequently progress in that order. She came to see grief as similarly evolving through these same stages.[32] Another stage model is that of John Bowlby and Colin Murray Parkes, who describe four common phases that grieving people experience: shock and numbness, yearning and searching, despair and disorganization, and reorganization.[33]

We should observe that these theorists do not intend for the stages they describe to be normative. Kübler-Ross and her coauthor David Kessler insist, "The stages were never meant to help tuck messy emotions into neat packages. They are responses to loss that many people have, but there is not a typical response to loss, just as there is no typical loss. Our grief is as individual as our lives."[34] Bowlby prefaces one of his early discussions of his proposed phases with the acknowledgment that post-loss behavior is varied and that the sequence of phases is only "in some degrees predictable."[35] Parkes and his colleague Holly Prigerson also point out that their framework should not be interpreted rigidly.[36]

Critics point out, however, that whatever the formulators' intentions, models involving stages have become entrenched in popular imagination and interpreted as norms. Scientific evidence for the existence of the stages and their purported sequence is lacking, and thus the popular idea that they represent the standard for grieving is deeply problematic.[37] Camille Wortman and Roxane Cohen Silver persuasively argue that phase models have become doctrinaire and are resistant to disconfirmation by evidence. The result is that grief behavior is typically interpreted in light of them, to the detriment of many bereaved people who depart from the established sequence.[38] Not just the public, but medical practitioners too, rely on the stage model, and this presents the danger that nonconformity may be interpreted as pathological in clinical settings. Wortman and Silver also argue that normative expectations about how grief should proceed encourage self-policing that only intensifies the sense of being out of step with the social world and its standards. In connection with the relation of aesthetics and grief, such expectations potentially pressure the bereaved to suppress their impulses toward emotional expression, discouraging even those strategies taking routes that are indirect.[39]

Stage theories may also obscure the grieving person's agency. Attig observes that the stage model takes grieving to be a quasi-automatic process with a fairly clear trajectory toward an end point.[40] He complains, "Thinking of grieving in terms of stages or phases (as something that unfolds in predictable sequences of experience) suggests that grieving happens to us after bereavement happens to us, simply takes time, and is choiceless."[41] Such theories neglect the individuality of the bereaved and "reinforce helplessness." In keeping with my purposes here, I would add that they conceal a precondition for engaging in aesthetic practices while grieving and fail to reflect the grieving person's potential for creative response.

A further criticism of the stage model focuses on the implication that the grief process will come to a definitive end. Wortman and Silver note that virtually all the authors who subscribe to the stage view anticipate a final phase of the grieving process that will bring it to a close. The idea that grief will terminate on its own has obvious relevance to the relation of aesthetics and grief. This expectation minimizes the importance of promoting adaptation through any means, since recovery can be expected to occur in any case.

The idea that grief normally runs its course to completion is a common view, whether or not a stage model is endorsed. Carolyn Price, who does accept a stage model, contends, "Grief ends when the subject has adapted to their loss."[42] Berislav Marušić also claims that grief ends, though prima facie he finds this odd in light of the fact that the beloved person remains dead and one continues to have reason to grieve.[43] Peter Goldie, while objecting to the social pressure to get over grief, nevertheless thinks that doing so is at some point appropriate and necessary.[44] Cholbi also thinks that grief typically resolves, sometimes very quickly.[45]

The expectation that in most cases time will heal was endorsed by Freud. He contends that grief will end when one has completed the "grief-work" of detaching libido from one's psychic images of the deceased. In his account of the difference between mourning and what we would now term depression, he acknowledges that the two have similar symptoms. Nevertheless, he observes:

> It is . . . well worth notice that, although grief involves grave departures from the normal attitude to life, it never occurs to us to regard it as a morbid condition and hand the mourner over to medical treatment. We rest assured that after a lapse of time it will be overcome, and we look upon any interference with it as inadvisable or even harmful.[46]

Freud dismissed the idea of medicalizing grief, but contemporary psychiatry has reconsidered. The prevailing view is that medical intervention is appropriate for alleviating the suffering of at least some grieving people. While that sounds like a plausible and benevolent position, considerable controversy has arisen over the question of which grieving people need treatment and under what circumstances.

Some worry that the current (fifth) edition of the *Diagnostic and Statistical Manual of Mental Disorders* (*DSM-5*) encourages the idea that grief itself is a cause for medical attention. In the United States, the *DSM* provides the standard that medical practitioners use for classifying mental disorders. In defining Major Depressive Disorder (MDD), the third and fourth editions had a "bereavement exclusion," maintaining Freud's distinction between clinical depression and grief, despite their similar symptomatology. The *DSM-5* in its original version eliminated the bereavement exclusion from the definition, although it did include a footnote urging caution in the diagnosis of bereaved people as clinically depressed. The decision to eliminate the exclusion was made after considerable controversy regarding the question of how to handle grief-related mental illness, often termed "complicated grief."

The *DSM-5* was updated in March 2022 to include "Prolonged Grief Disorder" as "a new diagnostic entity." This disorder is defined as "intense yearning or longing for the deceased (often with intense sorrow and emotional pain), and preoccupation with thoughts or memories of the deceased (in children and adolescents, this preoccupation may focus on the circumstances of the death)."[47] Paul Appelbaum, in his Physician Review of the diagnosis for the American Psychiatric Association, clarifies that prolonged grief persists "longer than might be expected based on social, cultural, or religious norms." The *DSM-5* specifies that the diagnosis should be applied no sooner than twelve months after the death (or six months when the patient is a child or adolescent). Appelbaum cites the following symptoms, the presence of three of which is sufficient for the diagnosis:

- Identity disruption (such as feeling as though part of oneself has died).
- Marked sense of disbelief about the death.
- Avoidance of reminders that the person is dead.
- Intense emotional pain (such as anger, bitterness, sorrow) related to the death.
- Difficulty with reintegration (such as problems engaging with friends, pursuing interests, planning for the future).
- Emotional numbness (absence or marked reduction of emotional experience).
- Feeling that life is meaningless.
- Intense loneliness (feeling alone or detached from others).[48]

The obvious challenge in constructing *DSM* diagnoses is to make them comprehensive enough that they capture patterns across individual variations, yet specific enough that atypical behavior does not automatically become pathologized.[49] The vagueness of many of the terms in the list of the symptoms for the new diagnosis accommodates individual variations in the manner and pace of grief. This vagueness calls for caution, though Appelbaum observes that the disorder category has been added for cases in which "the symptoms are severe enough to cause problems" that interfere with everyday life.[50] One would hope that clinicians would diagnose this disorder only when the severity of symptoms reaches this threshold of interference. Optimally, too, clinicians will simply view the one-year (or six-month) stipulation as a threshold, not a cutoff for grief.[51] The American Psychiatric Association itself defended the new approach to complicated grief by claiming that it wanted to remove the implication of the *DSM-4*'s two-month bereavement exemption for major depressive disorder "that bereavement typically lasts only two months when both physicians and grief counselors recognize that the duration is more commonly 1–2 years."[52]

In any case, the inclusion of the new diagnostic category may be reasonable given the pragmatics of the situation. For those bereaved patients who are suffering and facing severe difficulties in adjusting to their new situation, getting professional help may be dependent on there being an applicable *DSM* category.[53] Insurance companies often restrict coverage for mental conditions to those that have some "codable diagnosis" listing in the *DSM*. Still, Cholbi, among others, fears that the introduction of the new category may encourage the idea that grief itself is pathological. He worries "that medicalizing grief will disrupt, impede, or hijack the self-inquiry and self-reconstruction that make grief ethically significant to us."[54] This could happen, he fears, because it encourages regarding grief as a passively experienced disease rather than an active process that might contribute something positive to one's life. He acknowledges that there may be cases in which grieving individuals need medical intervention, for example, when grief precipitates depression or anxiety. But he sees grief as a stressor, not a pathological condition, and he opposes the *DSM*'s inclusion of such diagnostic categories as prolonged grief disorder.

I share Cholbi's concern, and I agree with him that experiencing grief in appropriate circumstances can be a sign of mental health, even if painful. If grief comes to be thought of as on a par with illness, this promotes its stigmatization, adding to the difficulties that the bereaved face.[55] The medicalization of grief reinforces the tendency to impose normative expectations on bereaved people, for whom these external pressures may add to their difficulties. It also has implications for the recognition of how aesthetics and loss are related. Art and music therapy are acknowledged as medicinal practices, but in an era in which medication to stabilize is often the first course of treatment in psychiatric cases, their role is likely to be understood as secondary. If medication is prescribed with the intended aim of reducing the intensity of emotional states, therapies that elicit emotional expression might even be considered counterproductive.

Cholbi is convinced that grief normally reaches an end, seemingly taking this to be desirable.[56] I am more convinced by Matthew Ratcliffe's suggestion that grief goes well when an equilibrium is attained. He maintains that we will not find a neat boundary between "normal" and pathological grief, but that we can nevertheless recognize potential pathologies if we attend to the temporal structure and interpersonal dynamics of different sorts of cases. Normal grief, on his analysis, involves "a dynamic engagement with one's lost possibilities, which involves eventually coming to inhabit a world that is largely consistent with the death." Grief inevitably involves a struggle to come to grips with the death and the possibilities that it has foreclosed, but in normal grief, the bereaved person eventually becomes somewhat reconciled to the situation. If an impasse results in pathology, according to Ratcliffe, this arises from a lack of the engagement he describes.[57] This lack of engagement may involve acknowledging the death but detaching from the living world or, alternatively, refusing to acknowledge the death and maintaining this refusal in all of one's interactions with the world.

Ratcliffe's model of dynamic engagement is open-ended, not aimed at any end point. As we have seen, Jonathan Lear comparably contends that grief ("mourning" in his terminology) involves ongoing imaginative engagement that keeps the absence alive yet renews a sense of hope as one goes forward. This multifaceted imaginative engagement with both the loss and the ways that we can build on the spiritual legacies of the dead is ideally ongoing, according to Lear, for it creates conditions for our own renewal. "In a . . . psychoanalytically informed sense of the term," he observes, ". . . mourning may continue on throughout a life and, indeed, constitute our humanity."[58]

What, then, should we make of the commonly expressed desire for closure after loss? My answer is that closure of a certain sort is important, but there are different kinds of closure. In aesthetic contexts, the term can refer to an artwork's being bounded, separated from what is outside the work. Understood through this spatial metaphor, the notion of closure furthers the notion of a sharp divide between art and reality. While such a divide is a traditional presupposition within Western aesthetics, it is hardly universal. Closure may also be understood in terms of fulfilling tensions that have been set up within an artwork. Closure in this sense is most easily seen in the case of a diachronically modeled process, in which tendencies run their course to completion.[59]

The felt need for resolution of tendencies, particularly those in tension with each other, characterizes not only many artworks, but also emotional life, as the characterization of emotions in terms of action tendencies suggests. Despite the previously discussed controversy among theorists about whether grief has action tendencies, the experience of bereavement is rife with chaotic feelings and desires that seem in tension with each other. Thus, a bereaved person who seeks closure might be wishing for as decisive a fulfillment of these tendencies as occurs in artistic resolutions of tensions. The expectation that the inner commotion of bereavement can be decisively resolved is, however, misguided, though more limited kinds of closure may be available.

We can differentiate closure in the context of artworks from that sought in connection with grief by noting the different kinds of tendencies involved in the two cases. In an artwork, significant thematic or compositional tendencies can be resolved so that no loose ends remain. Because these tensions are developed by the work itself and their field of play is circumscribed in advance, skilled arrangement of elements can result in a strong sense of closure. Emotional life is not circumscribed in a similar way, and only rarely do multiple tensions resolve simultaneously. In music, resolution is accomplished when further movement seems unnecessary. At that point, generally speaking, the piece is over. But to expect anything comparable with respect to grief would be strange, for grieving does not lead to a point at which tensions are all wrapped up. As Frijda puts it, "No death of a loved person ever fully becomes a settled fact. The tentacles of love continue to search for their object, the empty place remains, in bed, in feeling, in expectations, as in an ion split away from its molecule. . . . [T]his is proper to love."[60]

Death does not change one's love for a person or the action tendencies of love. Indeed, it sets up new tendencies in addition, such as what McCracken describes as the "dedicatory" impulse, the motivation to engage in activities that honor the deceased loved one.[61] The tendencies related to love, including the dedicatory impulse, are not resolvable while love persists. And love, with all its tendencies, continues beyond the death of the beloved. The desire to honor the person also has no obvious end point.

Funerals and commemorative events are often described as providing closure for those who mourn, but the idea that they should put a cap on grief seems out of keeping with psychological reality. There may be those who contend that they really felt no further distress at the loss after a loved one's funeral. If so, I suspect that either (1) they felt limited grief to begin with, (2) they are unusually adept at hermetically sealing off emotional reactions, or (3) they suppressed further grief reactions, most likely to their own detriment.[62]

I thoroughly disagree with Rev. Bernard A. Healey, the priest cited in an

Associated Press story about the policy imposed by the Catholic Diocese of Providence, Rhode Island, that "Danny Boy" should be banned from funerals. Noting that the song is evocative for Irish Americans and commonly performed at the funerals of Irish American men, the priest complained, "Part of what I do at a funeral Mass is try to lift people's spirits. But the song is emotionally manipulative. Everything I've spent the last hour working toward is gone within two minutes because everyone is reduced to tears."[63] Fr. Healey sees the song's effectiveness at bringing sadness to the surface as contrary to the consolation he seeks to provide. But I think it is wrong to see collective weeping as evidence that consoling efforts have failed. People may feel more capable of facing sadness precisely because the service has given them an emotional refuge. Psychologist George A. Bonanno offers evidence that grief typically involves emotional oscillation between consoling thoughts and pain at the loss:

> Relentless grief would be overwhelming. Grief is tolerable, actually, only because it comes and goes in a kind of oscillation. . . . We focus on the pain of the loss, its implications, its meanings, and then our minds swing back toward the immediate world, other people, and what is going on in the present. We temporarily lighten up and reconnect with those around us. Then we dive back down to continue the process of mourning.[64]

Viewing funerals in this light, one might say that they provide moments of comfort that give mourners strength for further bouts of intense grieving. I doubt that Fr. Healey actually thinks that ideally the grief is over once the funeral ends, and if that is the case, he would probably concede that the closure provided is limited.[65] But if he did think that funerals can and should eliminate further weeping, he would be applying the wrong conception of closure.

But what, we might ask, of the common claim that a funeral or other culturally prescribed ritual practices is necessary for closure? We should note that such comments are most often made when the felt need to engage in these practices is frustrated, or afterward, when the frustration has been relieved. Given the ubiquitous imperative to care for the dead and the detailed cultural specifications regarding how this should be accomplished, grieving people commonly feel distressed in the absence of the expected rituals. Their distress can be particularly acute when the circumstances of the death seemed to interrupt the deceased person's life. Alluding primarily to sudden deaths during wars, Frijda comments:

> Too often the business is unfinished because attachments that were cut off by the events had no natural termination point. Those left behind do

> not possess an image that can serve as such a termination point, to which the thoughts and feelings can return and find a moment of rest. It is as in mythologies that picture a wandering soul that only could find rest on its gravestone. Remember that the ritual function of funerals is to provide such a termination point.[66]

Although I do not accept the relinquishment model of grief to which Frijda's terminology adheres, I interpret his allusion to the lack of a natural termination point as referring to the need for emotional punctuation. Funerals do provide relative closure in the sense of emotional punctuation, and often they offer the feeling that one has completed certain necessary steps. However, this kind of "closure" does not secure an end to the grieving process.

Any sense of closure in connection with irrevocable loss will almost inevitably be incomplete and relative. To the extent that grieving people long for the revival of the deceased, satisfaction is unavailable. Even if other emotions eventually displace distress as the dominant affective tone in a person's experience, this does not imply that episodes of grief have been eliminated. Grieving people are often taken aback by sudden sharp attacks of grief that arise long after the loss that prompted it. Funerals do not result in closure understood as the cessation of all such episodes.

By offering emotional punctuation, funerals offer a type of closure. They can offer respite from a free-floating emotional condition in which episodes of one emotional character quickly give way to another by helping the grieving person to focus. They can also provide a ready-made outlet for emotional expression, shaping confused feelings into organized processes with points of cadence.[67] While in the grip of emotional chaos that is seemingly unending, grieving people can benefit from such opportunities for relatively clear and specific acts of emotional expression. Funerals provide a degree of containment of the chaos, and in offering bounded actions that focus and express emotions, they provide closure. However, understanding closure as a cutoff to grief strikes me as unrealistic.

CONTINUING BONDS

In later chapters, I will be suggesting that one of the benefits of aesthetic activity in grief is that it offers possibilities for accepting the death and reconnecting with the living world without surrendering attachment to the deceased. My view that attachment to the deceased desirably continues concurs with what has recently become the dominant view in grief theory, the idea that it is both common and healthy to maintain "continuing bonds" with the deceased. The term "continuing bonds" was coined by Dennis Klass, Phyllis R. Silverman, and Steven L. Nickman, editors of an eponymously titled 1996 book.[68] In opposition to the long-dominant Freudian view that relinquishing attachment to the dead is crucial to healthy adjustment, the book set out to defend the value of maintaining relationships with the deceased, albeit on a different footing than formerly.

Although they do not necessarily claim that grief should continue indefinitely, those adopting the continuing bonds approach see it as desirable that bereaved people maintain some sort of ongoing relationship with the deceased. Attig, for example, thinks that far from reaching a definitive end, grief (ideally) evolves into a way of life in which love for the deceased is integrated into a life-affirming attitude toward the future.[69] He thinks, in fact, that the developing this orientation is the best means of overcoming what may seem an unshakable sense of hopelessness in the wake of loss: "Seeing how lasting love is possible in separation is, I believe, the key that enables us to avoid the trap and despair that come with dwelling in a desire for an impossible return."[70]

The continuing bonds perspective strikes me as preferable to those focused on relinquishing attachments to the dead. It seems more realistic with respect to emotional ties with loved ones, for these do not evaporate even when we recognize that a beloved person is irrevocably absent. Moreover, while Freud's relinquishment model takes the grief process to be completed when one fully recognizes that the person is gone and withdraws attachment, it is hard to know how one would recognize the end of this process in practice. Grief does not dissipate in a linear fashion. Despite criticizing the attitude of "holding on to" grief, Cholbi "allows that its conclusion is sometimes provisional—that memories of the deceased can return well after the event of their death, sometimes prompted by unexpected and highly specific stimuli such as voices or colors."[71] By comparison with the relinquishment alternative, the continuing bonds orientation has a more open-ended conception of adjustment, and it helpfully acknowledges continuities as well as ruptures with the past.

This is not to say that there is a single continuing bonds approach. The idea that continuing bonds are valuable for adjusting to life after loss is consistent with a variety of perspectives on bereavement. Indeed, Klass has observed, "Continuing bonds are now regarded as a common aspect of bereavement in virtually all psychiatric and psychological models of grief."[72] Theorists do not all subscribe to a common account of continuing bonds. Instead, they interpret the agreed-upon thesis through various models. Given that a rejection of relinquishment theory was the shared starting point for continuing bonds theorizing, the diversity of accounts is hardly surprising.

The variety of models that have been conjoined with a continuing bonds approach are evident in the recent literature on grief. In 2018 Dennis Klass and Edith Maria Steffen published a follow-up to the 1996 volume, an anthology entitled *Continuing Bonds in Bereavement: New Directions for Research and Practice*, which includes essays that relate the continuing bonds approach to a variety of therapeutic and theoretical perspectives. Nurturing continuing bonds is a central focus in the two-track model of bereavement developed by Simon Shimshon Rubin. Track 1 concerns biopsychosocial functioning, and Track 2 is concerned with maintaining and transforming one's relationship with the deceased. Rubin criticizes earlier approaches to bereavement for equating successful functioning on Track 1 with successful adaptation to loss, and he proposed his model to draw attention to the importance of reworking the relationship with the deceased.[73]

Phyllis S. Kominsky integrates the idea of continuing bonds with an attachment theoretical perspective, which models grief on separation from one's caregiver in early childhood and interprets insecure attachment patterns as predictive of pathologies. She is among those who think that continuing bonds may be helpful or hurtful depending on the relationship, and she defends "the utility of attachment theory in identifying and strengthening bonds that promote healing and moderating the effect of those that do not."[74]

According to the "dual process" model of grief proposed by Margaret Stroebe and Henk Schut, grieving individuals oscillate between being loss oriented and being "restoration oriented" (engaging in practical tasks and making efforts to adjust to the new circumstances).[75] Both of these orientations produce stress, but Stroebe and Schut contend that they require different coping responses. Attention to continuing bonds is not built directly into the model, but Stroebe, Schut, and Kathrin Boerner recommend an integration of the dual process model's account of various coping styles with other theoretical accounts that directly concern relationships. Among these are attachment theory, with its categorization of relationships, and Boerner and Jutta Heckhausen's account of transformations in mental representations of the deceased. The latter approach considers the place of both disengagement and connection in the cultivation of continuing bonds and makes efforts to determine when these bonds are (or are not) adaptive.[76]

Few theorists, if any, would argue that continuing bonds with the deceased are always beneficial. Much depends on the character of the relationship before the death. If bereaved individuals feel that they have unfinished business with the deceased or if the relationship with the deceased was dysfunctional, a continuation of the bond may itself be maladaptive unless it is reevaluated and transformed. But such transformation can facilitate healing. For some, it may be optimal to learn to appreciate certain things about a loved one and the relationship but to dissociate oneself from others.

Those who accept a continuing bonds paradigm may differ over whether some modes of connecting with the deceased are conducive to complicated grief, either inherently or when maintained over a long period of time. One issue is whether "externalized" methods for maintaining bonds (symbolizing the person in some external form) are ideally short-term expedients.[77] Many theorists emphasize reflection and the value of internalizing one's relationship to the dead, that is, interpreting the deceased as "living on" within the person who grieves.[78] In light of this idea that developing internal representations of the deceased is desirable, externalized modes might be deemed deficient or symptomatic, at least when they take certain forms.

Life-size sculptures of the deceased have sometimes been erected as grave monuments. A bereaved person's behaving toward such a statue as if it were the deceased loved one (routinely embracing it or kissing it, for example) might be seen as an indication that the person has not assimilated the loss. Prolonged insistence on preserving a deceased child's room as it was when occupied might reveal that a person is remaining closed to the possibility of change, which is likely to reverberate through interactions with the larger world. These examples of externalized methods for continuing bonds might strike some as possible symptoms. They might be seen as contributing to pathological conditions if they help the bereaved to avoid acknowledging the death and revising the structure of life accordingly.

Perspectives on continuing bonds might vary depending on attitudes toward the possibility of an afterlife. Such attitudes might affect theorists' views about desirable ways of maintaining a relationship with the deceased, and they are bound to be relevant to how a grieving person regards the continuing relationship. In general, cultural and personal presuppositions affect the way in which the continuing bond is understood and the way in which it is thought to be real.[79] The continued existence of the deceased is taken for granted in many cultural and religious traditions. And while the rationalistic perspective that dominates Western scholarship has little room for such beliefs, this does not mean that Western populations are rationalistic in their behavior.

The practice of consulting psychic mediums is burgeoning in the United States, for example. Julie Beischel, Chad Mosher, and Mark Boccuzzi have noted that some theorists and practitioners have argued that "the primary issue regarding the experiences of the bereaved is not whether they reflect actual communication with the deceased, but how the experience can be used to aid in coping with the loss." They urge unbiased openness toward reported "after-death communication," which for them encompasses a broad range of phenomena, including

> sensing the presence of the deceased; visual, olfactory, tactile, and auditory (voices or sounds) phenomena; conversations; powerful dreams;

> hearing meaningfully timed songs on the radio or music associated with the deceased; messages from objects; lost-things-found; communication through electric devices (e.g., flickering lights); natural phenomena; symbolic messages; synchronicities; and other unusual incidents or unexplainable phenomena.[80]

Beischel, Mosher, and Boccuzzi contend that in light of the number of bereaved individuals who consult mediums and the alleviation of distress that may result, theorists and clinicians should accept reports of such phenomena as being in some sense real (at least to the person who experiences them). They propose that it might even be worthwhile for professional therapists to work in collaboration with credentialed mediums to help clients who might benefit deal with unresolved feelings, the urge to communicate, and other grief-related distress.

I anticipate that some readers may find this prospect itself distressing, perhaps enough to reconsider their own attitudes toward continuing bonds. But one need not endorse either mediumship or posthumous survival to see a benefit in maintaining bonds with the deceased. The idea of continuing bonds can be unpacked in secular terms, as I will consider further in chapter 7. One can certainly hold that deceased loved ones "live on" in our hearts and minds without believing that they are living anywhere else.

Reflecting on the fact that people often envision themselves engaging in extended conversations with the dead, Lear proposes that mourning occurs in a space of imaginative play, where one does not need to make sharp distinctions between self and other or inner and external life. He cites Donald Woods Winnicott's remark that "relief from the strain of relating inner and outer reality" is "provided by an intermediate area in which it is not challenged (arts, religion, etc.)."[81] Lear's claim that mourning awakens imagination seems plausible, certainly in connection with bereavement. Our certainties are interrupted in grief amidst an interplay of absences and presences, and so we resort to imaginative activity in response to this confusing experience. This may account for the wide range of aesthetic phenomena associated with grief that we considered in chapter 2.

Lear's stance strikes me as the appropriate perspective for considering the many ways that people regard deceased loved ones and relationships with them. One of the reasons there is no single continuing bonds theory is that any content given to the idea requires imaginative speculation or extrapolation. Even when people share some dogma about the dead (whether religious or secular), we cannot assume that they share an understanding of its meaning. What is obvious is that a person who has died is no longer present in the same way as prior to the death. This fact leaves open all sorts of questions about how to regard the deceased and the nature of one's connection with the person henceforth, and these can only be answered by playing with possibilities in an imaginative space of the sort that Lear and Winnicott describe. We have to play with possibilities if we are to contemplate these matters at all.

The vagueness of impressions of the deceased and the need to engage in a space of imaginative play may account for the multifarious ways that people envision the dead as relating to them. Ratcliffe suggests that impressions of the deceased being somehow "present" can arise from experiencing features of the environment as implying one's relationship with the person and the indefiniteness of envisioned possibilities in the circumstances. "Sometimes, it may be that possibilities ordinarily associated with perceptual experience and current activities combine with remembered and imagined possibilities. This would generate a sense of connection that straddles the boundaries between types of intentionality—a relationship with the deceased that is not experienced as unambiguously present or past, current or imagined."[82]

I suspect that with regard to reported experiences of the dead, most people differentiate between the plausible and the far-fetched, even though there may be little agreement about which category applies in certain cases. The itemized phenomena on Beischel, Mosher, and Boccuzzi's list are simply listed as "reported after-death communications," which does not address the question of whether any of them might plausibly be understood as actual communications. I think it is reasonable to take at face value that these reported phenomena correspond with experiences that some grieving people have had. As for their ontological status, I adopt the perspective advocated by Jack Hunter.

Hunter proposes an approach of "ontological flooding" toward the paranormal, which he defines as "any phenomenon that seems to exceed or challenge the limitations of current scientific understanding." By contrast with the strategies that seek to establish floodgates to "hold back the tides" of "those unusual events and experiences that seem to challenge our dominant explanatory models," the ontological flooding approach removes these barriers and begins with a stance of uncertainty.[83] I favor this strategy of not foreclosing possibilities in advance. Taking an agnostic stance strikes me as the best way of giving due respect to grieving people's imaginative efforts in thinking about their relationships with the dead.

The externalized forms of the reported communications should not lead us to ignore the fact that internalized representations of the dead can also be envisioned as involving communication, and thus the distinction between externalized and internalized representations of the dead may not be as sharp as it might appear. Many people think of their deceased loved ones as inner guides. Discussing cases of this sort, Sandra Dannenbaum and Richard Kinnier observe that even if the guidance is ultimately a projection from oneself, it may be enriching and expand possibilities for self-development.[84] They appeal to Hubert Hermans and Harry Kempen's theory of the "dialogical self," which holds that the self is relational and always involves an interaction among the voices of multiple people.[85] According to Hermans and Kempen, we understand ourselves in dialogical terms, bouncing our self-interpretations off various internalized impressions we have of other people. On their view, one necessarily relates to another person as a character within "one's internal scenario," but these internalized characters develop over time through interacting with actual individuals.[86] Relating to the dead in one's mind is on a par with relating to the living. We interact with internalized impressions of them in ways that help us understand ourselves. There may be some projection in our sense of what the deceased might advise, but the same is true of our sense of a loved one's perspective while the person is still alive.

I see the continuing bonds approach as bringing grief out of the closet, so to speak. Those who are grieving should not feel pressured to conform to external demands that they "accept reality" in relation to loss. They should be supported even in their seeming eccentricities, for they, like the protagonist of *A Portrait of the Artist as a Young Man*, are setting out to forge something new and humanly important.[87]

The aesthetic is an arena in which such forging can occur. It is a site of imaginative play where continuities and subtle connections are developed, where we work out answers to dumbfounding questions about how to proceed, where we address and respond to both the living and the dead, and where we savor our memories while nevertheless seizing the day. Such aspects of aesthetic life are valuable across the range of human circumstances, but bereavement presents challenges that make them especially felicitous. I have mentioned some of these challenges in passing, but I have yet to specify features of what the experience of grieving involves. I will proceed to do so in the following section.

THE PHENOMENOLOGY OF BEREAVEMENT

In this section I will consider the phenomenological character of being bereaved and experiencing grief. To reiterate a caveat made previously, the way I will characterize the experience of grief is bound to be influenced by my cultural context and background. I will draw on my personal experience, which may or may not be typical even within my context. Along the way I will therefore refer to accounts of others, both theoretical and literary, which I take to show that my characterization is not completely idiosyncratic.

I will describe grief experience in ideal terms as though longing for the loved one is the predominant response to the person's death, but I recognize that things are more complicated. Sometimes one grieves for a person with whom one had a troubled relationship, and probably any relationship has flaws and inspires a degree of ambivalence. Awareness of a relationship's flaws may sometimes make grief less intense, as when one has largely written off a person who was formerly close after a parting of the ways. Often, however, grief can be more painful when accompanied by the feeling that unfinished business with the person can never be dealt with. Responding to a death with ambivalence does not imply that one is not grieving. Nor does feeling emotions of varying character and valence. Any particular cases of grief will deviate from a generalized description. Nonetheless, I will describe some features of grief that are typical in relationships that are relatively happy, many of which are likely to characterize grief in more complicated relationships, too.

In grief the death of another person absorbs one's attention. This claim may be controversial, for some may think that we are mainly disturbed by someone else's death because it directs awareness to the prospect of one's own. No doubt, the death of someone else can bring one's own vulnerability into focus, and perhaps this is especially true in the case of a loved one. The possibility of dying yourself seems a lot more plausible after the death of someone you care about.[88] But one's own death is a secondary consideration in grief. Overwhelmingly, your attention in bereavement is drawn to the transformation of the one who has died, the changes in your relationship to the person, and the prospect of continuing to be *here* when your loved one is here no longer.[89]

Yet to describe the situation as a matter of distributed attention makes it sound as though one is sufficiently focused to contemplate these matters in reflective tranquility, a situation that is far from the case when one is grieving. Bereavement profoundly undermines the coherence of one's frame of reference. Guy Newland, describing his experience of grief over the loss of his wife, says, "I felt as though I were undergoing something extremely strange, like a secret LSD experiment."[90] The following subsections consider some of the factors that contribute to the incoherence of one's experience in grief.

Disbelief and Disorientation

The inability to believe that the person is dead typifies the frame of mind of those who have just suffered a loss.[91] This reaction is independent of whether or not one would affirm the abstract proposition that the person has died (certainly a rebuff to the philosophical dogma that knowing something implies believing it). Ratcliffe rightly claims it is an oversimplification to assert either that one believes or that one does not believe that the loved one is dead. One continues to rely on a framework of expectations which depends in some ways on the deceased, and one might say that one disbelieves in the death to the extent that one relies on that framework, even though one recognizes that the death has occurred.[92] The disbelief is not aimed at the abstract proposition, however, but at the aspect of the world that the proposition picks out. And it is the aspect of the world—the absence of the loved person—that cannot be psychically integrated.

The difficulty of processing the reality of the death is not simply wishful resistance. The disappearance of the person rattles one's most basic assumptions about how the world works.[93] One cannot absorb the sudden absence of a person who is central to one's familiar world. It is simply unintelligible. The world's fabric still appears to be intact, so how could one of the most evident people within it simply vanish? The stability of the whole time-space nexus seems doubtful if someone whose presence one has relied upon can suddenly pop out of it.[94]

Spatial Confusion

The disorientation of bereavement is reinforced by the fact that when we think of the dead, we inevitably envision them as somewhere in space. That the person is not present is not itself the issue. Our loved ones are not precisely where we are at all times, and we are accustomed to their being absent from our immediate location. This fact enables us to latch on to false comparisons when trying to make sense of the deceased person's absence. Things feel much as they do when the person has stepped out of the room or gone to work or some such thing. If not here, he or she must be elsewhere, one pre-reflectively supposes.

But where would the person be? Two common symptoms of grief seem geared to relocating the person. "Search behavior" is the tendency to expect to see the dead person, so much so that someone who even marginally resembles the deceased might be momentarily identified as the person.[95] "Introjection" is the tendency to take on the deceased person's traits or typical behavior, as if one were the person.[96] This tendency involves a strong identification with a person, so much that one does not—or does not desire to—distinguish oneself from the other. Introjection makes the question of locating the person less pressing. One cannot find the person in the external world, but that is because he or she has taken up residency inside oneself. One might imagine literally enabling the deceased to see and notice things by seeing and noticing them oneself.

The deceased may sometimes seem externally locatable independent of any search mechanisms. As previously noted, grieving people not infrequently have impressions of the dead person as being present, right here, right now. Thomas Fuchs, in fact, describes as grief's "core characteristic" the experience of a fundamental ambiguity "between presence and absence of the deceased, between the present and the past."[97]

C. S. Lewis describes having an impression of his deceased wife, which came to him unbidden:

> Something quite unexpected has happened. It came this morning early. For various reasons, not in themselves at all mysterious, my heart was lighter than it had been for many weeks. For one thing, I suppose I am recovering physically from a good deal of mere exhaustion. And I'd had a very tiring but very healthy twelve hours the day before, and a sounder night's sleep; and after ten days of low-hung grey skies and motionless warm dampness, the sun was shining and there was a light breeze. And suddenly, at the very moment when, so far, I mourned H. least, I remembered her best. Indeed, it was something (almost) better than memory; an instantaneous, unanswerable impression.[98]

The felt presence of the deceased is often described as reassuring, but when one feels it and for how long are uncontrollable. Perhaps this contributes to the impression that it is a real presence of the other and not a projection, for it seems to operate independent of oneself. Fuchs, while acknowledging that metaphysical and religious beliefs may affect how one interprets this phenomenon, describes what one encounters in such cases as an "as-if presence." Despite awareness that the person has died, such as-if presence is encouraged, he argues, by the fact that "the whole environment is permeated by affordances pointing to the lost person."[99]

On the other hand, often what seems present is not the person but the person's almost palpable absence. Sartre describes the potential for an absence to be experienced as a presence in the case of a living person, his friend Pierre.

> I have an appointment with Pierre at four o'clock. I arrive at the café a quarter of an hour late. Pierre is always punctual. Will he have waited for me? I look at the room, the patrons, and I say, "He is not here." . . . I myself expected to see Pierre, and my expectation caused the absence of Pierre to happen as a real event concerning this café. It is an objective fact at present that I have discovered this absence. . . . Pierre absent haunts this café.[100]

Such encounters with a person's absence, which are exceptional cases in relation to living persons, are rife in the case of someone who has died, particularly if proximity made face-to-face interaction habitual. In contrast to impressions of the person's presence, this presence of absence is disconcerting. Augustine describes this kind of experience in connection with a friend who had recently died: "My eyes were restless in looking for him, but he was not there. I hated all places because he was not in them."[101]

Felt presence and sensed absence reconnect the deceased person to a spatial location, but not consistently. Alternatively, the person might be related to space in a generalized way: one might sense that the person is everywhere (perhaps an unconscious corollary of the person seeming to be nowhere in particular). The association of the sky with the heavenly abode of the "good" deceased might be interpreted as a literalization of the idea that they now have a full range of vision of the earthly activities of their kin.

The common conception that deceased loved ones can now see into the hearts and minds of the living may be linked to this idea that their perspective is no longer restricted, as it was when they were "in" their physical bodies.[102] Perhaps the unconscious reasoning supporting this idea is that the dead now know what death is; but if they know that thing that no living person knows, they may have exceeded our other epistemological limitations, too. Or from the simple fact that they seem to be everywhere, they have no perspectival limitations.

The common belief in the quasi-omniscience of the dead may be bolstered by the elimination of most of our motives for subterfuge with respect to the dead, as opposed to living people. We often use dissimulation in efforts to coax each other into particular attitudes or behavior in the vignettes of daily life. This no longer seems purposive where the dead are concerned, for they are no longer involved in our vignettes. Perhaps the elimination of many motives for deception makes us feel more candid toward them, and reciprocally we may imagine that they can see without obfuscation because we are not hiding things from them. However, this attitude would only apply to the extent that one does not feel that one has anything important to hide from the person, and this may not be the case. The thought that the dead occupy a privileged epistemic position might make one feel exposed, revealing a continued desire to keep them unaware of one's secrets. Envisioning the deceased as having all-penetrating insight may also intensify the feelings of guilt toward the person that are often involved in grief.

Besides these varied effects on one's conception of the deceased as being in space, bereavement alters one's own sense of being situated in space, making it seem less secure. If it is possible for a loved one to slip off the spatial grid, the same can apply to oneself. One's sense of spatial reality is also affected by the fact that everyday activities that were basic to one's relationship to the environment seem deprived of meaning as a consequence of the loss. Typically, one relates to sites within one's sphere of operation on the basis of one's concerns, with those that entice or obligate looming large in one's locational impressions. In bereavement, places that ordinarily would be attractive or demand attention have lost their gravitational pull. One feels pervasive alienation from every location, with the effect that one lacks a sense of emplacement. Space can seem undifferentiated. St. Augustine's comment that he hated every place in his friend's absence expresses this leveled response to spatial reality.

Temporal Disturbances

Bereavement also transforms one's perspective on time. Ratcliffe describes a variety of temporal disturbances that may occur in grief, including the jumbling of past, present, and future, an untethered drifting from moment to moment, and the impression of temporal stasis. The last of these disturbances is aptly described by Denise Riley in her essay *Time Lived, Without Its Flow* as an "extraordinary feeling of a-temporality." She marvels that "the stopping of time can, for those who find themselves plunged into it, be lived."[103] Ratcliffe interprets this sense of atemporality as arising from "a diminished sense of *meaningful* change."[104] The person may recognize that changes occur, but these are not felt to have any significance.

The death of a beloved person represents a temporal watershed for the bereaved, and one's relationship to the past, the present, and the future seems irreversibly modified.[105] The time before the death, even that which was recently experienced, seems on the other side of a gulf. Recently past events also now have an aspect that they didn't have when they occurred—the last time you saw the person, the last time you had lunch with person, and so on.[106] A massive weight has been added to the memory of events that seemed inconsequential at the time.

The future has a strange aspect, too. One had envisioned it as proceeding under circumstances that no longer hold, for one assumed that the deceased loved one would also be present in the world. One has lost, with respect to that person, what Fuchs terms "intersubjective synchrony," the implicit sense of time passing in the company of others. Indeed, he observes, the movement of "world time," or time within the social world at large, "threatens to separate the bereaved person more and more from the lost object, which sinks back into the past." Like the ambiguity regarding spatial presence and absence, temporal ambiguity accosts one. Fuchs analyzes the situation as involving a dissociation between general time, which continues to flow, and the "dyadic time" that had been experienced intersubjectively with the deceased person. Dyadic time is now arrested but felt as a kind of timeless time in which the person remains present.[107]

Kurt Vonnegut characterizes his shell-shocked protagonist in *Slaughterhouse-Five* (a figure who has difficulty processing his experiences in Dresden after the bombing in World War II) as "unstuck in time." This phrase seems apt for the temporal strangeness in bereavement and the temporal ambiguity identified by Fuchs.[108] Time as most of the world experiences it seems inapplicable to oneself. Or one experiences it as exerting pressure that one wants to resist. The future is nowhere one wants to go in the absence of the one who has died.[109] One's life as an ongoing flux is derailed, for whatever continues as time goes forward does not seem to matter very much.

Disrupted Motivation

These incoherent conceptions of time and space and confusion about the deceased person's relation to them have multiple effects. One consequence is confused motivations. Many habits of interaction that have developed in relation to the deceased persist in an inertial state, though they have ceased to be supported by the situation.[110] These habits presuppose the deceased person, and so they reinforce one's inability to fully believe that the death is real. At the same time, they continually revive expectations of further interaction. (Interactive habits also affect the outlooks of many who have more casual relations to the person. How often does a colleague or acquaintance respond to news of a person's death with "But I just talked to her!")

The reality of the death, however, ensures that habitual actions premised on the assumption of ongoing interaction with the lost loved one will miss their mark. A typical consequence of having so many seemingly irrelevant habits is that one feels deprived of many of one's standing reasons for action. While not fully convinced that the deceased is gone, a bereaved person at the same time begins to anticipate what the absence of the person will mean.[111] Insofar as one can think beyond the present, one wonders how it will be possible to face being here without the other person. The far from uncommon suggestion by newly bereaved individuals that they would like to go with the departed is an indication of the seeming unacceptability of this situation and the irrelevance of former goals.[112]

Apathy and the feeling that nothing is worth doing typify bereavement.[113] One also feels a generalized numbness, what Matthew Ratcliffe terms "a comprehensive disengagement from the world of the living."[114] In effect, one feels dead to oneself.[115] Ratcliffe describes this disengagement as a "kind of participation in death," and he cites Denise Riley's description of her attitude toward her deceased son: "I tried always to be there for him, solidly. And I shall continue to be. (The logic of this conviction: In order to be there, I too have died.)"[116] Riley's comment reveals the strong feelings of loyalty and protectiveness that can motivate the desire to follow the deceased. The needs of the dead can seem more compelling than those of the living and to confront one with greater urgency.

Bereavement makes obvious how much the meaning we find in our pursuits derives from their connection with other people, especially loved ones. Our activities are in many ways done "for" particular individuals, in that we think of them as our audience or as beneficiaries of what we do. This is obvious in cases in which you do something that makes your parents or spouse proud of you or those in which your work earns money that is used in support of family members. But in less obvious ways, too, we consider loved ones a part of one's audience. Our loved ones are those we report to, in the sense that we tell them about our lives.[117] In bereavement, one becomes aware of how often we are motivated by the aim of impressing the deceased in some fashion. Soon after my mother died, I caught myself still storing up humorous anecdotes to tell her, since she enjoyed hearing stories of my antics. When I reminded myself that I could no longer reach her by telephone, I felt, "What's the point of even being funny if I can't tell Mom about it?"[118]

Altered Self-Impression

With previous motives seeming mostly inapplicable, much of one's energy in bereavement is expended in efforts to work out the nature of one's relationship with the deceased. This is made no less difficult by the fact that bereavement makes one feels something of a stranger to oneself.[119] The disturbed impression of oneself extends even to the perception of one's body, for grief has pronounced physical effects. Numbness is common, typically accompanied by various other symptoms. Fuchs cites feelings of "a heavy weight" on the body, "constant pressure on the chest, shortness of the breath and respiratory spasm intermittently relieved by sighing, crying or sobbing; frequently one feels literally 'choked with grief.'"[120] Guy Newland describes "intense shivering" and "a constant hollow sensation in my gut, something that felt desperate to be eased in a sigh," though sighing did not help.[121] Some symptoms are localized, while others are not. Fuchs describes pain "experienced as an oppression and constriction mainly around the heart (heartache)" and "a bitter or burning feeling of tightness in the throat," but also "waves of pain and distress which capture the entire body."[122]

The gestalt impression of one's body in grief may be only vaguely reminiscent of the body as one previously knew it. Its boundaries are unclear. One may feel as though the outlines of one's organs do not correspond to the outlines of one's skin. One's heart area, for instance, may seem to have become more prominent and exposed, as though one were literally wearing one's heart externally. Julian Barnes reports feeling as though he had undergone a fall "whose shock has caused your internal organs to rupture and burst forth from your body." He says of grief that it "makes your stomach turn, snatches the breath from you, cuts off the blood supply to the brain."[123] Grieving individuals often describe themselves as feeling mutilated or like amputees.[124]

The common idea that one has lost a part of oneself in bereavement reflects the fact that one's interactions with the environment have implicated the absent person, whom one implicitly took account of in one's behavior. Merleau-Ponty uses the term *intercorporeality* for the sharing of sensibility among embodied beings when they coordinate their physical behavior with that of one or more others. When we interact with another person for an extended period of time, this intercorporeality becomes basic to our sense of our own bodily engagement in the world. The death of someone with whom we have intercorporeally related to the world fractures our own sense of bodily engaging with the world.[125] Ratcliffe describes this impact of a loved one's death as follows:

> What I take to be my own perspective on the surrounding world does not incorporate a clear distinction between how the world appears to *me* and how it appears to *us*. . . . Something that was previously integral to one's ability to experience and engage with the world, to perceive things in structured ways that reflect a coherent system of projects, cares, concerns, and abilities, is now absent.[126]

The blow to one's relational framework contributes to one's disturbed impression of oneself.[127] Joseph Luzzi describes his state of mind in the days following the sudden death of his wife: "I was a ghost haunting what had been my own life."[128] One's sense of who one is has broken down, for the relationship with the deceased person importantly figured in one's self-conception. Allan Køster describes the situation as one in which one's self-familiarity has been compromised. This is because that impression is developed and maintained through interactions with others and the world. "I am not simply self-acquainted," Køster observes, "but continuously brought back to myself through my involvement with and inhabitancy in the things, people, practices, and places vital to my sense of self."[129] Sharing one's life with someone involves routine interaction that helps to ground our sense of who we are. For this reason, we find it difficult to recognize ourselves when that person ceases to be present in our world.

Although one's intercorporeal connection to the deceased has broken down, one is nevertheless accosted by a series of memories of interacting, many of which come to mind unbidden. This almost automatic inventory proceeds as though one were going through the entire contents of one's mental file on the person. According to Freud, this survey of images is part of the "work" of grief, and it is functional in helping one to recover. Freud explains this in connection with his theory that relinquishing attachment to the deceased is necessary for making psychic space for new attachments. This attachment is multifaceted, he contends, and one has a distinct attachment (libidinal cathexis, in Freud's terminology) to each of one's mental image of the deceased. As we undergo the spontaneous survey of memories, we come to recognize that the person we encounter in each of them is no longer here. Our minds present the images one at a time so that we can withdraw our libido from each of them, freeing ourselves up for attachment to some new object.[130] Although I reject the "relinquishment" model, I consider Freud's description of the parade of mental images of the deceased to be phenomenologically astute.

Freud's account of the spontaneous flood of memories does not rule out the possibility that the memories reassert the reality of the person before the reality principle takes charge and insists that the person is no longer present in the world. Even if the memories play a role in furthering adjustment, they may also contribute to the bereaved person's anguish. Proust provides a poetic rendering of such circumstances in *Remembrance of Things Past*, where his narrator describes his reaction to news of the death of a former lover.

> How could she have seemed dead to me when now, in order to think of her, I had at my disposal only those same images one or the other of which I used to recall when she was alive, each one being associated with a particular moment? . . . A little statuette as we drove to the island, a large, calm coarsely grained face above the pianola, she was thus by turns rain-soaked and swift, provoking and diaphanous, motionless and smiling, an angel of music. So that what would have to be obliterated in me was not one only, but countless Albertines. Each of these was thus attached to a moment, to the date of which I found myself carried back when I saw again that particu-

> lar Albertine. And the moments of the past do not remain still; they retain in our memory the motion which drew them towards the future, towards a future which has itself become the past, and draws us on in their train. . . . So great a wealth of memories, borrowed from the treasury of her life, such a profusion of sentiments evoking, implicating her life, seemed to make it incredible that Albertine should be dead. . . . It was not Albertine alone that was simply a series of moments, it was also myself.[131]

The narrator responds to the myriad recalled points of connection to his loved one in a complex manner. At first, he takes the sheer abundance of his memories as reason to think she cannot be dead. This is countered by his knowing that she is and that she is now *only* this series of pointillistic memories. His impression of Albertine is dispersed through the phantasmagoria, but each of them evaporates, and Proust suggests that his self-impression undergoes a similar fate. He may successfully emerge from the experience aware that Albertine is dead, but his reflections are an assault on his sense of self. If the person he has known is nothing but an amalgamation of such points, what has he himself become? His own ontological status is challenged by Albertine's death. For him, the review of memories becomes an aspect of the corrosion of self-image that bereavement involves.

Self-Accusation and Guilt Feelings

The difficulty bereavement imposes on one's ability to sustain one's previous impression of oneself can be intensified by another widespread phenomenon in grief, the tendency to identify oneself as a guilty party. While bereavement makes the value of the relationship to the lost loved one evident, one must come to grips with the fact that the relationship seems undermined by the permanent absence of one of the parties. When bad things happen in relationships, we frequently feel the need to assign blame. Perhaps this explains the fact that grieving people often blame themselves.

The simple fact of having failed to prevent the death is enough to provoke guilt feelings. Luzzi describes his experience: "I knew it was irrational, but I somehow felt responsible for my wife's death. I regretted that I wasn't with her that morning. And although I had tried to take good care of Katherine, I could not shake the feeling that I had failed to protect her."[132] Bereaved people often use considerable ingenuity to demonstrate ways that they were at fault: They should have recognized something amiss; they shouldn't have done something that figured in the causal sequence of events that led to the death; they should have intervened and thereby made the causal chain different.[133]

Social Alienation

One's social identity is foundering, too. Bereavement alters relationships across the board, and it introduces feelings of alienation toward others. Fuchs refers to grief's "exclusivity," meaning that "its gravity and authority do not allow for opening oneself to other, possibly competing feelings and related activities," which might connect one with other living people.[134] The often-noted tendency of people to withdraw may be in part a matter of avoidance of a world that seems to go on as if nothing has happened. To the bereaved, those who do not recognize that the world has changed seem entirely out of touch.[135] Others' continuing with their ordinary routines seems to rub it in. Bereaved people may feel distant even from those who offer their sympathy and assistance, feeling that however well-meaning, they do understand the extremity of one's situation.

Ironically, the death of a loved one often intensifies one's feelings of affiliation with the person. Even if this does not take the form of identification or introjection, the bereaved often feel strongly protective of the deceased, perhaps in compensation for the obvious failure to have successfully protected the person from death. This, too, puts pressure on relationships with other people. Any behavior perceived as a slight to the departed is taken to be inexcusable. Many a bereaved person has written off an erstwhile friend or a family member who is interpreted as showing insufficient respect for the deceased. And people may not be aware of their infractions. Patrick Stokes suggests that friends and family members of the deceased are often vigilant in assessing the attitudes that they ascribe to people's behavior, noting that many "become distressed by strangers assuming a too-easy intimacy" on internet sites.[136]

Social interactions are also complicated by the reactions of other people, however well-meaning. The intensity and distressing character of one's emotions in bereavement disposes one to confide in others. Folk psychology terms this the urge to "get it off your chest." The desire to communicate about emotional experiences seems to be especially pronounced in the case of emotions of great intensity, which are typically reported to more people and more frequently than less powerful emotions.[137] But those on the receiving end typically place caps on such interactions. Past a certain point, those who are approached do not want to hear any more. They can become frustrated with what they interpret as a seeming lack of resilience on the part of the confiding person. They may also want to avoid hearing reports that may result in their becoming upset themselves.[138] Subtly or unsubtly, they make it evident that they are not, or are no longer, receptive to what the person wants to say.[139]

This "ceiling effect," which attends any instance of communicating about a distressing emotional experience, is only one of many externally imposed difficulties a bereaved person may encounter in their interactions. One's social situation may have been adversely impacted by the death, particularly if the deceased was a family member, and this alters how one is regarded.[140] But even without major changes to one's social status, stigma is attached to bereavement, as Colin Murray Parkes observes.[141] Others' recognition that a person is grieving affects all their interactions with the person. Embarrassment and awkwardness are manifest in face-to-face conversations. Others feel uncertain of what to say, and they are fearful that they might say something wrong. Even when all parties approach interaction with the best of will, the atmosphere tends to be stilted.

Most people are sympathetic and feel they should offer condolences and assistance. But this sense of obligation itself can interfere with spontaneity in conversations, even when both parties desire connection. If the bereaved person is closely identified with the deceased in the mind of a third person, conversations between that person and the bereaved seem haunted by the absence of the deceased. The deceased is likely to be very much in mind, if only subliminally, for both parties, and this can disrupt feelings of rapport. The fact that those who offer sympathy are often individually grieving over the death can add further complexity to interactions because both parties are experiencing the disorientation characteristic of grief. Both are likely affected by the sense of fragility that bereavement brings, and they may apprehend each other, and other people generally, as powerless to dispel their sense of isolation.[142]

In general, what has hitherto been the social status quo has been radically altered, and even the most stable relationships with surviving people are up for renegotiation. This applies even to those who are very close to the bereaved. Bonds with those who provide support may be reinforced or intensified, while relationships with others may be curtailed or terminated. The idea of "finding out who your real friends are" in times of crisis certainly applies, and the recognitions involved can be momentous. They can result in a transformed sense of the relative significance of many relationships.

At the same time, grieving individuals can feel pressure from other people's reactions to their grief behavior, not only with respect to what they say, but also in connection with one's comportment more generally. As previously noted, negative reactions to a person's display of grief can prompt self-policing and emotional suppression. Newland, speaking as among the grieving, observes, "When we fail to don the mask, we invite being regarded as gloomy and self-involved."[143] Rinofner-Kreidl refers to the feedback loop in which others' responses affect the further behavior of the grief-stricken. "To a large extent, it is the intricate psychosocial dynamics involved in it that is responsible for grief's complexity."[144]

Disorientation and incoherence in one's experience are so pervasive in bereavement that Attig rightly describes it as a breakdown of a world. Kelly calls it "a second thrownness," alluding to Martin Heidegger's description of human experience as characterized by finding ourselves at every point already "thrown" into the world.[145] In the debilitated situation of bereavement, aesthetic activities are useful for addressing some of one's needs. In the chapters that follow, I will indicate ways in which aesthetic practices are beneficial for dealing with a wide range of obstacles that bereavement presents to moving forward in one's life. I will begin in the following chapter by considering ways that certain aesthetic practices can provide orientation and reassurance.

4
Aesthetic Resources for Orientation and Reassurance

Although often lacking motivation, the bereaved find themselves facing a massive agenda. This agenda may include dealing with many practical obligations, particularly if one is the next of kin to the deceased. One needs to plan for the funeral and the handling of remains, notify people, and begin to deal with the person's estate. But even to undertake these efforts, one needs to find some way to cope with the situation.

In this chapter, I will consider some types of aesthetic experience that facilitate coping. I will first discuss the basic aesthetic activity of attending to sensory objects and their features. Moments of aesthetic openness and appreciation of physical objects can counter the impression in bereavement that one's grounding presuppositions about the world have become fundamentally untrustworthy. Appreciation of certain physical objects and their features can also serve as a surrogate form of connection with the deceased. I will also draw attention to the reassurance offered by music, another kind of sensory "object," which has a tactile impact that can lend a kind of emotional support.

I will go on to consider resources that may be found in recollected interactions with artworks. These previous experiences almost certainly provided occasions for taking one's bearings in circumstances that differ from those of everyday life. To the extent that one succeeded in meeting orientational challenges in those experiences, they offer testimony to one's ability to navigate in unfamiliar circumstances, encouraging self-confidence despite the bizarreness of the current situation. Certain artworks can also provide templates that are useful for mapping aspects of this new terrain.

AESTHETIC REASSURANCE FROM SENSORY OBJECTS

Material Objects and Physical Properties

Bereavement, as we have noted, makes people doubt the reliability of much that they had previously taken for granted. Trust in even the most basic regularities in experience can be unsteady. Shocked by the deceased person's loss of physical connection with the world, one's own seems rather tenuous, and the lack of sleep that is common in bereavement may reinforce this impression. In these circumstances, tactile contact with physical objects can be experienced as grounding.

The mere physical materiality of objects can be appreciated and relished. Most of the time, the fact that a thing is physically existent does not command much attention apart from certain philosophical arguments. In bereavement, however, the situation is different. The absence of the deceased from the corporeal world and the impossibility of physical contact with the person is acutely salient. One is all too aware that living beings can pass out of existence, and this can make a thing's physical presence appear to be a matter worthy of notice.

It may seem odd to say that we can appreciate objects' physical materiality or consider this materiality as a property. Nevertheless, bereavement highlights the fact that whatever other properties an object has, its tangible reality—its having physical characteristics at all—is not to be taken for granted. One might regard material existence as a property in these circumstances, for bereavement makes it evident that material being is contingent. While it may require taking a rather unusual receptive stance, it is certainly possible to appreciate a thing's simple presence, its being in one's world. Although one may also value other specific features, an object's physicality itself can be attended to and treasured.[1]

One might attend to physical things with new eyes and ears and hands, regarding them now as fellow survivors in this strange new world. Such regard for the physical reality of objects, even if abbreviated and only occasional, strikes me as a type of aesthetic appreciation, albeit of a rather unusual nature. I recall, for example, picking up an apple while I was in deep grief over the death of a mentor. Its sheer tangibility seemed startling and rather moving, even before I took a bite.

Besides the welcome fact of persisting in the world, physical objects have properties that may render them aesthetically appealing or striking. The attention these attract may also prompt feelings of greater grounding in the material world. Objects that are experienced as beautiful along traditional lines (that is, having clear boundaries, with elements that are harmoniously interrelated) can be especially heartening. In a situation in which things seem to have fallen apart, such objects reassuringly demonstrate that at least some things still hang together.[2]

Objects that exhibit aesthetically appealing qualities are also well-designed to counter the tendency to feel while grieving that nothing is worthwhile. These objects strike one as deserving one's attention, and this is a step away from apathy. Aesthetic appreciation of well-constructed objects encourages the conviction that some good things in life remain. Taking satisfaction in such objects can also remind the bereaved, even though circumstances have left them feeling numb and somewhat deadened, that they themselves are alive. Beauty, as Kant contends, "carries with it directly a feeling of life's being furthered."[3]

Personal Effects

Independent of their aesthetically attractive qualities, physical objects that are associated with the deceased have a powerful and complex aesthetic impact. Solitude is often the context in which a grieving person attends to them, giving rise to poignant reflections.[4] The strong awareness that the deceased is now absent creates a situation in which these objects can seem to come forth from their surroundings on their own, forcing themselves on the bereaved person's awareness. Because the life that they accompanied has been broken off, personal effects now commandeer attention. In this respect, they are akin to the broken tool, discussed by Heidegger in *Being in Time*, that attracts a kind of notice that did not occur when it was functioning smoothly.[5] Personal effects similarly draw attention to themselves because they cannot recede into their various practical roles, as they did when the deceased made use of them.

Personal effects had a place in the daily life of the person, and their penumbra of significance derives from this association. They have evident relational value, independent of their intrinsic appeal. This is a reason they are often cherished even when they are damaged by years of wear. Yet interacting with personal effects can also be painful. They may strike the bereaved as disquieting, even if they are to some extent comforted by them, too.

Objects regarded as recently embedded in the deceased person's life can reinforce awareness of the person's absence. Consider the tossed-aside sweater or the empty boots lying where the person placed them, the pen on the desk that remains ready to hand, the sofa pillow indented by the last time the person sat there. All of these tangible reminders of the person's recent presence make awareness of his or her permanent unavailability particularly vivid. Thomas Attig describes the ambivalence of "relearning life with a father's chair," which involves "all at once . . . realizing that he will never sit in it again, feeling a range of emotions, deciding how to behave around the chair or what to do with it, negotiating with others who may have other preferences about the chair, and experiencing connection with father in a new way."[6]

Encounters with objects the deceased person used or handled may bring the loss of quotidian intimacy into focus. Noticing that the sofa pillow is still contoured from the lost loved one's having leaned against it may lead one to attend to the details of the pattern of indentation. This may sharpen one's anguish, as if one is dangling before oneself the still fresh evidence of the person's erstwhile presence while reminding oneself that he or she is permanently gone. Sonali Deraniyagala dwells upon such details in her grief memoir, *Wave*, written after she simultaneously lost her parents, her husband, and her two sons when a tsunami overtook the resort where they were staying in Sri Lanka. While acknowledging her growing ability to face certain items in their London home a few years later, she reports that others remained overwhelmingly upsetting. "I dare not open his cookbook. It would be too much to see a chili oil stain on a barbecued squid recipe or a trace of a mustard seed on the aubergine curry page of his *'Ceylon Daily News' Cookery Book*."[7]

Such objects are simultaneously seen as embedded in the person's life before the death and present in the aftermath, placing the person who beholds them in a position that Peter Goldie describes as the "agonizingly ironic" position of any grieving individual remembering pre-loss events. Such events are recalled from a standpoint that would have been impossible at the time they occurred, for they are now seen in light of the death.[8] So, too, are the objects that belonged to the deceased. They stimulate our memories of the person, but we see them as possessions of someone who has died and is accordingly absent.

Matthew Ratcliffe describes the complexity of the situation in terms of our sense of possibilities in relation to the person. Objects we associate with the deceased arouse memories of the pre-loss time when the person made use of them and our own possibilities bound up with the person were open. They ignite anticipations that are not sustainable in the post-loss situation. For us, these items point to the "actual or possible presence" of the deceased and thus arouse expectations in connection with the person, but the situation in the world undermines them. Objects that the person used continue to point "to possibilities *for* that person, but we experience those possibilities *as* negated." Such collisions of anticipations and actual circumstances reinforce the impression that the world is fragmented, prompting us to anticipate interaction with the deceased while simultaneously seeing all future possibilities in relation to the person as precluded. Personal effects give rise to expectancies that are recurrently disappointed, manifesting the "interplay of possibilities and their negation" that is pervasive in grief.[9]

Most bereaved people have probably found themselves startled when some seemingly innocuous object functions like an emotional booby trap. A to-do list scrawled on a scrap of paper, the person's cell phone, even some item of clothing that one might have long hoped would be discarded—any of these things can launch paroxysms of tears. A grieving person might interpret the whole environment as menacing because virtually any familiar object might be a site of emotional ambush.

Recall, however, Thomas Fuchs's comment that the "shortness of the breath and respiratory spasm" commonly experienced in bereavement is "intermittently relieved by sighing, crying or sobbing." Crying from time to time can be a release, alleviating physical and emotion tension. That beholding an object can precipitate tears is not necessarily an objection to such encounters. Nor is it an indication that such objects are negatively valued by grieving people. Quite often the fact of a close connection with the deceased is experienced as the basis for cherishing an object, and that link is a precondition for the item's overpowering impact. Being subject to unanticipated emotional eruptions is an unpleasant form of vulnerability, but the object that precipitates this reaction may still be experienced as precious by virtue of its association with the deceased.

In appreciating personal effects of a departed loved one, a survivor may interpret them as representing the person's entire life. Heidegger describes the shoes depicted in one of Van Gogh's paintings as calling up the entire world in which their owner made use of them. Heidegger's approach may not illuminate much about painting, and Meyer Schapiro has shown that the world of the peasant woman that Heidegger envisions is a rather fanciful projection onto a painting of Van Gogh's own boots.[10] Nevertheless, the suggestion that attending to an object can elicit a vision of an entire world is apt for the way that items regularly used by a departed person can evoke thoughts of the person's life, if also the rupture that has made it irretrievable.

The reference to the person's entire life can be consoling. Objects utilized by the deceased can revive memories of the person being in command of his or her powers, in contrast with the impression of the lifeless body the bereaved may have recently encountered. Items the person habitually used support recollections of him or her as active and lively, not as deprived of agency. Holding such an image of the person in mind can be a source of comfort.

A further positive aspect of interacting with personal effects is that they can provide openings for renewing one's bond with a departed loved one.

Nina Jakoby observes that the person's possessions represent "the self of the deceased" to the bereaved.[11] Handling such objects can serve as a proxy for physical contact with the departed, something that bereaved people often crave. Judith Simpson draws attention to this effect, particularly in connection with the dead person's garments. Because "clothes shape people and people shape clothes," she argues, "personhood comes to extend beyond the margins of the body to permeate clothing and valued possessions."[12] The object becomes a veritable medium for bodily connection with the person. It is as though by touching an object that the person used in life, one is virtually touching the person one loves. For many years after the death of my late husband, wearing his gloves seemed a consoling surrogate for holding hands. Simpson refers to the appeal of "heavy coats and jumpers previously used by the deceased: warm and comforting garments which '[mimic] the effect of an embrace.'"[13]

Personal effects draw one's attention more to their role in a relational matrix than to their specific aesthetic qualities as such. Their particular properties as objects may be noted and admired, but often as pointing to their connection with the deceased. The wrinkles in the leather of a parent's wallet or the tarnish on a grandparent's mirror can add to the sense that the object has "lived" along with the beloved person. These signs of aging are part of what is treasured, even though they might count as aesthetic flaws in relation to the object's original design. They, too, contribute to the aesthetic impact of these objects.

Personal effects of loved ones do not constitute the only class of objects whose aesthetic value can be enhanced by signs of wear. In discussing ruins, Carolyn Korsmeyer draws attention to their "age value" (dependent on "the marks of wear, damage, and deterioration"), which she sees as having "an immediate aesthetic impact" because it brings to mind much that is absent.[14] Leon Rosenstein similarly suggests that while the patina of age in an antique may either enhance or diminish the aesthetic impression of *formal* features, it increases "the object's material (as opposed to purely formal) aesthetic appeal" because it provides us with a sense of connection with earlier times: "In antiques, historicality is patently tactile—we feel, we can hold and caress, the age."[15]

Octavio Paz, too, sees the patina of age as an aesthetic enhancement in handcrafted objects, one linked with our sense that these objects share our finite temporality with us.

> The thing that is handmade has no desire to last for thousands upon thousands of years, nor is it possessed by a frantic drive to die an early death. It follows the appointed round of days, it drifts with us as the current carries us along together, it wears away little by little, it neither seeks death

> nor denies it: it accepts it. . . . Craftsmanship is the heartbeat of human time. . . . The craftsman's handiwork teaches us to die and hence teaches us to live.[16]

Speaking for all mortals, not just those who are bereaved, Paz sees handcrafted objects as comforting teachers. Because they live our temporally limited lives along with us, they serve as our companions as well as our servants, and they can also serve as guides to life, according to Paz.

While personal effects may not be guides, the wear they exhibit may remind us of the life they have been part of. They function now as traces that can make us mindful of the loved one actively embracing life. Although we might see this as emphasizing our loss, it might alternatively make us aware of the person's having lived a life with its own specific fullness. Or perhaps we hover between the two perspectives. Such reflections are bittersweet, and yet they can afford a degree of consolation.

Music as Sensory Object

Before leaving this discussion of aesthetic encounters with sensory objects in bereavement, let us briefly note the sensory impact of music. Music can play many valuable roles in the context of bereavement, a topic I will consider further in the following chapter.[17] But here we should note that it is sensory, whatever else it may be. Music is a different type of object than those we have been considering, which in many cases are items one can lift from a table. Despite these differences, however, we appreciate music in part on account of its sensory nature, and this contributes to its consoling power.

Philosopher Charles Nussbaum draws attention to music's haptic character, its effect on our sense of touch. Music's bodily impact is powerful, for it addresses our auditory and tactile senses as well as our motor system, and it literally enters the body through the ears and the skin. While music's effect on a grieving listener no doubt depends on the character of the specific piece and associations connected with it, Nussbaum suggests a partial explanation of why certain music can be soothing in these circumstances. "Fine musical sound has the characteristics of a loving touch," he observes, "not always gentle, but loving nonetheless." He adds that this "real touch effect of music" is what "endows it with its curiously immediate emotionally gripping quality," and when well performed it can give "rise to a delight in intimacy."[18] I will have more to say about music's potential effects on grieving listeners. But if Nussbaum is right, one reason that excellent music can reassure the grieving is that it has the effect of a loving embrace—an encouraging prospect for anyone who could really use a big hug.

AESTHETIC EXPERIENCE AS PRECEDENT

The use of the adjective *surreal* to describe the experience of grieving is far from unusual.[19] The term has become sufficiently commonplace that its reference to the surrealist art movement may go largely unnoticed, but this usage suggests that many have found some aptness in the implicit comparison. Surrealistic artworks are startling because of their bizarre juxtapositions of images that are hard to integrate. They clash with our expectations in a manner reminiscent of the disruption of presuppositions commonly experienced in grief.

I submit that recognizing comparisons between aspects of grief and experiences with artworks and other aesthetic objects can help bereaved people feel more comfortable with the unfamiliar aspects of their current frame of mind and the world as it now seems. The departures from habituated expectations, the unusual temporality, and the surges of disjointed memories commonly experienced in bereavement have correlates in aesthetic experiences. Recognizing this can encourage confidence in one's ability to function despite the many ways in which both oneself and the world now seem strange.

Many people who are grieving are so disoriented and have such disjointed streams of consciousness that they fear they are going crazy.[20] The impact of the loss on their mental processes unsettles them, and they flounder from despair over their perceived incapacities. I will discuss several ways that they might find reassurance through noting commonalities between the challenges of coping with the phenomenological strangeness of grief and certain cognitive tasks involved in engagement with aesthetic phenomena. The strategy of observing these similarities may seem bizarrely self-focused and second order, but I think it may be useful in the early stage of grieving, when one may feel that one's ability to function as an agent has been compromised by grief-induced changes to the character and contents of conscious experience. Recognizing that one has developed competencies in aesthetic contexts that one might draw upon in one's unusual frame of mind can help one feel capable of some degree of agency despite the many involuntary changes to mental functioning that bereavement has brought about.

Engaging with Unfamiliar Scenarios

Initially, bereavement involves a sense of unreality. One can scarcely believe that the loved one is gone, and yet one needs to engage in actions that are premised on this fact. Even while hovering in a liminal state between disbelief and unhappy awareness of the loss, one must function practically and deal with the perhaps unprecedented demands of the situation. And yet, in both subtle and obvious ways, the death of a loved one disrupts one's expectations and the standing set of goals, models, and schemas one has relied upon to navigate everyday life. One may feel incapacitated by this circumstance to the point of responding with alarm or despair.

Prior experiences with art can help one to defuse these self-critical reactions, which tend to compound one's difficulties. The challenges of adjusting to the world in the absence of the loved one bears comparison to the challenges of orienting oneself within the counterfactual "worlds" that are presented by many artworks. By recognizing the similarity between the two cases, grieving people can gain confidence that they have some resources for orienting themselves when encountering the unexpected.

Attending and responding to scenarios not taken to be actual is fundamental to engaging with many artworks. This has been the situation whenever one has entertained narratives that one recognizes as fictional. Enjoying a movie such as Robert Zemeckis's *Back to the Future,* for example, requires imagining circumstances that do not prevail in reality.[21] Marty McFly, the main character, goes back in time and interacts with his parents as high school students. He is warned that certain changes to the past would make his own existence precarious, and his teenage mother's attraction to him gives rise to the danger that she will not fall in love with his father and he will never be born. Ultimately, however, he changes the story just enough that all goes well, and present-day reality is altered for the better. When Marty returns to the present, a former bully has been subdued; his depressed, alcoholic, and slovenly mother has become lively, fit, and tidy; his pathologically underconfident father has become a self-assured, successful novelist; his parents' lackluster marriage has regained its spark; and a friend whose life had been at risk has protected himself by taking precautions based on information he'd learned in the past from Marty the time-traveler.

The film's over-the-top happy ending is enjoyable, but certainly not credible. To enjoy the movie, one entertains premises that one does not believe—that a machine in the form of a luxury sports car could enable time travel, that time travelers could selectively intervene in the past, that adverse side effects of meddling with the temporal sequence could be avoided, and so on. We simply entertain the film's counterfactual premises. Indeed, part of the pleasure of watching comes from following along to see how a story based on these premises might play out.[22]

Of course, the situation of a bereaved person is very different from that of the movie watcher. The bereaved person is not entertaining a counterfactual premise; the premise in view is all too real. He or she is trying on the belief that a beloved person has died but wavering in being able to hang on to it. While struggling to accept the new reality, the overwhelming impression is uncertainty as to what is what.

Yet second-order misgivings about one's inability to either completely believe or disbelieve can be alleviated if one recognizes the middle ground that is actually familiar from many experiences with art. Enjoying artistic presentations of fictional worlds that differ in marked ways from the real one builds on our ability to entertain possibilities without fully endorsing them. This entertaining of fictional circumstances has often been called "the willing suspension of disbelief," and recognizing this may help grieving individuals to regard their current frame of mind as less abnormal. Previous experiences of suspended disbelief in connection with narrative fictions provide precedents for taking on board what one does not fully believe. In both bereavement and engagement with fiction, what one has known about the world is partially deactivated. That one can linger in the experience of entertaining alternative realities while engaging with fiction makes it clear that one can entertain possibilities and formulate expectations without cognitive certainty or conviction.

Thus, reflecting on prior experiences with fictions might help a bereaved person to feel somewhat less panicked at the prospect of having to function with an unsettled framework of beliefs and expectations. The realm of artistic fictions has offered many previous occasions for proceeding on assumptions that one does not believe. That one has engaged with such works demonstrates that one *can* orient and mentally track developments in a terrain that is in some ways unlike the world as one has generally assumed it to be. This background can help to quell fear in the face of the bizarre character of bereavement and to instill confidence that one can cognitively function even in deeply unfamiliar circumstances.

Practice in Navigating Tensions

Self-doubt about one's ability to function in the face of the weirdness of bereavement can also be mitigated by recognizing that previous engagements with artworks have given one considerable practice in coping cognitively with tensions among various aspects of how things appear. Certain artworks present themes or characters that are sufficiently complex, for example, that we have conflicting expectations and attitudes toward what is presented. Prior interaction with such artworks has given us practice in contending with ongoing tensions.

Again, there are obvious differences between the willing engagement with tensions in art and the involuntary struggle with the many incompatibilities that seem present in grief (those between expectations and reality, between emotional responses of disparate character, between an abstract awareness of the forward march of calendar time and one's sense of time's total irrelevance, and so forth). Nevertheless, one can draw comfort from awareness that one is up to the cognitive challenge of keeping incompatible perspectives in view and navigating amidst tensions that are hard to reconcile. Again, recognizing that a comparison can be made between the kinds of cognitive demands in the two instances can bolster self-confidence.

Artworks that have developed our cognitive facility with managing tensions are particularly evident in the case of media involving temporally extended presentations, such as literature, film, music, and other performing arts. Works in these categories often involve tensions among themes, which may (or may not) be resolved by the work's conclusion. To make sense of such works, one's attention needs to float, so that one focuses at different moments on different aspects of the content, which may seem incompatible with each other and provoke quite different responses. Tracking and understanding the work's development requires holding these aspects together in one's mind, even at points when it is hard to see how the tensions might resolve.[23]

For example, many musical works in the Western classical tradition create both large-scale and small-scale tensions that are generated over the course of the music. Often tensions are heightened as patterns of contrasting character develop as a work proceeds. These tensions involve tendencies of conflicting character, and our attention is drawn to the contrasts that seem to require reconciliation. Typically, it is eventually provided, but complete resolution of tendencies occurs only at the end of a movement or work.[24] Such works (when well-constructed) provide occasions for practice in being patient with inconsistent or incongruent impressions. They have also encouraged recognition that resolutions can emerge after protracted periods in which they are unavailable. This realization can help grieving people to feel that patience can be warranted even through extended experiences that seem incoherent.

The appeal of many fictional narratives also depends on dissonant tendencies that are sustained over the course of the plot. *The Sopranos* television series projects its central character, Tony Soprano, as both a sympathetic family man and a cold-blooded killer.[25] The tension between these aspects of his character are hard to keep in view simultaneously, and yet the plot of each episode reinforces the premise that both apply and that each characterization needs to be qualified by the other. The fascination of the series stems in part from the instability of the viewer's reaction to Tony. If one has engaged with such works, one has gone along with premises and patterns that provisionally seem to clash and do not promise any clear resolution. Not only has one gone along—such knotty arrangements are often part of what one enjoys.

In television series, one season may end without a decision having been made about whether there will be another, and the season finale may involve only incomplete resolutions of themes and subplots.[26] Although it was clear in the case of the *Sopranos* that the sixth season would be the last, the tension between the two aspects of Tony reveals a fracture in his character that is not resolved. Presumably, it cannot be resolved if his psychiatrist is right in her judgment at the end of the series that he is a sociopath, a verdict that precipitates her dropping him as a patient. We may or may not be similarly willing to categorize him so definitively by the final episode. I am not arguing that we *should* take shifting views of him, though the series encourages us to do so. My point is that if we have cooperated with narrative works or series whose artistic effect trades on divergent facets of characters, we have managed to keep these facets in mind without settling on which is most important.

Reflecting on this fact can help us realize that we do not need to settle on a stable interpretation to make any sense of what is happening, and that we can let divergent impressions arise within us without a sense of complete orientational breakdown. To generalize, as we engage with temporally unfolding artworks, we are often prompted to reconsider earlier impressions by the introduction of inconsistent material. Awareness that such works have taught us to juggle seemingly inharmonious impressions can help us recognize that we have some practice in tolerating uncertainties for extended spans of time. This recognition on the part of those who are grieving might help build up their morale as they attempt to cope with mental contents that have conflicting implications.

Of course, the jarring inconsistencies in the experience of bereavement are unlike those in artistic encounters with tensions in transition. One anticipates that the artists have shaped their works so that the generated tensions will reach at least relative resolution. In fiction we might enjoy making guesses at various points about how the plot will unfold, but we need not act to work out tensions on our own as we do within bereavement. Tracking good artworks' developments can also be a source of satisfaction in itself. Artworks are often designed to make it somewhat challenging to monitor developments, and tracking them successfully confirms one's competence as a listener, viewer, or reader. Bereavement, by contrast, challenges any sense of one's own competence, and reckoning with experiential tensions must occur in the absence of any assurance that resolution can be achieved.

Even so, prior interaction with artworks that involve navigating dissonances and inconsistencies may help one to feel some degree of equanimity while facing the tensions involved in bereavement. Formally, at least, artworks are often designed to show that seemingly conflicting facets can be brought into an orderly whole. One's experience of relating to such works shows that one is able to navigate in unsteady circumstances and to keep track of developments that often seem disconnected or irreconcilable.

A possible objection is that feeling self-assurance in bereavement is not necessarily a good thing. Line Ryberg Ingerslev contends that grief calls us into question in a fundamental way. In grief we confront what she sees as "vocational" questions, such as "why must I live on without you, why must I live at all, how can I go on?"[27] This, she says, brings one to a halt, and the existential struggle of determining how to live in the absence of the beloved person is ongoing, though she thinks that one can find meaning in continued relational activity going forward. I think she is right about this.

The reinforcement of self-confidence I refer to in connection with artworks should not be construed as a safeguard against existential self-questioning. Here I am concerned with a more superficial kind of self-confidence, the opposite of the feeling that the situation is too much to handle. Having some level of faith that one can maintain a degree of composure while grieving can preempt the further burden of second-order, self-denigrating judgments about one's own inability to manage. Such judgments do not facilitate confrontation with the deep existential questions that bereavement raises. They can in fact forestall the kind of spiritual grappling that Ingerslev describes. Confidence that one can maintain a degree of poise in the face of certain symptoms of grief can, by contrast, help clear the way for dealing with the deeper existential issues grief involves.

The Temporality of Aesthetic Experience

Further reassurance can arise with the recognition of similarities between the unusual temporality that may be experienced in grief and the temporal character of aesthetic experience, which is often contrasted with the temporality of everyday life. As we observed in the previous chapter, grieving people often feel dissociated from time as ordinarily experienced. While this may be experienced without judgment, it is also possible that bereaved individuals may interpret temporal alterations in their experience as disturbing and as signs of personal incapacity. Such second-order judgments may be mitigated by the recognition that in connection with art one has often had experiences that do not involve the usual temporality of everyday life. Art is not unique in involving a nonstandard temporality. The temporality of religious experience, according to Mircea Eliade, is also distinct from everyday time, involving a time in which one is "present" at mythic events.[28] But most artworks also immerse us in a temporal field that is distinguished from that of daily life, and this does not depend on belief in a mythological reality.

Many thinkers, both historical and contemporary, have contended that aesthetic perception involves dislocation from our usual temporality. For some, aesthetic experience (which they do not confine to encounters with artworks) transports us into a *nunc stans*, a state in which time's movement does not apply. Arthur Schopenhauer, for example, asserts, "The person involved in this perception is no longer an individual, for in such perception the individual has lost himself; he is pure will-less, painless, timeless subject of knowledge." The aesthetically observant individual is pulled into a timeless state in which "it is immediately of no importance whether it is this tree or its ancestor that flourished a thousand years ago, and whether the contemplator is this individual, or any other living anywhere and at any time."[29]

Psychologists Nico Frijda and Louise Sundararajan also think that aesthetic experience (whether of art, nature, or everyday objects) involves a temporality that differs from the experience of time as a steady passage of causally connected events. By contrast with Schopenhauer's description of a timeless state, however, they characterize the temporality of aesthetic savoring as involving a distinctive kind of attentional pacing. "Savoring takes time. One dwells on one's object of interest and the experience it generates. Savoring involves a lingering that slows down or halts the pragmatic progress."[30] While Frijda and Sundararajan's account differs from Schopenhauer's, they agree that aesthetic experience involves a break from tracking the steady flow of everyday time, suggesting a basis for comparison with the atypical temporality that may be experienced in bereavement.

Recalling the temporal character of previous aesthetic experiences might help us, when grieving, to feel more comfortable with being in a temporally altered state. Aesthetic savoring or contemplation involves departure from our everyday synchronization with the social world's routine. In such experiences our position is somewhat resonant with that of the grieving person whose experience of time is anomalous. In both cases goal-driven focus and attunement with the temporal progress of consensus time are absent. We can recognize the situation of not moving along with routine time as actually familiar from aesthetic experience, and this recognition might make departures from a sense of time as a steady linear sequence in bereavement seem less bizarre than might otherwise be the case.

Besides the altered temporality of aesthetic experience itself, artistic use of nonlinear temporal sequences can also help diminish discomfort over seemingly disordered thought processes that may be experienced in bereavement. The interruption of the flow of an ongoing plot by a series of flashbacks is a conventional device across many artistic media (film, literary fiction, and graphic novels, for example), and this may make occasions when one's attention is disrupted by spontaneous floods of memories seem less confounding.

An effective use of flashbacks to portray the mental framework of the bereaved is available in both John Le Carré's novel *The Constant Gardener* and the eponymous film based on it, directed by Fernando Meirelles.[31] In one scene in the film, the protagonist, returning to his home on a rainy night soon after the death of his wife, sees through the glass of the front door as he inserts his key. He flashes back to occasions when he was at home there with his wife. The tone of the memories is happy, but he stops in his tracks, incapable of entering the house because he's overcome with tears. Even the most rapturous memories are as if behind glass, tormenting because he cannot reach them.[32]

This description of the scene may make it sound more oppressive than comforting, and it certainly is for the character. But as an external representation, this scene can help lessen the distress grieving individuals may feel about undergoing such upsurges of memories themselves. The inclusion of this scene in the film amounts to a kind of public acknowledgment of this type of phenomenon. This depiction might provide comfort to bereaved people who experience such memory flows by revealing that such experiences are recognized possibilities in grief. This artistic testimony that others have had experiences like their own can help grieving people feel less outside the range of normal humanity.

Of course, most nonlinear sequences in art are not designed to portray the parade of memories of the deceased that grieving people confront. But other kinds of nonlinear sequences can also help bereaved people to feel more comfortable with their experiences of this phenomenon. At the very least, they can help them to recognize that nonlinear ideation is not such a strange thing. In addition, artistic interruptions to the linear flow of time also provide at least a metaphorical means for describing the character of floods of images to others, a possibility that might ease feelings of isolation.

Perhaps nonlinear sequences also give one a foothold for starting to sort through one's impressions and emotions. One can recognize in one's seemingly chaotic thoughts and feelings a pattern that is familiar from art and popular culture. Coming to grips with the confusing way that one's mind is working in grief requires mentally stepping back and observing patterns that one can label and recognize when they recur. Even to be able to identify involuntary shifts of memories as nonlinear is to gain some reflective distance from these experiences. To be able to compare such parades of disjointed images with nonlinear sequences in artworks is to have at hand a model for thinking about these experiences. One regains confidence that one *can* put some order in one's experience by doing so, and making such comparisons can help in this effort. Even before that, one can draw reassurance from awareness that following such temporally disordered sequences in films has not (in most cases) caused one to lose the direction of their overall plots. The implication is that being assaulted by disorganized memories does not mean that one has lost the ability to think in organized sequences.

ARTISTIC TEMPLATES AND COMPANIONSHIP

Templates Mapping the Territory

In considering the benefits of comparing features of some kinds of aesthetic experiences and phenomenological oddities in grief, I have drawn attention to one's overall background of relating to artworks and other aesthetic objects. In this section, I will focus instead on prior experiences of specific works and their components. Certain artworks can provide templates that can help one to organize one's impressions of what is happening. They also offer testimony that some of the strange aspects of the current situation are not unique to oneself.

As an example, we might turn to Amy Tan's novel *The Hundred Secret Senses*. The novel recounts developments in the relationship between the narrator, Olivia, and her Chinese half-sister, Kwan, who believes that she remembers former lives and that she can see and interact with the dead. Olivia and Kwan are daughters of the same father, but Olivia is American born, while Kwan grew up in China and emigrated to the United States as an adult. After Kwan's immigration, Olivia has found her to be something of an embarrassment because of her poor English and her non-American ways. Part 3 of the novel ends with Kwan's disappearance after she steps into the recesses of a cave. By this point in the story, Kwan has persuaded Olivia and her estranged husband, Simon, to visit China with her, hoping to bring them back together. They have been exploring an area filled with rocks, ravines, caves, and mountains. Simon and Olivia have had a fight, and Simon has headed off on his own. Kwan attempts to comfort Olivia, and they have an extended interaction. Kwan says that she is going to go find Simon and that she will be right back, and then she heads into a cave that she and Olivia have climbed to. Before long, Olivia realizes that she no longer knows where Kwan is. As part 3 ends, Simon reappears, and Olivia sees that Kwan is not with him. Despite Kwan's absence at this point, as readers we still feel that we are in the company of the two sisters and their personal energies, which have become familiar over the course of the book.

When part 4 begins, this sense of personable connection with the women is gone. The narrator's tone is flatter than before as she details what happened. Now days are numbered in relation to Kwan's disappearance and punctuated by dealings with officialdom and disappointing updates from those searching for her.[33] The break between parts is the break between loss and the aftermath. Olivia's panicked horror when she realizes that Kwan has vanished is replaced with the somber rhythm and flat tone of what follows. This brings into focus the common shift after a loved one's death from being in a relatively normal (though possibly emotionally intense) condition to a deadened version of oneself, now confronting the affect-less approach of authorities and institutions that are unaffected by the loss.

Companion Artworks

Narrative presentations of situations that resemble one's circumstances can be a touchstone in bereavement, as we have already seen in connection with *The Constant Gardener*'s portrayal of a widower overtaken by memories. By intimating that others have been in similar circumstances, such representations encourage the impression that it is possible to survive them. In addition, the behavior of their characters suggest possible ways to think through and handle the challenges one is facing.

Arthur Frank uses the term "companion narratives" for stories used as points of reference in dealing with one's own situation. Such stories benefit a person because they "have primacy in conducting that person's perception and subsequent actions. Stories *conduct* persons . . . by indicating what counts as a perceptual foreground, how to evaluate what is perceived, and how to act in response."[34] Frank points out that companion narratives can be good or bad. Narratives can be bad companions when they are discouraging or overly simplistic. Good companion narratives offer consolation and hope, while nevertheless complicating one's thinking about current circumstances, suggesting new perspectives on how to respond. A good companion story helps a person to be him- or herself because in relating it to one's circumstances, one makes it increasingly one's own.[35]

One may engage with multiple companion narratives, and one may also find companionship with central characters. Frank describes a child who makes use of various companion stories, noting that "*Buzz Lightyear* is currently his privileged companion."[36] Companion narratives are particularly welcome when one's situation feels isolating. Like well-known friends, these stories can make suggestions and give one a sense of being understood, while leaving the further trajectory in one's own hands.

I see some similarity between Frank's account of the value of companion stories and Jonathan Lear's discussion of the importance of exemplars. Lear claims that exemplars help us to get an inkling of the elusive idea for which he uses the Greek term *kalon*, which means what is genuinely fine, noble, and beautiful. The *kalon*, when we glimpse it, is wondrous. Whatever exists of spiritual nobility in human actions and achievements is *kalon*. It is the touchstone for human flourishing and for all that makes us rightfully proud to be human beings.

The importance of exemplars, according to Lear, is that they alert us to ways of being and behaving that are *kalon* and to the possibility of embodying them ourselves. They help us to develop "confidence *here and now* in our own emerging powers with the *kalon*." Particularly important are "local exemplars," which he describes as "*the first responders*, as it were, to our need for the experience of something 'higher,' 'noble,' 'beautiful.'"[37] These are people we encounter in our own experience whose character and behavior enlarge our sense of what is possible and make us aware of how fine people can be.

Lear contends that fiction is no substitute for real-life exemplars that we can see as worthy of emulation. We can doubt the realism of a hero in a story, but we cannot deny the possibility of a real person's behavior that we encounter in our actual lives. While this seems undeniable, fictional stories can nevertheless have value as occasions for entertaining possible ways of acting and thinking that may be relevant in real-world contexts (a point that Lear acknowledges). Lear's own account of local exemplars draws attention to the way in which we circle back again and again to an occasion in which we recognized what is *kalon* in a local exemplar's behavior, giving a recalled incident the status of a story that we return to. He also emphasizes the way such incidents activate our imaginations toward elaborating on them, with a focus on *kalon* behavior. The exemplar is idealized in imagination so that the beauty of the behavior "shines forth in some kind of isolation, without the surrounding complexities of the wider world."[38]

This is precisely the kind of imaginative elaboration of something that one finds exemplary that Frank identifies in relation to companion stories. Focusing on some aspect of a story, the person who finds it a good companion uses it as a point of departure for finding a way of acting or responding to a situation that is personally useful. Frank points out that people who use stories as companions often imaginatively alter them in ways that suit their needs. The child who found companionship with Buzz Lightyear extrapolated from events in the *Toy Story* film to events of his own invention. The child had to have a series of surgeries, and in his elaboration of the story, Buzz had to have surgeries, too. Although achieving the *kalon* may not be the basis for all narrative companionship of the sort Frank describes, I can imagine that the dignified manner in which Buzz deals with challenges may have contributed to his attractiveness as a companion, something the child may see as worthy of emulation.

Frank mentions both *Toy Story* and the *Iliad* as companion stories, indicating that stories of various sorts can serve as companions. Joseph Luzzi's grief memoir about the death of his pregnant wife in a car crash, *Through a Dark Wood*, is organized around his relationship to two companion stories, both by Dante, *The Divine Comedy* and *La Vita Nuove*.[39] The latter is an anthology of Dante's poetry with commentaries connecting them to events his life, including his exile from his home city of Florence and his passionate love for Beatrice Portinari, which abides despite her early death. Luzzi compares his grief to Dante's recounted state of exile, and he finds resonances between Dante's devotion to Beatrice and his own enduring love for his late wife. Luzzi's title alludes to the opening of *The Divine Comedy*: "In the middle of our life's journey, I found myself in a dark wood."[40]

Comparing his situation to Dante's (both as epic narrator and as one who has been sentenced to exile), Luzzi speaks of the way the poet's works provided sustenance: "I felt that her death exiled me from what had been my life. Dante's words gave me the language to understand my own profound sense of displacement. More important, they enabled me to connect my anguished state to a work of transcendent beauty."[41] Frank's description of companion stories "conducting" a person aptly describes the role Dante's works served for Luzzi. Consider this passage, in which Luzzi cites a passage from *Paradiso* that served him as "a mantra":

> *You will leave behind everything you love*
> *Most dearly, and this is the arrow*
> *The bow of exile first lets fly.*
>
> No other words could capture how I felt during the four years I struggled to find my way out of the dark wood of grief and mourning. And yet it was only because of his exile that Dante was able to write *The Divine Comedy*. . . . Only in exile did he gain the heaven's-eye view of human life, detached from all earthly allegiances, that enabled him to speak of the soul.[42]

The Divine Comedy, with its tale of traversing hell and purgatory while en route to heaven, helped lead Luzzi through grief, for it provided him with a model for successfully transfiguring heartache. Dante served him as an exemplar for dealing with grief and transforming his suffering into insight.

Although Frank talks about stories, I do not think aesthetic companionship is restricted to stories per se. Artworks in other media, including the visual arts, can also provide companionship and guidance, as Laura Cumming demonstrates. She describes overcoming the depths of grief after the death of her father through her encounter with a painting by Velázquez. Her father had been a painter, and for a time after his death, Cumming could not bear to look at any paintings but his. Later on, she felt it would be appropriate to go see the work of her father's favorite painter, El Greco, while she was on a trip to Madrid. On her way to the part of the Prado where the El Greco paintings are hung, she caught sight of a painting in a room she was passing, and even though it was mostly eclipsed by a tour group, she was mesmerized. The painting she beheld was Velázquez's *Las Meninas*, with its "mirror-bright vision of a little princess, her young maidservants and the artist himself, all gathered in a pool of sunlight at the bottom of a great volume of shadow, an impending darkness that instantly sets the tenor of the scene." She was transfixed by the awareness that all the people depicted are "already dead and gone," yet alive in one's encounter with the painting.[43] Cumming goes on to describe the impact of the painting on her grief:

> The painting I saw that day seems to hold death back from the brink even as it acknowledges our shared human fate. It shows the past in all its mortal beauty, but it also looks forward into the flowing future. Because of Velázquez, these long-lost people will always be there at the heart of the Prado, always waiting for us to arrive; they will never go away, as long as we are there to hold them in sight. *Las Meninas* is like a chamber of the mind, a place where the dead will never die. The gratitude I feel to Velázquez for this greatest of paintings is untold; he gave me the consolation to return to my own life.[44]

Las Meninas served Cumming as a companion artwork, one that reframed her thinking about her relation to her deceased father. So powerful was the painting's impact that she decided to compile "a book of praise for Velázquez." In the course of her research, she discovered a tradesman whose life was turned upside down by his love for a painting he had acquired, which he believed to be Velázquez's missing portrait of Charles the First of England. Her book recounts the story of this man, John Snare, and his love for the painting, but this does not represent an abandonment of her ambition to compile praises of Velázquez. Encomiums on the artist are woven through the book's tale of Snare's fortunes and misfortunes, and the story of the man who let his love for the painting drive (and arguably destroy) his life epitomizes the highest reverence for the artist.

Yet perhaps Cumming's own highest praise is to summarize the vision that *Las Meninas* inspired in her. At the close of the book, she itemizes the deaths of some of the key figures in *Las Meninas,* including that of the artist himself, deaths that come breathtakingly soon after the work was painted. The work is "piercingly sad in its representation of these lost children . . . dead and gone for centuries" and in its hint of what is to come, suggested by the figure in the back, who is on the verge of stepping out of the room and into "that other light, hovering between this world and the next." "But," Cumming follows in the next sentence,

> he does not go, and they do not fade. . . . The figures of the past keep looking into our moment as long as we keep looking back at them. Everything in *Las Meninas* is designed to keep this connection alive forever. The dead are with us, and so are the living consoled. We live in each other's eyes, and our stories need not end.[45]

This understated suggestion is that *Las Meninas* can serve as a companion work for us all. Cumming's account demonstrates the quiet way that a companion work can fortify the grieving. *Las Meninas* gave Cumming a mission that reconnected her with her father, while at the same time renewing her sense of purpose going forward.

The narrative companionship that Frank describes is also available in traditional myths and legends, which might be seen as companion stories shared across entire cultures. Frank is cautious about the way that such stories have sometimes been employed, noting "the Nazi use of Nordic myths as legislated companion stories in political mobilization."[46] Surely, he is right that "legislated companion stories" can be terrible company. Besides their obvious potential to do harm on the broad social scale, they may be poor companions on a personal level, too, since dictated interpretations may supplant the personal interaction that enables one to make these narratives one's own.

Alexander Nehamas suggests the converse case, in which engagement with artworks is comparable to the interaction of true friends. In the case of friends, each is open to being affected and changed by the other. Nehamas describes the impact of artworks in similar terms: "Interacting with works of art changes us in ways we cannot anticipate completely; and it also changes them because, ideally, our interaction, which consists in interpretation, establishes new and previously unknown features of theirs, and gives them to us and perhaps the world with a new face."[47]

Nehamas observes that two friends see each other in ways that are unlike the way anyone else sees either. Similarly, companion narratives need not reveal the same aspect to everyone, any more than a person has the identical place in the lives of various close friends. Even collective companion narratives can potentially meet each person where he or she is, so long as this is not impeded by the imposition of doctrinaire interpretations.

I will close this section with an example of a collective companion story with facets that can facilitate insights of various sorts. The story I have in mind is one in which grief is the central theme, the Buddhist tale of Kisagotami. Kisagotami is the mother of a child who has died. She is crazy with grief, and she carries her child's corpse from house to house, asking everyone she encounters for medicine to revive it. Someone directs her to the Buddha, and she repeats her request to him. He says that he can heal the child if she brings him four or five mustard seeds from a house where no family member or slave has died. Kisagotami goes to every house in her village, but she does not find a single one in which no one has died. She returns to the Buddha, recovers her sanity, and becomes one of Buddha's disciples.

One common interpretation is that the Buddha has led Kisagotami to realize that death is a universal part of human experience, not an exceptional tragedy visited upon her. She is healed by this realization because she learns to put her own sorrow into perspective. Her story is every else's story, too. Guy Newland's elaboration of the story follows this interpretation: "Repeatedly looking into the eyes of others who had borne terrible pain, her heart unclenched. Looking down on the town at the end of the day, she knew the pervasiveness of loss. One thousand doses of empathy purged Kisa Gotami of her psychotic grief." Yet Newland also interprets the story from another angle, focusing on the Buddha's role in the story. The Buddha does not dismiss Kisagotami as a crazy woman, but gives her his full attention, skillfully guiding her toward insight. Those of us who want to help the grieving, do not know whether our words will be helpful, Newland reminds us. But "from within that not-knowing we can offer our presence, our fullest effort and attention," and if we say or do something that goes wrong, we can "acknowledge that, forgive ourselves, try again."[48]

Peter Hershock, drawing inspiration from the Ch'an school of Buddhism, interprets the story in still another way. He sees it as drawing attention not only to the pervasiveness of impermanence, but also to the network of human relationships.

> We have to recall that Kisagotami is not just "a woman," a faceless player in a generic tale, but someone known with greater or lesser intimacy by

> everyone in her village. When she knocks on a door and asks if a death has occurred in the home, rather than being answered with a brusque yes or no, her own pain will call forth that of the people she meets.[49]

In Hershock's reading, as Kisagotami visits one home after another, she renews her intimate connections with other members of her community who share their stories with her. Through reconnecting with her social world, she is restored to mental health.[50]

Even in talking with other people in her village, Kisagotami recognizes that she is not as isolated as she had seemed. "They are friends and relatives whose life-stories include and are included in her own," says Hershock, and their mutual involvement in each other's lives becomes increasingly evident as they converse. But he sees the moment of awakening as occurring when she returns to the Buddha and relates to him the stories she has heard. As she does so, she "actively understands that suffering is never merely objective or subjective but profoundly and irreducibly interpersonal, shared." In reporting the stories of her neighbors' fortunes, "including them now as a part of her own, she opens herself to the unlimited reciprocity of true community. It is in that moment of profoundest narration that 'one' and 'many' dissolve. That is her awakening."[51]

Hershock's interpretation emphasizes the healing potential of interpersonal communication. For a grieving person to regain the sense of inhabiting the world, reintegration with the social world is essential. This is another area in which aesthetic practices can be helpful. Indeed, the interactions that Hershock sees as the means to Kisagotami's enlightenment are themselves steeped in an aesthetic practice, that of storytelling. Aesthetic means for reconnecting with the social world, including storytelling, will be the focus of the following chapter.

5
Aesthetic Modes of Reconnecting

The reassurance that others have been in similar circumstances is especially important at times, such as bereavement, when one feels disconnected from others. But alone it is an insufficient means for overcoming feelings of alienation. That requires reintegration with the surrounding world of living people. In this chapter I will consider aesthetic resources that can assist this effort.

I will begin by considering music's potential for helping grieving people to surmount social isolation, briefly considering the social functions of lamentation and noting how music of other sorts can function somewhat similarly. Lamentation invites the participation of other people, and when this participation occurs, it reassures the mourner that the loss is not a private affliction. I will proceed to consider other practices in which the participation of many individuals has a powerful effect, both aesthetically and emotionally. When practices of this sort are used in contexts of mourning, they can offer the bereaved gestural testimony of others' support and concern. I will conclude the chapter by considering ways in which storytelling can connect the bereaved with other people, whether the stories are narrated by the grieving person or are produced collaboratively.

MUSIC AND FELT CONNECTION

Feelings of Solidarity

In an era in which music is often consumed through headphones or earbuds, it may not seem obvious that it is a sociable activity. But music is a powerful means for generating camaraderie, and this makes it serviceable as a tool for developing social bonds. Even when accessed privately, music entrains the bodies of both performers and listeners, synchronizing the movements of those who engage with it together. Rhythmic entrainment may be conscious or subliminal, but it creates feelings of solidarity either way. These feelings can be intensified by the awareness that other people are participating in the same musical experience. When one is in physical proximity to others engaging with the same music, this impression is especially pronounced. But even when listening or playing music in solitude, the experience creates the impression of human connection, either through a sense of being in contact with the performer(s) or through awareness that one's own performance transmits the music into a world where others might hear it.

Because it is propelled into an environment, music is accessible to an audience that is potentially very wide-ranging. All within earshot can listen, regardless of whether they are present for a performance, hearing a broadcast, or using recording and playback technology. Music is also physically intimate, pervading the body while also resounding in the external world. The listener not only hears but feels the music. And given that the world is filled with other people, music draws attention to our ability to attune our consciousness and bodily rhythms to theirs. Simple awareness of being in a physical world shared with others is not sufficient for assuaging feelings of social isolation, but it can be a first step, which music facilitates.

Social Signaling through Music

A more direct way in which music can counter feelings of alienation is by serving as a means of social signaling, in which the emotions expressed are taken to be interpersonally understood. This function of music is particularly evident in lamentation, which we considered briefly in chapter 2. Greg Urban describes ritual wailing as signaling "a feeling of grief," and he sees it as useful for helping to mediate between the wailer and the larger social group. "The signal is emitted in a way that other actors consider appropriate," he observes. "Hence the sadness itself is rendered socially intelligible, and it is through this intelligible sadness that the basic intelligibility and acceptability of the social actor emerges."[1] Wailing involves improvisation, but it is nonetheless stylized and thus easy to recognize. Others in the community interpret the wailer's emphatic emotional outburst as warranted, for it is sufficiently conventionalized to alert them to the nature of the situation to which the wailer responds. While extreme behavior might prompt social ostracism in other situations, lamentation helps the distraught individual secure the understanding of the larger community.

Lamentation is socially intelligible, but it also serves the wailer as a vehicle for distinctively personal emotional expression. According to Urban, its expressiveness derives from the tension between regularity (the social standardization of its conventionalized elements) and irregularity, which "signals the individual or unique aspects of the emotion." The primary function of wailing, as Urban sees it, is expression of the grieving person's turbulent emotions in a way that others can understand. For this reason, he describes it as a form of communication that positions the community in the role of listeners.

> Wailing is a process of making public the feelings of the person who is wailing. It is intended not to be heard, in the ordinary linguistic sense, but rather to be *overheard*. Ritual wailing purports overtly not to engage an addressee, but to allow anyone within earshot access to something that would otherwise be private.[2]

Steven Feld challenges this characterization of lamentation as monologic. Describing the wailing practices of the Kaluli tribe in Papua New Guinea, Feld observes:

> The otherwise privacy of the message is not the issue; wailers are speaking out to the deceased, other wailers, and the present collectivity. Their mode of expression places them forcefully in the social domain as performers. Their words are in some sense very much meant to be heard rather than overheard in that they function as an invitation to others to collaboratively enunciate felt thoughts about the death at hand and the social position of the deceased.[3]

Feld suggests that a key function of lament is to elicit the participation of others.[4] While it does serve to signal the community, it also invites the community to join in the lament. If others do join in, this signals back that both the wailer and the person mourned remain within the community's embrace.

Each of these accounts draws attention to a benefit that lamentation serves in linking mourners to other people. Urban emphasizes its usefulness for generating community awareness and acceptance of the mourner's emotional state. Feld draws attention to its role in eliciting the participation of others in responding to the death. On either interpretation, the community adopts a supportive role, though the wailer may be more aware of it when others actively join in.

Lamentation is far from ubiquitous, and it is becoming less common even in those societies where it is still practiced. Nevertheless, the signaling functions that Urban and Feld describe are also operative (if less obvious) in other employments of music in connection with mourning. In funerals and other commemorative events, suitable music reminds those gathered of the loss and signals the appropriateness of the emotional responses of those who are grieving. It also invites the community to share in this emotional response by inducing moods that are deemed appropriate in context, such as somber sadness.

Reflective Distance and Externalized Emotion

Some music that is utilized in commemorative events and mourning-related settings (such as funeral homes) differs from lamentation in being aimed at calming the grieving person's violent emotions. G. W. F. Hegel saw this as a key function of funeral practices and expressions of condolence, which help the distraught person get some distance from the grief. Interestingly, in this connection Hegel mentions wailing that is performed by people hired for the purpose:

> It was a good old custom at deaths and funerals to appoint wailing women, in order to bring the grief before the mind in its utterance. Manifestations of sympathy, too, hold up the content of man's misfortune to his view; when it is much talked about he is forced to reflect upon it, and is thereby relieved. And so it has always been held that to weep or to speak one's fill is a means to obtain freedom from the oppressive weight of care, or at least to find momentary relief for the heart. Hence the mitigation of the violence of passion has for its universal reason that man is released from his immediate sunkenness in a feeling, and becomes conscious of it as of something external to him.[5]

Hegel considers the effects of wailing by others on the overwrought individual, suggesting that this allows the person to recognize that the emotional state can be the focus of reflection. When a grieving person gains reflective distance from overpowering feelings, this alleviates their pressure. We should note that Hegel sees gestures of sympathy as also facilitating this shift to a reflective stance. Of particular interest for purposes here is that Hegel sees reflective distance as freeing the grieving person from being submerged in a feeling understood as being private. Instead of being oppressed by feelings interpreted as disconnected with others' affective reality, one can recognize that one's state is not intrinsic to oneself, but potentially a part of others' experience as well.

Vicarious Emotional Expression

Hegel's reference to professional wailers suggests a reason that grieving people might be musically enabled to recognize that others may share their feelings, which otherwise seem to pull them into a purely private subjectivity. Grieving individuals take the lament of these wailers to be expressive of their own emotion. This vicarious emotional expression has an effect that is akin to that of direct expression, alleviating the sense of being submerged in one's feeling. But additionally, it testifies to the interpersonal intelligibility of one's state. If professional wailers can express it, it does not close one off from intersubjective emotional reality.

In contexts in which the hiring of professional wailers is a common practice, employing them may simply accord with cultural scripts; it need not imply felt grief. However, that such a practice even developed seems to reflect the conviction that vicarious displays can manifest one's own emotions and do so appropriately.

One hardly needs to be grieving to find reflections of one's own emotional states in music. For most of us, musical reflections of emotions we have experienced adds to our pleasure and our feelings of intimacy with the music. Kendall Walton has suggested that poets and songwriters may consciously intend for their works to provide opportunities for others to express their attitudes, thoughts, and feelings. In this respect, they are like speechwriters, who write texts for others to deliver, and he describes their activity as "thoughtwriting." Regardless of their conscious aims, many do in fact provide formulations that others find pertinent to their own situations. And among the satisfactions people take in poetry is the feeling that it beautifully expresses sentiments they have experienced but could not put so well.[6]

Demonstrating the benefit of engaging with songs and poems as vicarious emotional expression is not a main goal of Walton's article, which is aimed at proposing an alternative to the view that expressive poetry and music should be interpreted as expressing the psychological experience of a postulated persona. However, Anna Christina Ribeiro, drawing on Walton's idea, elaborates on the therapeutic value of poems, especially sad poems written in first person. One of the benefits she sees in such poetry has some similarity with the one that Hegel associates with lamentation: it can facilitate reflection. Ribeiro observes that poetry can help to give clarity to feelings that are unstable or inchoate. "Sad lyric poems, that speak to us in our moments of grief," says Ribeiro, "give us the formal space in which to feel the emotions that may yet be formless within us."[7] In this respect, she points to a way in which poetry can help one to order one's feelings, suggesting a value it can have for bereaved people who have difficulty sorting out their impressions and emotions.[8]

More relevant to the topic of overcoming isolation are other therapeutic benefits of poetry mentioned by Ribeiro. She argues that lyric poetry written in first person offers an invitation to engage with the poem "in the first person as well, that is, in my own person." When we do so and recognize that the poem expresses feelings we have had, we take it as giving voice to our feelings. This makes the experience of engaging with it both relieving and "peculiarly *personal*."[9] Ribeiro emphasizes the individual's enjoyment of the poem, but this notion of that the poem invites others to participate in its expressive gesture demonstrates that one's emotional experience is not privately encapsulated. Ribeiro's third explanation for why she sees sad poetry as therapeutic makes this further evident. She observes that such poetry provides social validation for one's feeling. As she puts it, sad poems help us "feel that we belong in this world, because we feel the way others do or have felt, and we can commune with them via their words."[10]

Ribeiro describes therapeutic benefits of poetry that apply to grieving people, but her points about sad poetry apply also to expressive music. Although making music oneself can obviously serve as a form of emotional expression, relating to music composed or performed by others can also be unburdening when it is expressive of emotions that resemble one's own. We find music to be a source of comfort because it offers an outlet for expressing our emotions, even when this is accomplished vicariously. This ability to relate our own emotions to music made by others, in fact, is especially valuable for helping grieving people feel connected with the social world. Expressive music can demonstrate that our emotional experience is not idiosyncratic, and it gives testimony to the social world's acknowledgment and validation of emotion of the sort that we ourselves have experienced.

Music, with its physically penetrating character and stimulation of the motor system, may extend an even more obvious invitation than lyric poetry to be experienced in first person. Unless we find an instance of music to be an abrasive stimulus, we easily identify with it and its movements and experience its projected emotions as our own.[11] Through its broad address in social space, music invites others to identify at the same time it invites us. The experience to which we are invited is ambiguously both first-person singular and first-person plural. Music gets inside us and makes our experience seem profoundly personal, but we also experience it as shared (at least in principle). And its presence as simultaneously both inside and outside us makes its intersubjective character conspicuous.

Shared Space for Private Reflection and Experienced Temporal Flow

The upshot of the discussion so far is that engaging with music can be valuable to grieving individuals on many counts, particularly as a means for generating awareness of one's continued connection with the social world despite the sense of isolation that grief tends to produce. This point is reinforced by two further considerations. First, music can further feelings of companionable togetherness apart from verbal communication of specific statements. For this reason, it is useful for creating settings that encourage collective experience of inward, meditative thought without the interpretive constraints to which verbal messages might give rise. In such musically supported settings, one joins with others to engage in meditative reflection, even though the specific thoughts of the individuals involved are bound to be quite varied. Instrumental music used in many Western funerals and in funeral homes seems aimed at supporting reflection on the part of those who gather, and this socially validates engagement in reflective thought and recollection, even making it seem a shared activity of collectively remembering the deceased.

Second, music disrupts one of the causes of felt isolation in bereavement, the temporal disturbances that dissociate the grieving person from the social world's time. We have observed that grieving people often experience a sense of atemporality, or dissociation from time's ongoing flow. Musical experience can offer the grieving person a reprieve from this condition, for to engage with music is to feel connected with its ongoing development and to feel that others share in it, too. Thus, experiencing music involves one in a temporal flow that is recognized as intersubjective.

Importantly, this sense of immersion in an interpersonally shared, flowing reality does not require resumption of everyday activities or pursuits. As previously noted, grieving people often resist such engagement, both because everyday projects seem pointless and engaging in them would suggest an ever-growing distance between themselves and their deceased loved ones. Because the social world in general is flowing toward the future, the resistance grieving people feel to engage with social time contributes to the sense of disconnection from the world of the living. Musical experience diminishes this sense of disconnection because, by immersing oneself in the music as it develops, the bereaved person attunes to a temporal flow that others (at least implicitly) share. But music's temporality is virtual, distinct from that of everyday life and its projects. While one listens or otherwise engages with music, one is in a shared temporal space that does not involve problematic reengagement with consensus time.

Experiencing music thus cancels the sense of temporal alienation from the experience of others. One hitches a ride, as it were, on flowing temporality that is felt as being intersubjective. Even though afterward one returns to the temporal conditions of bereavement and its lack of forward momentum, the experience of music demonstrates that dissociation from temporal flow is not irreversible and that one's present disturbances are not a complete divorce one from shared temporal experience. This musical reconnection with social reality is temporally limited, but its impact can be powerful. It provides reason to believe that the experiences of collective flow do not necessitate abandoning the deceased, a conviction that may be necessary if one is ever to reengage willingly in the temporality of social life.

CUMULATIVE AESTHETIC PRACTICES

In the previous section, we considered ways in which music (and some kinds of poetry) invite participation and observed that this participatory aspect can help grieving people feel less isolated and more aware of social support. In this section we will look at other practices that involve social participation. I have in mind those mourning activities that utilize some form of accumulation to aesthetic effect, and thus manifest *cumulative aesthetics*. This term was coined by artist Sarah Canright in reference to phenomena in which aesthetic impact is achieved through the accumulation of numerous instances of an image, gesture, or token. Especially when the accumulation is the result of many individuals' contributions, it can suggest a powerful tendency, commitment, or emotion. It can also testify to an outpouring of responses to some phenomenon on the part of the social world. I will suggest that cumulative aesthetic effects give the bereaved a forceful impression of being emotionally accompanied and supported in their grief.

The Character of Cumulative Aesthetics

To convey an impression of gestures that fall into the category of *cumulative aesthetics*, I will describe the context in which Canright proposed the term. She and I had visited a shrine associated with healing in Chimayó, New Mexico, at the site of a reported miracle. Looking around, we observed a proliferation of crosses, rosaries, candles, and milagros positioned in virtually every available space within the precinct of the shrine. Seeing them prompted Canright to note the distinctive aesthetic character of items amassed in such great numbers. The aesthetic impact derived mainly from the accumulation, not so much from the features of the individual objects.

For the most part, the items deposited at the shrine were made of humble materials. Often they reflected resourcefulness rather than resources. Many crosses were improvised by tying two sticks together. That crosses were plentiful in the church and chapel connected with the shrine was not particularly surprising, but we were struck by their abundance throughout the area within sight of an outdoor altar. Makeshift crosses hung from trees and rocky constructed niches; they were attached to fences; they stood at the base of large ornamental crosses around the perimeter. We had the impression of multitudes coming to visit the shrine, each adding another token to those already in place. The profusion of tokens testified to the stream of pilgrims who had passed through, and the site suggested that the flow was ongoing, given the numerous people who (like us) continued to visit.

The Chimayó shrine undergoes continual transformation. A hole in the floor of the chapel at the shrine is supposed to be the place where a crucifix kept miraculously appearing, and dirt contained in the hole is believed to have healing properties. Visitors are invited to gather a small amount of this dirt and take it with them in small containers. Gesturally, they amplify the site of the miracle and extend its healing force through the world.

Significantly, the aesthetic impact of the shrine does not stem from a particular artist's creative activity. Instead, it stems from many, often tiny gestures made by countless people at various times. The myriad votive offerings testify to innumerable personal gestures, gestures that are expressive but not exhibitionistic. Presumably, the devout who make them seek to be seen by God, but not other people. The offerings include milagros that are shaped to indicate particular concerns, such as body parts that need healing, but to human visitors (if not to God) they are anonymous tokens once installed.

The Chimayó shrine, like others that welcome votive items, conveys an open-ended invitation to participate. Anyone can join in, and any given arrangement is temporary since additions may be made at any time. The flow of new additions, along with the individuality of each of them, enhances the impression that the assemblage has built up over an indefinite expanse of time. The site-specificity of such shrines makes them cumulative in another way, too. The accumulation bears witness to the journeys of the many people who have sought out the site as a pilgrimage destination, and our awareness of this fact may have an impact on our aesthetic impression as well.[12]

Noteworthy aesthetic features of the tokens at the Chimayó shrine are thus: (1) their relative smallness in relation to the whole; (2) their personally expressive character; (3) their humble materials; (4) their non-uniformity; and (5) their serving as markers of many people having traveled to the site. The accumulation as a whole also has the distinctive features of (1) being the result of many small gestures of various individuals over an extended period of time; (2) the lack of coordination among the individuals who contribute to the effect; (3) its continually changing and open-ended configuration; and (4) its invitation to participate.

Not every case of cumulative aesthetic phenomena involves the characteristic features of the Chimayó site. Canright observed that the amassing of tokens occurs in formal artworks, too, noting that many major artists from Cubism on had made works featuring accumulations of images or objects. Petah Coyne's work, for example, often makes use of natural materials that are themselves found in aggregation (such as hay, black sand, hair, wax, soil, wood, white powder), materials that she takes to suggest the precariousness of life. Nancy Rubins, Lari Pittman, Mike Kelley, and Zoe Leonard, similarly amass types of objects in their works. Rubins, for example, has made assemblages of mattresses, cakes, and canoes. Reiteration of images is another form of accumulation, evident in Robert Kushner's patterned paintings. However, these artworks have a different cumulative character than the tokens at the Chimayó shrine, in that they are intentionally produced by individual artists, who control the decisions that determine the configuration. They are not the products of non-coordinated gestures on the part of numerous individuals. The material accumulated in these works is sometimes humble but not necessarily. The tokens or images can be uniform. The works might not be personally expressive, and most do not invite participation.

Formal artworks can, however, use accumulation in various ways. Félix González-Torres's candy installations have certain cumulative aesthetic aspects that resemble those of the Chimayó shrine. Their impact relies on many individuals engaging in actions that have a collective effect, and they invite participation. These works consist of large piles of wrapped candies, from which visitors are encouraged to take a piece. Again as in the case of Chimayó shrine, González-Torres's candy installations invite visitors to take something home with them.

González-Torres explicitly aimed to commemorate his deceased lover, Ross Laycock, with his candy installations. The participation invited by these works evocatively echoes the fate of the loved one being honored. As the visitors successively remove candies, they enact the dissolution of the form. This echo struck some critics as a morbid reminder of Laycock's life force being drained away by death. However, these installations can also be interpreted as suggesting the dissemination of Laycock's life force into the world, which continues to feel its impact. One might recognize the same formal principle at work in the ritual of the Christian Mass, which commemorates the death of Jesus. While the Mass is designed to help participants recall his resurrection, it also memorializes his death, and it symbolizes his spirit being dispersed throughout the congregation by way of the Eucharist, to be carried forth into the world.

Cumulative Aesthetics in Mourning

The Chimayó shrine manifests a burgeoning devotional tendency, the tokens materializing a growing wave of accumulating prayer. Many phenomena related to mourning similarly convey the impression of an outpouring of love and sympathy by way of cumulative gestures and actions. Because I am mainly interested in this chapter in the way that cumulative aesthetics helps bereaved individuals to feel connected with the larger social world, I will focus mainly on phenomena that utilize the cumulative aesthetics of addition (à la Chimayó). Nevertheless, cumulative aesthetics through subtraction can also be used to moving effect, as González-Torres's candy installations demonstrate with their enactment of growing absence.

We need not search far to find instances of cumulative aesthetics in relation to loss. Consider the spontaneous shrines that arise after the deaths of well-known people (for example, Princess Diana) or events in which many people are victims (among them the many shrines in the United States to commemorate the victims of the 9/11 terrorist attacks). Roadside shrines that incorporate many personal artifacts sometimes have a cumulative character, too, though it is often unclear whether the objects placed at a shrine have been positioned there by many people or a single person or family. The same can be true of accumulated objects at a grave site, which may be items that belonged to the deceased or symbolic offerings that seem to reflect the person's sensibilities (for example, teddy bears placed on a child's grave).

The amassing of items at grave sites or roadside shrines may not be intended as an open-ended invitation to add more, and some of these accumulations may be more planned than spontaneous. However, I think even these cases extend a kind of open-ended invitation to the social world, for these accumulated displays are located in public, presumably with the aim of summoning witnesses. In effect, the accumulation directs passersby to pay attention and to join those who mourn in remembering the person who has died. In this case, the physical proliferation of objects may produce a spiritual amplification, one in which those who witness contribute by helping to maintain the person's continued place within the memory of the community. The extent of this kind of amplification is not aesthetically verifiable, but it is the effect that I think these displays encourage.

Cumulative gestures are also part of certain mourning-related performances, in which the repeated acts of numerous individuals have a poignant emotional potency. Funeral processions come to mind. So do those conclusions of burial rites in which many individuals each drop a flower or a clod of earth onto the casket that has been lowered into a grave. These particular gestures can only contribute to a cumulative effect while the rituals to which they contribute are in progress. Flowers sent to a funeral home or church might also contribute to a short-term cumulative display, though whether a significant accumulation occurs depends on timely elective decisions, and probably these are rarely made with cumulative aesthetic impact in mind.

Another loss-related practice displaying cumulative aesthetics, however, does imply an open-ended invitation in the manner of the Chimayó shrine. This is the laying of small stones on a grave, a long-standing Jewish tradition. The gesture of laying a stone is a tribute, but one that serves as a precedent for others to do likewise. To see a grave or tomb decked with many such stones is affecting. Traditionally, the stones are brought from elsewhere, effectively marking the grave as a pilgrimage site. We rarely know when the most recently placed stone was positioned, but the typical haphazardness of the placement suggests that the arrangement is, in effect, a work in progress. The stones appear to attest that the person's memory lives on.

Formal commemorative artworks, too, sometimes make use of cumulative aesthetics, especially when the aim is to make people aware of the enormity of some loss. The NAMES Project AIDS Memorial Quilt is a case in point. Officially begun in 1987, the quilt is made up of panels, most of which have been contributed by survivors of individuals who have died from AIDS to commemorate their loved ones. The dimensions of the panels are three by six feet to approximate the size of a grave, and the quilt rapidly became too large to display in any usual exhibition space. It has been several times displayed on the National Mall in Washington, DC, although in 2012 it had to be shown in segments, with different groups of 1,500 panels being shown on different days over a two-week period. Virtual space currently seems to be the one exhibition space that is capacious enough for the AIDS Memorial Quilt, which as of July 2020 was reported to have some 48,000 panels, weigh 54 tons, and extend to 1.2 million square feet. It is currently possible to see all of these panels online.[13] Other memorial quilt projects have followed the lead of the NAMES project to honor groups who have died from particular causes or in particular circumstances. In addition to physical quilts, some virtual memorial quilts have developed (one, for example, to honor victims of suicide).

The AIDS Memorial Quilt was begun as an activist effort, asserting the grievability of those who died of the AIDS epidemic and demanding social justice for those affected by the disease, who were often targets of stigma.[14] In this respect, it is something of an objectified public demonstration, utilizing cumulative aesthetics with political aims, as demonstrations characteristically do. Certain other memorial quilt projects also seem geared to combating the stigmatization of those who are memorialized, for example, the virtual quilts organized by the American Foundation for Suicide Prevention and by Survivors of Suicide Loss. Such projects are aimed at attracting public attention to a cause, even if the public that observes them is largely self-selecting.[15]

Virtual quilts are only one category of virtual memorializing activities that utilize cumulative aesthetics. Memorial websites (such as those supported by Legacy.com and those based on various social media platforms) typically solicit comments from visitors to the sites. The accumulation of relatively brief contributions by many individuals can have an effect that resembles what I have described as the impact of many tribute stones on a grave (except that the recency of an online post is often evident).[16] This case, too, suggests that a host of people, though spread out in time and space, have visited this same site with the goal of honoring the person.[17]

Collective gestures of mourning and commemoration in response to a death can be moving to witnesses, regardless of whether they are directly affected by the loss themselves. What particularly interests me here, however, is the way that they can help grieving people feel less isolated. Practices involving the accumulation of gestures of the sorts we have been considering offer evidence that many people are moved to express a sense of loss and pay respects to the person who has died. Those who make the gestures may be grieving themselves or displaying solidarity with those who are. Either way, bereaved individuals can see the accumulations as direct evidence that other people are also affected by the loss and moved to display their love and respect. Cumulative gestures demonstrate to the grieving that they are not alone in recognizing the loss and feeling the need to assimilate it.

Funerals and related gatherings have a cumulative impact, too, that can help those who are bereaved. The very fact of many individuals coming together helps to demonstrate that the loss is a collective concern. Such events are designed to be intersubjective spaces in which all present, though related to the deceased in different ways, share the activity of mourning and honoring the dead. At such events, grieving people can also feel the supportive presence of those who have gathered with them.[18]

Memorial shrines and other physical sites with cumulative aesthetic effects give less palpable impressions than do gatherings that other people are "with" the grieving person. But sensory tokens have an immediacy of their own. And when one attends to the fact that each is a proxy for a person participating in the loss and commemoration, these sites can also offer reassurance that one does not grieve alone.

STORYTELLING IN BEREAVEMENT

In the previous two sections, we have focused on aesthetic practices that reassure bereaved people that they remain a part of the social world. Let us now consider storytelling, an aesthetic form that involves active efforts at communicating. Storytelling can take the form of either individual narration or collaborate construction. Either way it can help bridge the perceived distance from other people that the grieving person may feel.

Social Sharing by the Bereaved

The need to express one's emotions and to communicate about one's experience is typical among the bereaved, as we considered in chapter 3. Most people who have suffered a loss, like most who have had any type of harrowing experience, spontaneously tell others about their experience, a phenomenon social psychologists term "social sharing."[19] Social sharing may not sound obviously aesthetic. Yet telling other people about one's experience most often involves editorial selection and arrangement of details, and one often gears the account to the person being told. These are aesthetic choices, although this may not be the narrator's focus of attention.

Even an incoherent story might be interpreted as having an aesthetic character.[20] I doubt I am the only bereaved individual ever to be startled by the thought, "What I'm saying is not making sense—I'm positively raving." Yet undirected narrating has its own aesthetic features, and it can even precipitate breakthroughs in which one reveals oneself more authentically than in most ordinary conversations.

Actress and playwright Anna Deavere Smith, explaining her interest in imitating the speech and gestures of people she interviews, claims that if allowed to speak to a nonjudgmental listener, ordinary people are moved to poetic eloquence when they describe emotionally powerful events. As she sees it, the shift to poetry occurs through the breaks and hesitations, when routine patterns of speech get interrupted, and the speaker's character struggles to appear.[21] Such moments can be stunning and revelatory. According to Smith, the lack of editorial restraint is precisely what gives such speech its poetic power. Given the strong emotions experienced in bereavement, we might expect such poetry within everyday speech to emerge when grieving people confide their feelings without any deliberate effort to shape what they are saying.

The aesthetic character of such spontaneous poetic expression, however, may be evident only to the listener, not to the person narrating the loss.

In any case, this unbridled mode of storytelling is probably not typical in bereavement past a certain point in time. As we have considered, grieving people adjust their behavior in response to reactions from others, and given the limited tolerance most listeners have for repetitive accounts or emotional outbursts, grieving narrators are likely to feel motivated to structure what they say.

Excessive self-editing in social sharing can limit the degree to which it reinforces interpersonal bonds, but even then, the process of shaping one's account may have certain cognitive benefits. Organizing the details into some type of presentational whole can help give some order to experiences that are confused and hard to integrate. Jerome Bruner proposes that storytelling serves an especially important function in the case of circumstances that violate our expectations, for it gives them form that helps to make them understandable.[22] The mental organizing required to narrate one's experience is an activity of sorting through what has happened, a preliminary step toward orienting oneself in any new situation. Counseling professors and practitioners Lorraine Hedtke and John Winslade see storytelling in bereavement, in particular, as a creative process that can help grieving people to reclaim agency and give order to their thoughts and feelings.[23]

Bernard Rimé contends that those who tell others about their upsetting emotional experiences are seeking some kind of assistance, and they typically tailor their stories to specific listeners and structure them in ways that can be expected to elicit desired responses.[24] Cognitive assistance would help the storyteller to examine the experience in ways that might facilitate processing emotions and ascertaining ways of avoiding further distress. Ideally, it would help narrators to "abandon their frustrated goals, reorganize their hierarchy of motives, accommodate their models and schemas, re-create meaning, and reframe or re-appraise the episode." Socio-affective assistance would involve emotional support that helps alleviate "insecurity, anxiety, helplessness, loneliness, and so forth."[25] When such support is provided, feelings of relief result, but this effect is more temporary than the benefits secured by conversations that help the storyteller think things through. Ideally, conversations elicit both cognitive and socio-affective assistance, but Rimé's experimental evidence suggests that affective support is by far the most frequent response to social sharing. This provides short-term relief, but little help with emotional processing.

If sympathetic responses predominate over more practically oriented ones in the case of bereavement, this hardly seems surprising. When a grieving person tells someone about the loved one's death and its aftermath, emotional need is often quite evident, while the primary "problem" the person faces (adjusting to the world in the absence of the loved one) cannot be readily solved. Telling someone about one's experience of grief is not so unburdening that it resolves the need to share, and the felt need to elicit emotional support from many people seems proportionate to the massive life-altering impact of grief.

Cues from the bereaved also tend to indicate that they are seeking socio-affective attention. Even under routine circumstances, according to Rimé, persons who verbally share their emotions about an upsetting experience are more typically seeking moral support than strategic advice, at least initially, when they usually "do not feel ready to reframe it, nor to change their perspectives."[26] Even if a confidant has some practical ideas that might be useful, moreover, it may seem inappropriate to present them to a person who is in obvious emotional pain. Some people do offer sympathetic commonplaces that suggest a reframing of the situation, for example "s/he's in a better place." Yet however well intended, remarks of this sort often sound offensively superficial or spurious to someone who is grieving.

As for more well-considered suggestions, newly bereaved people are especially unlikely to be ready to reorient their lives. They are almost invariably fatigued. In addition, when many of the bereaved person's habits are premised on the presence or central role of the deceased in their lives, retaining them may seem a matter of loyalty or a means of preserving connection with the person. For a conversational partner to focus too much or too directly on how the bereaved might reorganize goals may seem insensitive in this context, and it would ignore the affective importance the bereaved person likely places on lingering in their sense of loss.

Wolfgang Stroebe, Henk Schut, and Margaret S. Stroebe question the usefulness of social sharing in bereavement. They contend that the evidence does not establish that it "facilitates adjustment to loss in normal bereavement," though they think it may be helpful in many cases.[27] Yet to focus on adjustment as such may be to miss the fact that sharing stories signals openness toward other people. If we focus on the social dissociation that is common in grief, the bereaved person's confiding in another person is an active move toward maintaining interpersonal connections. It shows that the person has not given up on the social world entirely, even if the motive of not abandoning the deceased predominates.

When grieving people tell others about what they have been experiencing, this does not necessarily accelerate their adjustment. It may, however, prompt emotional support from those they tell. Parties on both sides of the conversation are active participants in the exchange. Although practical problems remain unresolved, such conversations nevertheless maintain open channels of interpersonal connection at a time when all the bereaved person's social relationships seem up for renegotiation.[28]

Collective Storytelling

Social sharing is not a foolproof means of nurturing relationships with the living. Not everyone whom one might approach will be a willing listener, particularly if the person selected is a target for repetitive sharing. The reactions of certain individuals may intensify feelings of being disconnected and misunderstood. We should notice, however, that many studies of social sharing emphasize unidirectional storytelling, in which one person narrates and another person listens. This is not the only way in which storytelling is practiced in bereavement, and it may not even be the most common.

In many conversations, as Peter Hershock notes in connection with the story of Kisagotami, one person's account reminds those who hear it of stories from their own experience. Through mutual sharing, the bereaved person might come to recognize that his or her dissociation from the living community was never as extreme as it may have appeared. Telling stories with one's friends and other associates makes it evident that one is supported by a network of other people and that one's own role is reciprocal in numerous relationships.[29] Although grieving people are sometimes annoyed when their interlocutors seem more intent on telling their own stories than on listening, reciprocal sharing can result in mutual benefit.

Sociologist Tony Walter points out that collective storytelling is often spontaneous among people who are sharing a loss, particularly when gathered for formal memorial observances. Their conversations typically involve interactive discussion of the death, the person who has died, and the participants' various relationships to the person.[30] This can have many benefits for grieving individuals. Besides demonstrating that the person's death is not a purely private loss, collective storytelling can also facilitate cognitive processing of the type Rimé describes. Hearing other people's contributions may lead one to consider alternative ways of framing events and thinking about the deceased and the relationship. Others' stories can also help one to see previously unnoticed facets of the loved one's personality and life, and this may result in novel insights.

Walter identifies another cognitive benefit of collective storytelling that is relevant to the topic of reconnecting with the social world. He thinks collective storytelling can help people to socially situate the deceased. A whole community has suffered a loss, and this needs to be assimilated collectively. Through storytelling the community endeavors to establish a place for the deceased in its collective memory. Walter describes this process as the attempt to construct a "durable biography."[31]

When I first read Walter's account of the durable biography, I was a bit dubious about the notion of durability.[32] The word *durable* seemed to have too much the connotation of something fixed, so sturdy that it can be considered almost indestructible. But I suspect that Walter intended the term to mean something more like *steady* than *rigid*. As we have noted, those who are suffering from a loss are often overwhelmed by disconnected memories of the deceased. In this situation, some steady sense of the person is likely to be stabilizing. And if the community is to acknowledge that he or she is still valued, it seems important that there be some shared notion of who the person was. The need for collective construction of a stable account of the person's identity may seem all the more pressing when those closest to him or her find their impressions so fugitive.

Yet here we again confront a problem that we considered in chapter 2, the one that Derrida describes as the danger of covering over the actuality of the person with one's somewhat fantastic image. Although he considers it impossible to have a true vision of a friend who has died, he is wary that one will divert attention from the real person toward one's own imaginative construction. If this is a risk even for a eulogizer who is motivated by the desire to honor the real person, it is surely more extreme when motives of self-justification or self-aggrandizement are prominent.

Milan Kundera describes a flagrant case of this sort in his novel *Immortality*.[33] His narrator describes what he has in mind as the "quite earthly immortality of those who after their death remain in the memory of posterity."[34] Kundera recounts the story of Goethe's affectionate relationship and falling-out with the much younger Bettina von Arnim. Von Arnim compiled an edition of their letters to each other after Goethe's death, and she took considerable liberties with Goethe's tone, the dates of letters, and their content. "For three years she kept correcting, rewriting, adding," says Kundera. By means of the edition she presented to the world under the title *Goethes Briefwechsel mit einem Kinde* (*Goethe's Letters with a Child*), von Arnim accomplished her ambition, which she made evident to Goethe as his death approached, "to take his immortality into her hands."[35]

Von Arnim's letters were published in 1835, but her falsifications were exposed only in 1900. By that time, Kundera suggests, she had indeed gotten her hands on Goethe's immortality. The impact she had on posterity's impressions of Goethe had become all too durable. This aggressive pursuit of a personal agenda through meddling with the social world's memories of a person seems egregiously improper.

If Kundera is right that von Arnim influenced how Goethe was remembered, this only reinforces Walter's point that collectives develop enduring biographical accounts of deceased persons who lived in their midst. Collective storytelling does not seem immune from serving as a platform for some participant to steer community memory off course. Precisely because it is collaborative, however, such storytelling may be resistant to any effort by a single individual to enshrine self-serving accounts in collective memory.

Still, the question remains as to how durable the collectively developed biography should be. I am sympathetic to Arnar Árnason's criticism that the idea of a "durable biography" sounds too much like an objective account. He thinks it ignores the creative character of storytelling and underemphasizes the relational context in which both the deceased and those telling stories are ensconced. According to Árnason, grieving people tend to focus in their stories on the relationships between themselves and the deceased, and they typically make use of conventional models available within a cultural tradition.[36] He draws on Paul Ricoeur's notion of emplotment, "the operation that draws a configuration out of a simple succession." Making a plot from a sequence involves situating events in a way that suggests an explanation for the way it unfolds, typically making use of established genres and story types.[37] Árnason contends that grieving people "emplot" the stories of their relationships with the deceased, making use of models from other stories. In so doing, they position themselves and the deceased and endeavor to make their relationships understandable to others.

To illustrate, Árnason provides a detailed analysis of a grieving man's remarks about his wife, drawing attention to the way the man describes their relationship and how he designs his narrative in a way that justifies his current attitudes and behavior. The man provides a kind of argument through his account.

> The argument goes something like this: when we were married marriage meant something, it was for life. People were faithful and devoted to each other whereas now people divorce as soon as they have an argument. Simultaneously we had a particularly close marriage, we thought a lot of each other and were never parted even to the extent that other people found us "sickly." I am aware of the possibility of remarrying but because of the very close relationship I had with my wife, because of our mutual love and devotion, and because of the meaning of our marriage when we actually married, I will not marry again.[38]

Árnason focuses on the artistic aspects of storytelling in connection with loss and the way artistic models may prove useful in these creative efforts. He also notes the operation of personal motives in shaping the way that stories are told. Given that bereaved people are often gripped by self-doubts, storytelling of this sort might help defuse them, particularly if the story told is reinforced by the narratives of others who are grieving.

One might wonder whether the type of storytelling that Árnason highlights is especially susceptible to willful distortion of the sort that Kundera identifies. Those who tell stories to justify themselves are trying to influence listeners and win their approval and admiration. Narrators who are in some way blameworthy may be especially inclined to misrepresentation in their accounts. Obviously, narratives of any sort can incorporate lies, and lies are sometimes persuasive to others. Probably we are all adept in the strategy of convincing oneself of one's own merits by first persuading others.[39] We might hope, however, that efforts at self-justification through stories about one's relationship to the deceased will usually be unsuccessful if the stories are largely fabricated.

Árnason's idea that grieving people make use of conventional forms for narratives reinforces the point made in the preceding chapter that models from literature can offer precedents of use for dealing with one's situation. They can help one to see one's own role in relation to the deceased as having its own kind of narrative dignity.[40] They also help reintegrate the narrator into the social by appealing to others to accept the presented interpretation of themselves and to sympathize.

My emphasis in this chapter has been on the value of certain aesthetic practices for renewing feelings of connection with other people. Collective storytelling among mourners is among these practices. As they hear various stories and contribute others, participants conjure up a vision of the person. This view is "durable" enough to counter the shakiness of fleeting images that may confuse impressions of the deceased. Instead, it offers a clear impression of the person that participants knew, reminding them of his or her unique specificity.

Mourners involved in collective storytelling share the experience of bringing to mind an impression of what that deceased was like. But their conversations also help them recognize that other people knew the same person they did. This helps them to feel connected with each other through the person that touched all their lives. The experience produces feelings of social bonding that do not require anyone to divert attention from the deceased. Participants reveal their shared respect and love for the deceased by collectively remembering the person fondly, producing feelings of social connection without arousing the resistance to social interaction that bereaved people so often feel.

Are Narratives Overrated?

Before I end this consideration of storytelling in bereavement, I should acknowledge that not everyone sees narrative accounts of one's experiences as necessarily desirable. Galen Strawson opposes this view, arguing that narratives make one's grasp of the past too deterministic and that they privilege temperaments that are geared to organizing experiences diachronically over those who organize more episodically.[41] He formulates his argument in response to Peter Goldie, who encourages taking a narrative perspective on oneself as a means of making sense of one's experiences over time and coming to grips with aspects of one's past.

Strawson rejects both the psychological thesis that human beings tend to experience their lives as narratives and the normative thesis that a well-lived life requires this. Not everyone organizes their lives in terms of narrative, and there are serious reasons to avoid doing so. Overarching narratives can interfere with making sense of one's life and living well because they inevitably incorporate inaccuracies. As Strawson puts it:

> My guess is that it almost always does more harm than good—that the Narrative tendency to look for story or narrative coherence in one's life is, in general, a gross hindrance to self-understanding: to a just, general, practically real sense, implicit or explicit, of one's nature. . . . [T]he more you recall, retell, narrate yourself, the further you risk moving away from accurate self-understanding, from the truth of your being.[42]

My discussion of storytelling as an aesthetic activity that can benefit bereaved individuals should not be construed as an argument that it is indispensable for their ordering their experiences. Nor is this the implication of an argument I made elsewhere that thinking in narrative terms has advantages when attempting to navigate bereavement.[43] I do not think that narrative interpretations are essential for self-understanding or for making sense of one's relationship to a person who has died. Nevertheless, I think narratives can help people find coherence in their experiences.

Any way of emplotting experiences involves interpretation, but narratives are not objective in the way that Strawson seems to prize when he calls for accuracy. Some of the value of stories told in bereavement stems precisely from their being creative products that can make use of the full range of narrative techniques that we observe in literature. Like more straightforwardly artistic narratives, the stories constructed in grief can emphasize details and developments. These can reflect the singular individualities of the deceased and highlight various facets and complications of relationships with them. Thinking in narrative terms does not require deterministic interpretations or oversimplifications, any more than narrative accounts in literature are necessarily deterministic or excessively simplified.[44]

Nor is any given narrative construal of one's experience unrevisable.

Contemplating the temporal unfolding of a life or a relationship can enable attention to its various facets, and stories can support this effort. At times, they might even help a grieving person gain fresh insights about the deceased or the relationship, despite the person's absence.[45] If one recognizes stories as revisable, one is open to reconsidering the significance of something one remembers the person saying or doing. Perhaps some comment by the person rings differently in light of a new experience in one's own life, leading one to wonder if the person had a different take on matters than one had ever imagined before. Telling stories that artfully accentuate and idealize can help keep one's relationship with the deceased person alive in the sense that what they said and did continues to reverberate in one's life, sometimes in unexpected ways.

One need not see stories as definitive. They can be aids to remembering the deceased and taking joy in the relationship. And at the same time, they can help us envision the deceased as a member of a social network. This can remind us that others also knew and cared for the person and that we ourselves are members of the social network, too.

In this chapter, I have focused on aesthetic practices that can help reconnect the bereaved with the social world. However, I have thus far not considered the impediment to communication that the weird aspects of bereavement pose, especially communication with those who have so far been spared grief-provoking experiences in their own lives. In the following chapter, I will consider some ways that artworks can expand the bereaved person's communicative resources and help bridge the experience gap.

6
Artworks as Communicative Resources

The experiential gap between the bereaved and those who lack comparable experience creates a communicative challenge for both. I have earlier suggested that specific artworks may provide sufficient resonance with a grieving person's experience to make them suitable companions. We noted that they also attest to the fact that one's situation is not unprecedented and that the social world includes some people who do understand it. In this chapter we will consider artworks' potential usefulness for assisting communication despite the difficulty grieving people may have in describing their current perspective.

I will begin by considering the empathy gap that can occur because of different experiential backgrounds. I will then suggest that companion artworks might provide a source of common symbols that can help bridge the gap. I will go on to suggest examples of artistic devices and works that can convey aspects of the experience of bereavement. One common feature of grief experience that is difficult to describe is the ambiguous sense of presence and absence that tends to characterize it. I will suggest that art that strategically employs absence can hint at how this ambiguous condition might feel. I will also contend that the figure of the ghost, at least as characterized in many mainstream Western artworks, can be communicatively useful because it suggests some of the weirdness of the experience of grief. I will conclude this chapter by considering two artworks that feature ghostly figures as cases in point.

THE EMPATHY GAP AND COMPANION ARTWORKS

Besides helping the bereaved to orient themselves in their new situation, companion artworks can help them communicate and help their interlocutors to empathize. The notion of empathy that I am assuming here involves imaginatively taking the perspective of another person. This is a common idea in the field of philosophy. Murray Smith defines empathy as "a type of personal or central imagining" that involves mental simulation of another person's experience.[1] Amy Coplan similarly characterizes empathy as "a complex imaginative process in which an observer simulates another person's situated psychological states while maintaining clear self-other differentiation."[2] Stephen Darwall contends that "empathy consists in feeling what one imagines [another person] feels, or perhaps should feel (fear, say), or in some imagined copy of these feelings."[3] The idea that empathy involves perspective-taking is so widespread in the philosophical literature that it almost goes without saying.

However, researchers in psychology often classify emotional contagion, the subliminally prompted behavioral mirroring of another's emotion, as a subcategory of empathy. Such externally observable behavioral indicators can be monitored in experiments and correlated with physiological markers, making it possible to compare the conditions of the empathizer and the target of empathy. Defining empathy so broadly that it includes emotional contagion also enables researchers to make affective comparisons across wide ranges of subjects, including those who are incapable of self-reports. Stephanie D. Preston and Frans de Waal, for example, defend the "Perception-Action Model" model of empathy, which focuses on somatic and automatic affective responses to perceptions of another's state.[4] Some of the advantages they claim for their model are that it helps explain empirically observed patterns, predicts empathy disorders, suggests the evolutionary background of empathy, and allows for comparisons across species, age groups, and societies. De Waal's research deals primarily with primates, so he is particularly interested in cross-species comparison.

The kind of empathy that grieving people seek, however, is not unconscious mimicry of their emotional behavior. They need emotional support because their world has fallen apart. The result is that they are typically doubtful of much that they used to take for granted, including the comprehension of their fellow human beings. Comprehension, in fact, may be especially hard to come by. As human beings we are empathetic and particularly attuned to the feelings of others in our social group (because of being socialized to have a common emotional repertoire), but we may have difficulties understanding the experiences of a person who is grieving unless we have had similar experiences ourselves.

In the first place, the bereaved person is extremely disoriented and often has wildly fluctuating emotions. Getting a fix on the person's emotions is impossible because of their extremely transient nature. Moreover, in comprehending the emotions of others, we usually assume a set of "normal" reactions, based in part on what we take to be the person's goals, beliefs, position in the social network, and so on. All of these are now uncertain matters in connection with a grieving person.[5] In addition, the specific emotions experienced in grief depend to a large extent on one's singular relationship with the deceased. The dense texture of feelings and emotions connecting individuals who have a close relationship is accessible only to those involved (and differentially for each of them).

Those who lack comparable experience are likely to find themselves quite limited in their ability to vicariously feel their way into the bereaved person's state. Even if it is granted that empathizing does not require having a psychological state identical to the other's, any kind of perspective-taking requires some familiarity with what the target perspective involves.[6] Graham McFee makes this point in connection with literary fiction, claiming that the reader has limited ability to imaginatively enter the world of a person whose experience is too distant from her own.[7] The bizarreness of bereavement, described in chapter 3, is likely to be similarly alien for those who have not experienced it and comparably hard to imaginatively enter. The seeming "irrationality" of the bereaved when regarded by many who are not directly affected by a loss speaks in support of this contention.

In the face of this difficulty, artworks and devices used in them can supplement potential empathizers' personal experiences with virtual ones, expanding the range of perspectives they can imaginatively assume. The features of companion artworks that make them serviceable touchstones in bereavement also recommend them as vehicles for making sense of those who grieve. This is another use of companion artworks: they can sometimes provide a taste of an experience that is in some way comparable to what the bereaved person is undergoing, making the bizarre world of that person seem less foreign. At the same time, grieving people can appeal to such works as resources for describing their experience in terms that others may understand.

I will attempt to illustrate what I mean with an example from my own experience, though perhaps I should provide the trigger warning that my report could be upsetting. My husband, Bob, died from a sudden heart attack while we were in transit in the Zurich airport. In the aftermath I had difficulty explaining to other people why I kept obsessing about how he must have felt abandoned. "But you were there," they kept telling me. "He must have been comforted by your presence."

I would tell them that I had been completely oblivious as to what was happening. I could make that much sound reasonable. Bob collapsed in the waiting area at our gate shortly after disembarking from a flight. First the flight crew and then a medical team made efforts to stabilize him. I assumed they would succeed and that we would go to a hospital in an ambulance. That was my expectation when the team decided to defibrillate, and I was told to step away from the patient.

The scene to this point was easy to describe. I remembered the events clearly, for I relived them every night when trying to sleep. In every reiteration, I imagine that things are headed in the right direction. The defibrillation will regularize Bob's heartbeat. I'm just waiting for them to finish and wondering what course of treatment Bob will need. I slightly shift my position on the bench where I am sitting, and then I see a monitor showing Bob's vital signs. I also see a regular pattern to the graphs. Lines go up and down, and then they don't. Then they go up and down again, and then—I realize that they only go up and down when electricity is being applied. Whenever the current isn't flowing through Bob, the lines go entirely flat.

Oh no—

This experience continued to haunt me. I very much felt the urge to tell people who were close to me about it, and I did. But I kept feeling that although I could describe the situation, I couldn't communicate the emotional aspect. It was hard to explain and why my being oblivious compounded my sense of horror—and that was the part that I wanted to get off my chest. In this context, I found a helpful companion artwork, and not one that I would have anticipated. It was Stanley Kubrick's *2001: A Space Odyssey*.[8]

I found artistic companionship when I thought of the scene in which the spaceship's HAL 9000 computer (known affectionately as "HAL") kills several members of the crew while they are unconscious. These crew members are scientists whose expertise would be needed only when the spaceship reached its destination, so they have been put into artificial hibernation to save resources. Step by step, HAL terminates these astronauts' life functions. The camera moves to the area with the hibernation units, and we see that each has a monitor presenting a stack of regular waveforms tracking the vital signs of the person inside. As the scene proceeds a warning light on each unit starts to blink. One by one, the lines showing vital functions become less rhythmic. The warning light messages become more dire as the lines gradually become irregular. Then one after another, lines go from irregular to flat. Eventually, on each monitor, we see a new pattern—the variously moving waveforms we saw at the beginning have vanished. Now all we see are stacks of flat lines flashing by.

What has long fascinated me about this scene in *2001* is how quietly chilling it is. The monitors and warning lights are the only indication that the sleeping scientists are being killed. The one conscious astronaut within the film, trapped in a modular pod without a space helmet, is as powerless as the film's viewers to stop HAL from murdering his slumbering colleagues. Worse yet, as you watch with horror, you cannot really see what is happening. Three deaths take place right in front of you, yet you see, essentially, nothing. The monitors alert us only retrospectively to the fact that the scientists are dead.

The perspective the film induces in the viewer was much like my own at that dreadful moment in the Zurich airport, and it helped me to make some sense of the admixture of alarm and incapacity that overcame me along with more obvious grief emotions. The film conveys the experience of helpless horror while seeing someone die right in front of you, something I certainly felt. But it also conveys the added gruesomeness of not registering what is happening until it is too late. As viewers, we realize that we have missed the astronauts' deaths. We know that they happened, but we do not know exactly when. The dying astronauts have missed their deaths, too. Their final conscious experiences happened long ago, just before they underwent induced hibernation. It is as though they were dead before we met them. They missed their own deaths, and so did we, but in a way that compounds our sense of being separated from them by an unbridgeable distance. This, too, resembled my situation in Zurich. I felt that even though I had been there, I was so disconnected with what was happening to Bob that even to be there was to be hopelessly far away. Making this comparison enabled me to convey to friends how I was led to feel at fault, despite my powerlessness, when I realized that all I had left were . . . flat lines.

The resemblance between the scene from the film and my experience may not sound comforting. Yet recognizing the comparison was. The scene in the film enabled me to see that there was a precedent in my life for my bewildering feelings. It helped me to make sense of the paralyzing horror that was part of my emotional state. The scene also gave me a reference point for explaining to others why I felt that I had so entirely failed Bob in his final moments, a reaction that people I had spoken with found baffling.

My friends (most of whom had seen the film) could use the scene, too, as a means for explaining to me that my inattention during defibrillation could not have caused feelings of abandonment. By the point that the monitor was attached, Bob had already died, as was confirmed by the flat lines on the display when electricity was not flowing. The scene from the film, in other words, was communicative currency at a time when verbal explanations left my confidants and me feeling that we simply could not get through to each other. The film was an excellent companion, not competing with my friends, but in solidarity with all of us.

ARTISTIC EMPLOYMENTS OF ABSENCE

That *2001: A Space Odyssey* offered me and my puzzled friends a common language in my bereavement depended on our specific background of having seen this film. Whether an artwork can serve as a bridge will depend on whether those attempting to communicate have common experience of the work in question. Fortunately, artistic tropes, devices, and images used in myriad works can also serve as bases for communicating, and because they are so familiar, they tend to have greater common resonance than particular works. Often, too, they are sufficiently underspecified that they correspond in general ways with a broad range of individual experiences.

Artistic techniques that suggest absence are among the devices that help communicate a certain aspect of bereavement. Artistic reflections of the experience of a beloved person's absence can be powerfully affecting. The experience of being disappointed in the expectation of encountering a particular person is familiar to virtually everyone from infancy, when one sometimes makes the troubling discovery that one's caregiver is not present. This may be one of the reasons we can find a poem or ballad about a person's absence so haunting, even when we believe that both the persona expressing emotion and the absent person are fictional.[9] We relate to the protagonist not as a personal acquaintance, but as a human being experiencing an ache of longing that is endemic to our common condition.[10]

The theme of longing for someone who is absent, or love in separation, appears frequently in narratives and non-narrative works (such as paintings) that illustrate or allude to them. But absence can also be symbolically indicated by formal techniques, as well. One of these is the use of negative space. Empty space does not always signal absence, but context can show that absence is the intended meaning. So can incomplete compliance with expectations associated with the work's genre or other hints conveyed through judicious use of a well-known formal vocabulary.

Works using negative space to convey the impression of a deceased person's absence can be evocative in part because such works play on observers' anticipations. The absence marks the site of something they might have expected to find, but do not. This is a feature of the experience of negative space in the Oklahoma City National Memorial. Part of the memorial is the Field of Empty Chairs, which includes an empty chair for each person killed in the bombing of the city's Alfred P. Murrah Federal Building. In general, an empty chair suggests the possibility of someone sitting in it, and sometimes it is understood as setting a place for a particular person. The empty chairs that are part of the memorial do set places for particular individuals, but individuals who will never sit in them. Particularly haunting are the tiny chairs honoring the children who died. Seeing these little chairs for perpetually absent children is heartrending, particularly because they are positioned outside in a grassy area that might otherwise be suitable as a place for children to run.

The site draws further attention to the victims' absence because the chairs are located in the footprint of the Murrah Building. Even the structure of the place where most of them worked or attended day care has been annihilated. The building now fits the category that Jeannette Bicknell terms "architectural ghosts," "human-made structures that no longer exist and can now be known only through traces they have left."[11] The empty chairs standing vigil within the ghost of the building assert the absence of an entire bustling community that was suddenly erased.

Architect Michael Benedikt notes another case in which absence is conveyed by negative space in his discussion of what he describes as "the relational grouping" evident in a picture of a North African grave site that was "published by Dutch architect Aldo van Eyck in 1953." The grave is shown as taking the form of a low-built quadrilateral structure that frames the space. The structure has walls on the four sides that occasionally veer up to form points, reminiscent in a stylized way of the heads of people sitting in a circle. There is a lowered, flattened area on one side and an especially prominent heightened point directly opposite it. Benedikt sees this as manifesting absence and presence simultaneously. He urges the reader who is consulting the photograph:

> Notice—feel—the gravesite's dipping gesture at entry and notice—feel—the fifth, mid-wall element, i.e., the honorific rise directly across from the entry dip. This rise both marks the whereabouts of the deceased's body, and the gone-ness of the actual person. Is the hole his absence? It is not in us too? And yet the departed presides, paternal, eternal, in a posture of greeting, accompanied by the ring of his friends.[12]

This may be an imaginative construal of the grave's design, but one that its shape certainly invites.

Formal devices in music, too, can convey the presence of absence, as musicologist Scott Schumann points out. In his analysis of Stravinsky's *Élégie* for solo viola, Schumann emphasizes the composer's repeated avoidance of the tonic, making it an absent presence in the work. Similarly, Stravinsky focuses on the pitch A in the early part of the third movement of his memorial work *Ode*, but then avoids the pitch when earlier material is reiterated at the end of the movement. This strategy, says Schumann, results in listeners experiencing an absence in the movement's final musical gesture.[13] Those who have enough experience with Western classical music to be oriented in works, such as this, which present a return of material heard earlier, will be expecting the basic shape that was established by structurally significant pitches to be preserved. The avoidance of a salient pitch in the later presentation will be felt as an absence because listeners will be missing it.

THE FIGURE OF THE GHOST

Artworks of the sort I have been describing use formal means to convey impressions of absence by emphasizing places in which the presence of something was expected but not delivered. The simultaneity and ambiguity of presence and absence in grief can also be conveyed by a converse approach, that of rendering something that is absent as an obtrusive presence. This is the strategy employed in many works featuring the image of the ghost, which literalizes the idea of an absence as present.

The topic of literal ghosts is not in vogue among contemporary intellectuals, but this was not always the case. Thomas Laqueur points out that for centuries, many in intellectual circles considered how one could distinguish real ghosts from fake ones and whether spirits appeared with divine sanction or by virtue of the activity of satanic forces. He cites even utilitarian reformer Jeremy Bentham as remarking that the "subject of ghosts had been among the torments of his life."[14]

Things changed in the eighteenth century, however, when the rise of science resulted in skepticism toward the spectral (though interest in the occult flourished at the same time, as a kind of "return of the repressed").[15] The scientifically respectable view of ghosts that developed was that they were projections of the psyche. "Ghosts became thoughts," Laqueur contends, and he cites the literary critic Terry Castle as aptly describing the consequences: "By relocating the world of ghosts in the closed space of the imagination, one ended up supernaturalising the mind itself."[16]

I will consider ghosts from this contemporary point of view, though my argument does not depend on disbelief in literal ghosts.[17] I'm inclined to observe, facetiously, that if ghosts did not exist, bereavement would compel us to invent them. In any case, the figure of the ghost economically condenses many features of the bizarre phenomenology of bereavement into an external image. Regardless of our credence or our skepticism, we can make use of the image of the ghost, which is familiar from cultural tropes, ghost stories, and other art forms that make use of it. And given its reflection of some of the uncanny features of the experience of grieving, I think it is no wonder that the ghost has staying power (so to speak).

From the standpoint of the artist, the figure of the ghost offers opportunities for creative elaboration, for the characteristics of ghosts are vague at best. Artistic variations abound. A wiki site devoted to television tropes offers extensive lists of possible characteristics that presented ghosts may have, whether they appear on TV, in other sorts of artworks, or the folklore of religious traditions. The site considers alternative motivations, powers, limitations, ways of interacting with the living, ways of appearing, and vulnerabilities as noteworthy variables.[18] Filmmakers, among others, have worked with quite different sets of ground rules for how ghosts are supposed to act. For example, in the film *A Ghost Story* (2017), directed by David Lowery, ghosts can communicate with each other, but seem to be anchored to particular places. In the film *Beetlejuice* (1988), directed by Tim Burton, the ghostly realm has numerous rules and practices, so many that the ghostly protagonists are issued a *Handbook for the Newly Deceased* upon arrival in their posthumous existence. Both films emphasize the situation from the point of view of the ghost, but they do it in very different ways. *A Ghost Story* is deeply melancholy in tone, while *Beetlejuice* is a comedy.

Despite this artistic license, widely known artworks and media productions have popularized ideas about what ghosts are like and what sorts of behavior one might expect from them. I will be suggesting that the figure is useful for suggesting aspects of the phenomenology of bereavement to those who have not experienced it. Even variations in ghostly features often correspond to different phenomenological aspects of grieving. This is so much the case that I suspect that many ideas about ghosts' behavior and capacities derived initially from bizarre experiences people had in bereavement that were then projected onto a figure that helps to contain them.[19]

The following are some relatively common views about ghosts promoted by mainstream media and art (at least in the United States and other Western societies, but probably many others, too): Ghosts are the spirits of the dead returned to earth. They appear from time to time, and they come and go as they will. The living cannot make them appear, and usually they cannot detain them against their will. Ghosts are not bound by ordinary material constraints; they can dissolve or vanish through walls. But often they can manipulate material objects. A. O. Scott, reviewing *A Ghost Story*, refers to the display of "some of the usual haunting behaviors" by the ghost in the film: "He knocks books off shelves, makes light bulbs flicker, opens closet doors in the middle of the night and subjects a terrified family to a full-scale, crockery-smashing supernatural tantrum."[20]

A ghost's continuity with the person who has died is complicated. It both is and is not the beloved person. A ghost may have hostile attitudes out of keeping with those displayed by the person during life. Ghosts may in fact be menacing, out to avenge themselves on the living. They may be attached to places, springing on those who, innocently or not, wander into their precincts. Ghosts seem to know more than the living, and sometimes they are in a position to offer revelations. When they do, however, their messages are not always clear or complete, and the living are often left uncertain about what to make of some ghostly utterance.

Such popularized ideas about ghosts and their behavior externalize features of the phenomenology of bereavement. First, ghosts restore the deceased to space and time. The unfulfillable wish that the deceased person be returned to our world is partially satisfied by the figure of the ghost. Encountering the loved one's ghost would fulfill the desire to see the person. In fact, as we have considered, the bereaved are on the lookout. Search behavior is undertaken automatically. If you see a ghost, you often see what you were looking for.

But then again, you don't. The dead person has not really rejoined us, because the ghost both is and is not the person. Commonplaces about ghosts reflect the reality that bereaved people know but usually don't want to assimilate—they haven't come back to us. Ghosts come and go capriciously, and this reflects the fact that although one sometimes has a strong impression of the dead person's presence, one cannot summon or control it or do anything to ensure that it abides. We might recall C. S. Lewis's account, cited in chapter 3, of his surprise when he felt the sudden arrival of his wife's presence at a moment when he was paying no particular attention to his loss. Ghosts, like such apparent visitations, go where they will, walking on air, passing through walls. Sometimes they pay a visit, but just as often they give us the slip—particularly if we want to hold on to them.

Ghosts' power to appear and then evaporate contributes to their supposed scariness. This power seems superhuman, and thus alien. But perhaps even more unnerving is the idea that the dead are aware of much that was hidden from them while alive, which we considered in chapter 3. There I mentioned the common impression in bereavement that the deceased know what is in one's hearts and that one is culpable in relation to him or her. The idea of the knowing ghost externalizes the frequent impression among the bereaved that the deceased loved one now knows the survivor's secrets. Hamlet's father in spectral form epitomizes the quasi-omniscient ghost. The fact that he did not prevent his own death is evidence that he lacked the knowledge of the plot against him while alive, but as a ghost he knows the identity of the guilty parties and is able to describe the details of his murder to Hamlet.[21] This conception of ghosts' privileged epistemological position is also a premise in the pilot episode of the HBO television series *Six Feet Under*. An aging mortician is killed early in the episode when a bus runs into his car. After his wife has been informed of his death, she retreats to their bedroom and while looking at herself in a mirror, sees him standing next to her. She tells him she knows that he knows. She subsequently confesses to her sons that she was unfaithful to her husband for years, adding "and now he knows."[22]

The impression that ghosts can see the ugly truths that we managed to keep from their living counterparts gives them a potential reason to be hostile, though our failure to have prevented their deaths gives them motive enough. The idea that ghosts are often ill-disposed toward those who are close to them is geographically widespread, and many cultures engage in mourning practices aimed at placating ghosts, who might otherwise attack the living. The fear of ghosts' hostility parallels a common perception in bereavement that however close we were to the person in life, they might be unsympathetic or alienated in their altered condition (assuming a continuation of their consciousness). Particularly if one's last encounter with the person was less than perfect (as inevitably it will have been), it is easy to imagine that the person ultimately viewed one harshly and that this perspective is now a definitive fact about the relationship.

At the very least, grieving individuals may imagine the deceased loved one as being somewhat alien or estranged. In bereavement, a person is faced with trying to put the ideas of the loved one and "deceased" together, and this is hard to do. The emotional detachment often associated with ghosts may reflect the difficulty of combining the feelings of emotional rapport that attended thoughts of the loved one while alive with their current inaccessibility. It is as though the awareness that they are not "present" in an ordinary sense is interpreted as emotional aloofness.

Perhaps the widespread fear that a loved one's ghost is hostile is also grounded in the difficulty of bringing the various aspects of the person together in one's mind. The spontaneous mental review of disconnected images underscores the fact that aspects of our thoughts of the person are not bound together in our thinking, and we now confront impressions that seem incompatible with emotional closeness. One faces, to begin with, the impossibility of reconciling one's impression of the lifeless body with the hitherto vibrant loved one. The inertness of the loved one's body can be associated with unfriendliness. Someone who was responsive to you as a particular individual lies there, apparently indifferent. We can no longer have confidence that the person is on our side in any sense. And perhaps the ambivalent response we may have to seeing the corpse, in which repugnance mitigates the longing we might feel, gets transferred onto the ghostly figure. We cannot rely on the ghost's affection, and we might anticipate being rebuffed or otherwise maltreated, given our own reaction toward the cadaver.

In artistic presentations, the motivations that prompt a ghost to appear vary widely. Some are concerned to ensure that they are properly mourned or buried.[23] Some have unfinished business on earth, completion of which may require some action on the part of a living person. (One of the ghosts in M. Night Shyamalan's *Sixth Sense* seems to need the help of another character, though perhaps another ghost, when she seeks to alert her father that her mother had poisoned her and is attempting to visit the same fate on her younger sister.[24]) Some appear with the motive of helping the living, perhaps by warning them of a danger (as is the case with Jacob Marley's ghost in Charles Dickens's *Christmas Carol*). Some want justice for themselves (as does Hamlet's father's ghost) or all-out vengeance (as seems to be the aim of the ghostly figure in *High Plains Drifter*, directed by Clint Eastwood[25]).

One can see these various ghostly motivations as reflecting motives the bereaved themselves feel. Grieving people usually feel driven to ensure that the proper mourning rituals are performed. They often feel that it behooves them to take up some project or pursue some unfulfilled wish of the deceased. If they are in the position of executing the person's estate, they are also legally compelled to enact the person's wishes. If they believe that someone is responsible for the death, they are likely to seek justice or revenge. The ferocity with which bereaved people may feel such motivations may be hard to grasp for those who have not been similarly situated, but the unrelenting aims of fictional ghosts, undiluted by mundane preoccupations, can imaginatively convey something of the sense of urgency that grieving people typically feel.

Ghosts in art can also raise a question that parallels the historical debate about distinguishing real ghosts from fake ones. As audience members, we are sometimes left in doubt about whether a ghost is to be considered "real" or whether the person who sees it is hallucinating. This uncertainty might be seen as mirroring another that often afflicts people who are bereaved. Many sense the presence of the bereaved from time to time or experience apparitions. Regardless of their beliefs regarding spiritual survival, they may well wonder what to make of this. Even those who believe in the existence of ghosts may still doubt that what they are experiencing is more than wishful thinking. And those who view ghosts as projections from the psyche may wonder whether their experiences are potentially revelatory communications from the unconscious or whether they are simply a function of their imaginations running wild. We do not really know what to make of ghosts, whether or not we believe in them. They are embodied manifestations of the condition in bereavement of not knowing what to believe.

Those who are skeptical about the existence of ghosts are not immune from the power of the ghost as a figure. To disbelieve in ghosts is beside the point of the ghost story. Even to entertain the idea of such beings involves resisting set convictions about what is so. This mirrors the eerie condition of bereavement in which belief and knowledge get pulled apart. Ghosts demand that we bracket our skepticism. We are free not to do so, but the idea of ghosts endures in cultural and artistic space, potentially rattling our commitment to our disbelief. And to get anything from ghostly figures, whether considered as external visitors or as projections, we must go along with their program.

But to give in to them is to be haunted, if only fictionally so, and to be haunted is to be on the verge of collapsing into an unknown world that is disconnected from ordinary social reality. This, too, may contribute to the impression of ghosts as scary. To see ghosts is to cease to be grounded in the down-to-earth reality in which our social world has confidence. It is to be partially outside the world that is here and now and to occupy an isolated alternate reality. But this is just the condition in which the bereaved person currently lives.

Ghosts have power only to the extent that we relinquish a sense of clear division between our own world and theirs. Ghosts demand, if one encounters them, that one enters their liminal space, leaving behind the comforting normality of life as we think we know it. Artworks involving the figure of the ghost invite us to imagine being within this in-between world, where unusual perspectives can be entertained and, perhaps, yield insight.[26] I am convinced that they can assist exploration of the liminal state involved in grieving. To give an impression of the kind of exploration I have in mind, I will proceed to consider two examples.

ZEAMI'S *IZUTSU*

Izutsu (*Well*),[27] a classic of Japanese Noh theater written by Zeami Motokiyo (c. 1363–c. 1443), presents the story of a Buddhist priest who has traveled to a location where a temple formerly stood. The site is associated with a pair of famous lovers, the poet Ariwara no Narihira and a woman identified as the daughter of Ki no Aritsune, and the priest prays for the repose of their souls. He then meets an old woman who tells him the story of the lovers, who had been childhood playmates and married when they became adults. At a certain point, the male member of the couple began a dalliance with another woman, but he was drawn back to his wife when he observed her in secret and recognized the sweetness of her love for him.

Before the old woman vanishes, she reveals her identity to the priest. She is the ghost of the daughter of Aritsune. When the priest goes to sleep for the night, the ghost appears in his dream, now undisguisedly the female member of the famous pair. She recites a poem about the transience of cherry blossoms and then performs a dance that expresses her tender feelings for her husband. At the end of the play, dawn breaks. The priest awakens as the ghost disappears.

The climax of the play occurs in the scene depicting the priest's dream. The dream ghost puts on the robes of her late husband, performing a dance that expresses her longing for him. She wistfully refers to "this world where nothing stays except this keepsake, these robes of Narihira, which I have put on." She recites the poem he sent her at the beginning of their romance, a poem in which the central image is their looking at their reflections in the well together as children. Then, strikingly, she dons her husband's hat and looks into the well. In the reflection, she glimpses the hat above the face and momentarily imagines that she sees her husband's countenance. "I see! Oh, how dear he is!" she cries, and the chorus echoes, "Though it is myself, Oh, how dear he is!"[28]

What makes the play especially relevant for purposes here is that the ghost in *Izutsu* is presented as a widow. Indeed, her widowhood seems to be the basis for the attachment that pulls her back to earth from the spirit world. We see her taking on characteristic behaviors of bereavement. Her seeing her husband's face in the well suggests search behavior. Her donning of her husband's clothing is a familiar gesture of introjection. Her experience of the reflection in the well—seeing him through seeing herself—testifies to her sense of their inseparability. But when the spell is broken and she becomes aware that it is her own face she sees, she is a prototypical mourner, whose brief impression of the loved one's presence must collapse as she confronts the reality of his absence.

This scene, presenting a dream about a ghost who is herself bereaved, hints at the intensity with which bereavement forces the relational character of one's identity into view. We might have expected that, as a ghost, the woman would be in the same "place" as her late husband, but, instead, she is bereaved in her ghostly state. Her identity is bound up with her love for her absent husband, as perhaps befits a romantic heroine. But her condition resembles a common situation in bereavement, that of being overwhelmed by longing for person who is absent. In this state, one can feel that one has passed somewhat beyond this life to the atemporal place where the dead person is. And yet having entered this liminal state, one does not find that one's longing is satisfied. Instead, that longing becomes one's ever-present reality.[29]

Bereavement's unsettled condition, characterized by opposite tendencies such as presence and absence, is reflected in the many layers of liminality in the play. The framing of the dancing scene is liminal on multiple levels. The priest himself is in transit, pausing in his journey to reflect and pray. The location is the site of an architectural ghost, the former temple. The dream is prompted by a waking encounter with a woman who is actually a ghost, and the dance is performed by a ghost within a dream. The story is also multiply refracted through the priest's recollection, the ghost's narration, the dreamed ghost's enactment of the movements of her absent husband, and her experience of the husband's presence and absence. The extreme liminality of the play's framing makes it clear that any effort to distinguish reality from the imagined is utterly beside the point, something that may be as true in bereavement as it is in making sense of the play.

Wells themselves are liminal, conjoining the upper and the lower world. The ghost first appears to the priest in waking life as an old woman coming to draw holy water from the well, bringing water from the lower world to the upper world where the living dwell. (Her statement that she does this each day also confuses temporality in that ghosts are presumably outside of time.) When filled with water, wells create conditions for confusing what is real with what is only reflection. Yet in the play, the well is also a site that had nurtured the real relationship between the lovers. It serves as an objective correlative of their relationship, harboring memories of their shared childhood, the kindling of their romance, and the renewal of the husband's love. The poem the ghost recites, in which her lover conveys his feelings for her, begins with reference to the well-curb, against which they measured their heights as children. The well arouses thoughts of both transience and permanence. Though enduring itself, its content, water, epitomizes flow. It is a persisting symbol of the evanescent children who used it to mark their successive attainment of various ages, a practice that draws attention to the passage of time. The fleetingness of time is underscored by the fact that the poem about the children was composed by one of them in adulthood, and the fact that his life has ended long before the presented scene in the play.

The lovers are never presented together. The events in the play are ensconced in an atmosphere of absence. The actual lovers lived in a time far removed from the present reality of the priest. The ghost is a reflection of only one of them, who is herself overwhelmed by the absence of the other. Bereaved in life, she remains bereaved as a ghost. Catching sight of her husband in the well, she replays the children's joyful game of viewing their faces in the well, but while the children's game pointed to their future life together, her sighting of her husband briefly blocks her ability to discern her own face. She cannot see their faces simultaneously, but only one at a time.

And yet, I hesitate to say that what occurs when the ghost sees her husband is presented as merely a misperception. Recurrently, the ghost within the dream observes that memory enables the past to endure. "How true that whatever comes / leaves its memories / in the minds of those who love / within this changing world."[30] Although she refers to her husband's robe as a mere "keepsake," she is also stirred by his clothing. By putting it on, she reanimates it. Her own movements while wearing it enliven it so convincingly that for a flicker of a moment, she believes that she sees her husband himself. And perhaps for a moment, she really does see him within the liminal space.

Those who read or see Zeami's play are prompted to imagine and explore the terrain of grief as it is enacted by the ghostly figure. In this respect, *Izutsu* can serve as an artistic means through which those who have not experienced bereavement can gain a sense of the emotional and reflective currents that are involved. The play's sustained poetic exploration of love and emotional attachment makes *Izutsu* available to mourners and non-mourners alike as a basis for reflection about the relationship of living people and their deceased loved ones. Is the priest's whole encounter with the lovers' story just a passing reverie in this lonely place? Or can physical remnants of former lives enable the dead to speak to us? Does the priest's recollection of the lovers when he comes to the site revivify them? Do they continue to "live" as long as they are carried in someone's memory? Is there a sense in which the dancing ghost brings back her husband when she misidentifies her own face? And is the free flow of identity from old woman to ghost to dream figure to transfigured dancer to the reanimated beloved a revelation of the truth (implied by the Buddhist no-self doctrine) that we are not separate selves, but participants in a dance that is shared by the living and the dead? Does the ghost within the dream remain apart from her deceased husband only because she does not recognize that the separation is the illusion? And does she grasp the truth at that moment when she cannot tell them apart?

The play can stir reflections on these matters and the aspects of the human condition to which they refer. It raises questions about how we relate to each other, to transience, and to those who are no longer alive. These questions are relevant to all of us, whether or not we have personally experienced grief. The play might make it possible for those whose lives have not yet presented occasions for grieving to gain some sense of the in-between character of the experience.[31] But even if its liminal framing makes comparisons with lived experience seem difficult, the existential questions that it raises might enable those with different experiential backgrounds to marvel together at the mysteries of human life and death.

TARKOVSKY'S *SOLARIS*

Let us now turn to a contemporary artwork making use of ghostly figures, Andrei Tarkovsky's film *Solaris*, based on Stanisław Lem's science-fiction novel of the same name.[32] The film affords opportunities for as-if experiences that can help those who have not yet grieved to understand their grieving counterparts, though, like *Izutsu*, it is fertile in many other ways that I will not touch upon in my discussion.

I am not alone in seeing Tarkovsky's film as a meditation on grief. "As a haunted ode to lost love," says film critic Chris Barsanti, "*Solaris* has few equals in all of cinema."[33] Phillip Lopate observes, "Unlike *2001*, . . . Solaris is saturated with grief, which grips the film even before it leaves the earth."[34] Hospital chaplain Joey Armstrong more or less recommends the film as a companion work. He comments, "As a hospice care specialist, I can assure you that rarely in film will we get as close to grief as with Andrew Tarkovsky's *Solaris*."[35]

The basic plot of film, following the novel, concerns the experiences of a psychologist, Kris Kelvin, who is sent from Earth to investigate a space station near the planet Solaris after each of its crew members has experienced an undiagnosed emotional breakdown. Kelvin arrives to discover only two living crew members on the station, Dr. Sartorius and Dr. Snaut, neither of whom is forthcoming about what has been going on. A friend of Kelvin's, a crew member who has killed himself, has left Kelvin a video message that refers to the problems on the station.

Kelvin gets some rest in his quarters, and when he awakens, he finds his wife, Hari, in his room even though she died of suicide a decade before. The present Hari's status as a replica becomes evident when she asks Kelvin to help her remove her dress and he discovers that the dress has no fasteners. He persuades this replicant Hari to get into a space capsule, which he launches into space.

One of the crewmates explains to Kelvin that all the crew members have been receiving such visitations, which had begun when they made contact with the planet Solaris. He claims that Solaris creates these "visitors" by tapping into each crew member's memories. He also says that the crew has developed an annihilator that can stop the visitors from returning. He proposes that they beam Kelvin's brainwaves into the planet to convey the message that the visitors must stop, for Solaris is obviously an intelligent being.

Hari reappears in Kelvin's room, despite his having shot a previous "Hari" into space. This time, Kelvin embraces her, and they fall asleep. Kelvin and the new Hari soon fall in love with each other, and this makes Kelvin hesitate to assist in any effort to put an end to the appearances of visitors. Kelvin and Hari jointly attend a birthday party for one of the crewmates, and when she is reminded that she is not the real Hari, she kills herself by drinking liquid oxygen, though she revives a short time later.

Kelvin retreats to his quarters in a feverish state, and he stays there for several days. When he emerges, he discovers that Hari has gone. She has left a letter to Kelvin in which she explains that she had asked the other astronauts to destroy her. Neither Hari nor the other visitors appear again. Nevertheless, Kelvin is undecided about whether to return to Earth. Armstrong puts Kelvin's quandary as follows: "Should I return to Earth and all that is present there or should I live on Solaris, where all of my memories, both happy and sad, will be with me forever?"[36] In the next scene we see Kelvin back at his aged father's country home, which is where the film had opened. His father opens the door to let him in, and Kelvin drops to his knees and hugs his father's legs. The camera zooms out, and we come to recognize that Kelvin is not on Earth as he seems to be, but instead on an island on Solaris.

Much in the plot conveys aspects of the experience of grief. Lopate points out that the way the film is cut contributes to feelings of liminality and "ontological instability." He notes the jittery camera work, which is "suggestive of a seizure." He also highlights Hari's body "jerking at the threshold of being and nonbeing" during her suicide attempt and a temporary loss of gravity that Hari and Kelvin experience together, which Lopate sees as "another stylized representation of this transcendence borderline," which is the obsessive focus of people who are grieving.[37]

The blocking of scenes on the space station also conveys a perceptual sense of bodily unease that is reminiscent of grief experience.[38] The camera angle on locations within the space station makes the environment seem oppressive. The curvature of the walls is pronounced, the portholes have disparate sizes, and physical objects are often only partially within the frame. Even a seemingly symmetrical view of the space station's hallway is set off-center. The curving hallway has no horizon, its apparent continuation unalleviated by visual punctuation. The dark beams and walls in many places make the rooms seem confining, cramping the human figures who appear. Rooms are disheveled, with tossed-aside bits of equipment and larger machinery standing off-kilter. As we accompany the film's protagonist through his experiences on the space station, we absorb his feelings of physical distress and disorientation. The entire environment, along with events in it, create a sense of uncanniness in which one's very body feels tyrannized.

The most central parallel with grief experience is Kelvin's fluctuation between loving the vision projected from his memories and his recognition that he is not relating to the real Hari. This recalls the situation in bereavement in which one lurches between the consoling sense of the absent person's presence and the reality principle's flat insistence that the person is no longer there. Kelvin's situation also reflects two aspects of grief that

Lewis emphasizes in *A Grief Observed*, the inability to control impressions of the deceased person's presence as well as the fear that one's memories are becoming clouded over with one's own fanciful projections.[39] The film draws the viewer into empathizing with Kelvin in this precarious position, which Lopate sees as the source of the film's poignancy: "The real power of the film comes from the anguish of Kris's reawakened love for Hari—his willingness to do anything to hold on to her, even knowing she isn't real (. . . this is a story about falling in love with ghosts)."[40]

Indeed, the film draws attention to a danger of ghosts that is ignored when we envision them as frightening. The greatest threat of ghosts may be that they are too alluring. The film forces viewers to recognize that the prospect of seeing our deceased loved ones, especially when they conform to our imaginative view of them, is nearly irresistible. Kelvin falls in love with the visiting "Hari," even though he and she both realize that she is not really his dead wife. She is gone by the time Kelvin decides not to return to Earth, but since she has been revived many times, he may harbor hopes of seeing her again. In any case, he responds to a replica as his actual father at the end of the film, and his behavior suggests that he feels the satisfaction that a real reunion with a loved one might inspire, even though he will never again see his real father, who (being very elderly at the start of the film) is most likely already dead.

Kelvin's decision to stay on Solaris may meet with audience dismay. But if his opting for a life of dreams over engagement with reality seems tragic, we nevertheless understand his choice. *Solaris* allows us to explore the appeal of choices that doom real interaction with living people by ensnaring one in memories and fantasies. In doing so, it can help us relate to actual grieving people who feel detached from worldly projects or express the wish that they could follow their dead loved ones to the grave.

I do not mean to reduce Zeami's *Izutsu* and Tarkovsky's *Solaris* to therapeutic aids. These works are among the masterpieces of their respective genres, and their many valuable facets recommend extended and frequent engagement with each of them. I draw attention to these works in this context because I think they generate especially powerful as-if experiences that can make the experience of grief more socially comprehensible than it otherwise might be. These works can occasion intersubjective reflection that restores grief to our common attention, something that is particularly important in cultures like my own that do not provide much social space for grieving.

Anyone who has experienced bereavement is aware that the commotion of this state cannot be envisioned in advance, no matter how much a loved one's death has been anticipated. This commotion contrasts with the relatively tranquil state that is usually involved when one approaches an artwork, even one that takes distressing material as subject matter. Nonetheless, artworks that explore grief, memory, and continuing love provide audience members with imaginative experiences that can familiarize them with some of the emotional complexity and uncanniness of the grief experience. Such works can therefore provide training for interaction with the grieving people and for experiencing grief oneself. They can also serve the bereaved as points of reference for comprehending their own experience and for making their condition somewhat intelligible to others.

I have suggested that artistic representations of ghosts might be particularly helpful for suggesting certain features of the experience of grief because these features are reflected in characteristics associated with the ghostly figure. Nothing I have said, however, should be construed as implying that the figure of the ghost is domesticable. Representations of ghosts are serviceable for reflecting the experience of grief because they suggest uncanniness, stubbornly resisting our efforts to assimilate them into our world. The uncanny amalgamates what is well-known with what is bewildering, recasting everything that is familiar as being potentially bizarre. Because it defamiliarizes even the most routine features of one's world, we can think of bereavement as uncanny through and through, and the ghost figure as a fictional incarnation of the uncanny.

Perhaps the most important way that ghosts reflect grief is by reflecting what is not contained and not containable within the grieving experience, the ambiguous presence-absence of the deceased. If bereaved people are to be understood, this dimension of their condition must be recognized. Artworks that give those without comparable experience a taste of what this condition is like can help bridge communicative divides that might otherwise strain relationships between them and those who grieve.

In this and the previous chapter, I have focused attention on artworks and artistic practices that can help grieving people reintegrate into the social world, from which their loss often makes them feel dissociated. Relationships with the living, however, are not the only ones that grieving people need to recalibrate. The relationship between a bereaved person and the deceased also requires renegotiation. In the following chapter, I will consider this project and the way that aesthetic practices can help one accomplish it.

7
Dealing with the Dead

The dead can be lively presences. To discover this can be unsettling, as James Joyce brings home in his *Dubliners* story "The Dead."[1] The tale describes a holiday party given by three elderly sisters and its aftermath. It is told from the viewpoint of the sisters' nephew, Gabriel Conroy. The final scene is set in the hotel room where Gabriel and his wife, Gretta, have retreated to spend the night.

Gabriel is eager to make love, having been aroused by Gretta's emotional reaction to a song sung at the end of the party, but she does not share his amorous aspirations. She tells him that the song had reminded her of a youthful love, Michael Furey. The boy had died of consumption at the age of seventeen after keeping vigil outside her window on a cold, rainy night just before she was to leave her home in Galway and move to Dublin. Weeping, Gretta confides that she has always felt responsible for his death. After a bout of sobbing into her pillow, she falls asleep, and Gabriel broods over the fact that his wife has carried this long-dead teenager in her heart the entire time he has known her. He is convinced that Michael Furey loved Gretta more zealously than he ever had or ever would. But he recognizes the pointlessness of competing with a dead loved one held in memory. He somberly reminds himself as the story draws to a close that before long, all of them—his aunts, Gretta, and he himself—will be but memories themselves.

The dead, for those who grieve them, can seem more psychically powerful than the living, sometimes with damaging effects. Experienced as absent, they diminish one's sense of being present oneself. We internalize their voices, which can still seem to be making demands.[2] And they can threaten to disrupt relationships with the living, particularly when maintaining a connection with them seems to require abstinence from goal-directed activities.

Aesthetic practices can help us to navigate these treacherous waters. They can help us retain a concrete impression of the deceased as a distinct individual, and they provide vehicles for comporting ourselves toward that person. They provide outlets for our desire to communicate with the dead and help us to renew reciprocal relationships with them. They serve as means for commemorating the dead, helping us to attend to them while renewing engagement in the world of the living. I will defend these claims in what follows.

SELF-FAMILIARITY AND A FELT SENSE OF THE DECEASED

As we considered in chapter 3, one's self-impression is often disturbed in bereavement. When we have interacted on a daily basis with a person, many of our habits and ways of orienting ourselves in the world refer to him or her, and one's own impression of oneself is partially based on habits of interacting with the person. Allan Køster draws attention to the extent to which our interactive habits involve sensory experience. Our sense of our own bodies reflects our receptivity to those with whom our life is intertwined as specific individuals, each with particular characteristics that are registered across sensory modes. As a consequence, when one of those individuals dies, our own embodied being is disrupted, for we are oriented toward responding in multisensory ways to a person who is no longer there.[3]

According to Køster, in order to sustain a continuing bond with the person, one must have an embodied, preverbal sense of the person as a "concrete Other." Our sense of a person is given concreteness through impressions of the person's distinctive "sensory qualities (auditory, olfactory, tactile, visual), his kinaesthetic rhythms, atmospheric presence, etc." We must sustain an impression that meets a certain threshold of clarity if engaging with "typical mediators of continuing bonds such as visual and object representations, rituals, narratives, and social practices" is really going to function in helping one to maintain the bond.[4] Thus, Køster considers a concrete sensory impression of the person a precondition for benefiting from these typically aesthetic means that help us to keep a sense of the person alive.

I agree that mediating objects and practices aimed at helping one feel a link with the deceased will not be useful for those who lack any sense of the person as a distinct embodied presence. Køster describes the case of a woman who lost her father as a child and does not feel any connection with video images of him because she did not retain any memory of him as a specific embodied being. However, the retention of such a felt sense of the person can be supported early on in bereavement by means of sensory contrivances, as can a degree of self-familiarity.

Representations of the deceased such as photographs and videos, for example, can conjure up the felt sense of the concrete person that Køster describes. The person's physical stance and embodied attitude can come through in a way that brings a fuller impression of the person to mind. Aesthetic activities making use of them can also afford symbolic opportunities to behave in ways that reflect an attitude of receptivity toward the deceased. Such representations can thus help us retain impressions of the way deceased loved ones occupied their bodies, and we can also use them as focal centers for symbolically comporting ourselves toward them.

Photographs of the deceased positioned in memorial halls and funeral homes, for example, serve this double function. They offer sensory surrogates that symbolically emplace the person in our world. They also allow mourners to adopt a bodily orientation toward the person despite the person's physical absence. Photographs thus enable mourners to engage in behavior in which they regard themselves as active participants in an ongoing relationship with the deceased.

Funeral rituals and other commemorative events allow for sensory immersion that is reminiscent of immediate multimodal engagement with the deceased, who has been summoned as an implicit "presence" at the proceedings. Such rituals focus the mind on the person as a distinct individual, and the sensory involvement helps us retain a felt sense of him or her by enabling us to bodily relate ourselves to the person. Funerals typically activate vision and hearing, but often other senses as well. Movement, which involves the kinesthetic sense, may be part of the scripted program, as when processions are part of the service or when those present are called on to rise at certain moments. Incense, which addresses the olfactory sense, is used in some funerals, and the scent of flowers may permeate the environment. The haptic sense may be involved, too, as is the case when flowers or handfuls of dirt are tossed into a grave, or when a person serves as a pallbearer. Through the multisensory experience in the ritual, we engage in a surrogate interaction with the person. Such rituals can also reinforce a sense of ourselves as agents by involving us in the performance of gestures directed toward the deceased. This counters the corrosion of self-impression that the loss has brought about. Rituals thus enable us both to recognize ourselves as active, responsive beings and to relate to the person, even if only symbolically.

THE URGE TO COMMUNICATE

Part of the shock of a loved one's death stems from the abrupt elimination of the possibility of conversing with the person. Particularly when the person has been central in one's network of relationships and one's everyday interactions with the environment, his or her abrupt departure is harrowing. The shock is compounded if the person you would ordinarily consult during crises is the very person who has died.[5] The desire to check in with the person is an "action tendency" that grief seems to provoke in many people.

In fact, many people literally act on this impulse by speaking to dead loved ones, whether aloud or in imagination, at least for some period after the person's passing.[6] But many also envision the deceased as witnessing their aesthetic gestures and activities, which to some extent provide outlets for the urge to communicate. Funeral rituals, creative projects dedicated to a loved one's memory, and more informal aesthetic practices that defer to the person's tastes make at least oblique reference to the dead as a part of the intended audience.

Many grief counselors and psychotherapists see value in relating to the dead through aesthetic activities. Sandra Dannenbaum and Richard Kinnier encourage grieving people to engage in "imaginal relationships with the dead," typically involving some form of conversation, but often making use of props designed to add a sensory dimension to the interaction.[7] Among these is the "empty chair" technique, developed by gestalt therapists. Unlike the empty chairs in the Oklahoma City National Memorial, which draw attention to the bombing victims' absence, the empty chair in this case affords an impression of as-if presence. It serves as a proxy for the absent person, and clients are encouraged to address the person as though he or she were actually sitting there.[8] Two therapists interviewed by Dannenbaum and Kinnier also encourage the use of photographs to "deepen the imaginal conversation" with the deceased, a recommendation reiterated by some counseling clients interviewed in the same study when asked what advice they would give to others.[9]

Grief counselors frequently encourage their clients to engage in creative artistic activities as well. Often the ostensible purpose is to externalize feelings and impressions that enable clients to notice things about their experience or their relationships that can serve as new bases for finding meaning. For example, Nancy Gershman and Barbara E. Thompson encourage grieving people to construct (physical or virtual) collages that flesh out stories that build on memories that they have revived. These "dreamscapes," which utilize photo images as materials, are then used as the basis for discussion within therapy, and efforts are made to shift the emotional tone associated with disturbing memories to more positive feelings and forward-looking attitudes.[10]

However, some grief therapists explicitly utilize art therapy as a means of directing communications toward the deceased, even if it may also serve other purposes.[11] For example, in certain forms of therapy, the grieving person engages in verbal and gestural enactments that express feelings and reassurances that they wish they had communicated to the deceased while alive. Describing her therapeutic work with clients whose loved ones have committed suicide, Diana C. Sands describes enactments that offer "opportunities . . . to hold and rock the loved one, symbolically represented by a pillow, saying unsaid words."[12] Shanee Stepakoff describes involving expressive writing in grief therapy, some of which is structured (for example, composing a letter to the deceased).[13]

Gestures of communication incorporated into therapy can be elaborate. Yu-Chan Li and Cypress Chang describe therapies involving a "Grief Healing Garden" at the National Taipei University of Nursing and Health Sciences, which was developed to help the bereaved, particularly parents who had lost children. The garden is used in a variety of ways, but Li and Chang mention several that take the form of directing messages to the dead. When grieving clients appear "ready to say something to the lost loved one," they are asked to write letters or poems that might be read aloud or to make drawings or collages. Whatever form the creative production takes, it is placed in a transparent, inflated plastic bag that is tied with a ribbon, and then it is set afloat in the "Wish Pool," connected to a waterway that flows through the garden. The plastic bag represents a "grief bubble," symbolizing the grieving person, who is visible to others but may feel incapable of reaching anyone.[14]

At some stage, when the grief bubble has been stopped in its progress by a dam set up in the Wish Pool, the grieving person is able to pick up the bubble "and help it leap across the dam." The therapy also involves making "blessing bottles," designed to represent "the true blessings received from the deceased person," which would then "become a linking object between the client and the lost loved one." This suggests recognition of a reciprocal relationship between the grieving person and the deceased. At some stage, the client might set a tea candle on a small raft and set it afloat, at the same time removing the grief bubble. The letter or artwork might then be taken home or burned "as a way of symbolically sending the message to the deceased," a common Chinese tradition.[15]

Grieving people also direct communications toward the dead through aesthetic means apart from therapy, as we have already considered in connection with lamentation. While lamentation is a culturally scripted practice, grieving people sometimes come up with innovative aesthetic practices for addressing the dead. Itaru Sasaki, a resident of the Japanese coastal town of Otsuchi, lost his cousin in 2010 and felt the need to talk with him. To satisfy this urge, he bought an old-fashioned phone booth, painted it white, and put it in his garden. Inside is a disconnected rotary phone, and

Sasaki would use it to speak to his deceased cousin. He described his thinking to Miki Meek, a producer at Public Radio International's *This American Life*, "Because my thoughts could not be relayed over a regular phone line, I wanted them to be carried on the wind. So I named it the wind telephone."[16] Sasaki's town was especially hard hit by the 2011 earthquake and tsunami, which killed more than 90,000 people, and in the aftermath of that tragedy, many of his neighbors who wanted to speak to their deceased loved ones started to make use of the phone booth. Word spread, and the phone booth has become a pilgrimage destination that attracts grieving people from all over Japan.

Meek's moving story describes some of the conversations that NHK Sendai recorded in the course of making a documentary about the phone booth. Some people actually dial the phone. Some use the phone regularly to update their relatives on what has been going on. Many attempt to reassure the deceased that their living loved ones are okay. Others use it as a chance to express their love or their regrets for what they now perceive as hurtful behavior toward the deceased—or for not being able to save them. Some use it simply to cry in the virtual presence of the loved one.

Using a physical prop in gestures of communication toward the dead is not an idea that is original to Sasaki.[17] I have mentioned the traditional Chinese idea of burning a letter as a way of posting it to the dead, and burning money (joss paper) or other paper images is also traditionally considered a means of conveying these items to the deceased for use in the afterlife.[18] Grieving people do not seem to feel that a physical prop is required, since many talk to the dead in imagination or out loud, even when they do not believe that their deceased loved ones can actually hear them. And yet when entertaining the idea of getting some message across to the dead, it may be reassuring to use what is seen as a proper vehicle. I dreamed once soon after my mother died that I had written her a letter and was looking for a "dead letter box" to get it to her. Tangible devices or established gestural practices can fortify the fantasy that we can get the dead's attention and persuade them to attend to what we say.[19]

Use of the wind telephone is a good example of an aesthetic practice that is well-designed for directing communications toward the dead. The phone is a physical prop that involves sensory engagement. People use it to send out messages of all sorts without any expectation of the kind of back-and-forth associated with everyday conversation. They accept that vast distances separate them from their dead loved ones, but the phone seems a plausible means for traversing them.

The framed ritualistic context also offers the opportunity for regarding the communication as a complete, accomplished act. The power of the wind telephone derives in part from its enabling straightforward and bounded acts of communication.[20] By making the ersatz phone call and carrying it through to a point at which one deems that enough has been said, one can feel that one's message has been sent. This can provide a sense of relative closure despite the lack of evident uptake from the party envisioned on the other end of the line. The definite nature of the gesture also offers a sense of punctuation within the torrent of emotion that grief involves. It facilitates the impression that one has encapsulated a specific message toward the deceased instead of discharging an affective tumult.

Sasaki began using the wind telephone as a personal ritual in grief, but the proliferation of the practice gave it social validation as a mode of grieving behavior. While most wind telephone conversations are not overheard, the sense that other people endorse the practice of using the phone may enhance its emotional power. Others' acceptance of the practice as intelligible and appropriate reinforces the impression that this is an effective symbolic mode for acting on the desire to speak to the dead.

Aesthetic activities may thus providing surrogate satisfaction for the desire to communicate with the dead, a satisfaction that is enhanced if relative closure is available within the chosen form. But not everyone takes such practices to be symbolic or the communication to be surrogate. Some people believe that the dead in fact hear their statements and see their gestures. Patrick Stokes points to the growth of second-person address of the deceased in the context of postings on the Facebook pages of people who have died. He notes that quite a few of those making posts "report that they *do* take themselves to be communicating with the dead" as well as living Facebook users, "without necessarily having an idea of how that could be possible."[21] Some readers may be dubious of this attitude, viewing it as irrational, intellectually negligent, or psychologically harmful.[22] From that perspective, the suggestion that we can and do communicate with the dead might itself seem worrisome. Because I am viewing the desire to communicate indulgently and praising the role of aesthetic activities in satisfying it, let us pause to consider further what might be going on when people direct messages toward the dead.

COMMUNICATING? REALLY?

I suspect that most of us who have experienced grief have also envisioned the dead as witnessing our doings, even if we reject the possibility. This idea is probably unsurprising to believers who have participated in religious funerals. While funerals do not necessarily involve directing messages toward the dead, they often encourage those gathered to feel that the dead are present and aware of their ritual actions. Religious funerals are designed to direct participants' attention away from ordinary concerns and to engage them in a shared practice of being present together and attending to what is said and done.

According to Mircea Eliade, religious rituals enable participants to enter a reality that is so distinct from that of daily life that they enter a distinctive "ritual time" in which they reenact and/or witness mythic events and deeds.[23] His account works well as a description of the Catholic Mass from the standpoint of the devout, for example. The Mass is a reenactment of the events of the Last Supper, in which Jesus is supposed to have transformed bread and wine into his body and blood. Those who absorb themselves in the ritual are not just commemorating these events but living through them. Sacred rituals generally, Eliade claims, allow participants to experience themselves as present for such important "mythic" events. The ritual gives them access to a liminal realm of experience, in which both the living and the dead are in attendance.

Eliade's account suggests an explanation for why funerals can be so important to those who are grieving. Understood as sacred rituals, they can comfort because they seem to enable entry to a spiritual reality that is envisioned as encompassing the deceased. Sharing the experience of these rituals with others also provides social validation of this mode of being with the dead.

This conception of connecting with the dead through ritual may make sense from the standpoint of those who believe in an afterlife, but what of those who are skeptical? Many people do not believe that souls survive physical death and do not take seriously the idea that rituals give us access to spiritual beings. I think most of us at times imagine the dead as witnesses to our communicative gestures regardless of our metaphysical beliefs, but I anticipate that some will balk at this idea. To regard the dead as witnesses seems to presuppose that we think they can perceive us. Many reject this idea outright, and some think that failing to do so is delusional.[24]

And yet, no lesser an unbeliever than Friedrich Nietzsche seems to have envisioned his father's response when he had words from St. Paul inscribed on his father's headstone: "*Die Liebe höret nimmer auf*," "Love never stops."[25] Nietzsche used money he had won in a court settlement with a publisher to buy a headstone for his long-deceased father, who had been a Lutheran pastor. His selection of the quotation from St. Paul is beautifully ambiguous. It defers to his father by citing scripture while making a statement that, naturalistically interpreted, expresses something that Nietzsche might (and apparently did) mean—love never ends. Considering that Nietzsche often presents himself as an adversary of St. Paul, it seems implausible to view his gesture as aimed at promoting pious sentiments on the part of passersby. It strikes me as most probable that he was engaged in an imaginal relationship with his father when he chose the inscription, considering how his father would regard it. Like all inscriptions on grave markers, the engraving is ostensibly directed toward the world at large, but it also represents a gesture directed toward Nietzsche's father. And it asserts that whatever the distance between them, love continues.

What might we make of the fact that many people address the dead in some fashion or envision the deceased as their witness while being committed to denying that the soul survives death? Are they simply behaving irrationally? I think we should hesitate to criticize. If we follow Jonathan Lear's suggestion that mourning should be viewed in a space of imaginative play, efforts to shore up the boundary between reverie and intersubjective reality in this context are beside the point. Ontological questions are philosophically important, but largely irrelevant to those who are grieving. Early in bereavement, when the environment seems filled with intimations of the deceased person, they may be incapable of settling on a determinate view of the person's status. They certainly may not have any second-order view about what they are doing when they envision the deceased as a witness or recipient of messages. If Lear is right, abstaining from judgment is fully appropriate.

For those would subject their behavior to norms of rationality, I can see several ways in which skeptics might consistently direct communications toward the dead. First, they might address the dead as a matter of rhetorical convention. Apostrophe, in which speech is directed at someone who is not present or who cannot respond, is a common vehicle for expressing strong emotions. It need not imply the conviction that the target will receive the message. If grief is an emotion that has moved many to poetic expression, then for a grieving person to engage in this conventional poetic practice seems fitting. Doing so does not presuppose any specific view about the status of the dead. If we want to rationalize this phenomenon, we might interpret it as intended for being overheard by living people, in the manner Urban describes as "monological" in connection with wailing.

A second possibility is that a skeptic who addresses the deceased is defying death by asserting that the person remains one of us. We might recall Steven Feld's description of ritual wailing as addressed to the entire social world, including both the living and the dead. Treating the deceased as we treat the living signals our continued intention to include them as part of our community. Hegel analyzes the impulse to bury a dead loved one as the living family's collective embrace of the person as a member.

> The Family keeps away from the dead the dishonoring of him by unconscious appetites and abstract entities, and puts its own action in their place, and weds the blood-relation to the bosom of the earth, to the elemental imperishable individuality. The Family thereby makes him a member of a community which prevails over and holds under control the forces of particular material elements and the lower forms of life which sought to unloose themselves against him and destroy him.[26]

Hans Georg Gadamer offers a similar suggestion as to why we bury the dead.

> The burial of the dead is perhaps the fundamental phenomena of being human. Burial does not refer to a rapid hiding of the dead, a swift clearing away of the shocking impression made by one suddenly struck fast in leaden and lasting sleep. On the contrary, by a remarkable expenditure of human labor there is sought an abiding with the dead, indeed a holding fast of the dead amongst the living.[27]

These passages from Hegel and Gadamer suggest that as human beings we take a rebellious attitude toward death, shown by our refusal to hand the remains of our loved ones over to the elements. Our practices assert their continued place among us. This view does not imply that we think that they survive as conscious beings. A skeptic could consistently engage in gestures directed toward the dead, taking them to express our commitment to continuing to view them as respected and beloved community members.

A third possibility is that skeptics are taking an "as-if" stance. They might entertain the idea of communicating with the dead or of the dead observing us while nevertheless not believing it. This would be a stance akin to the one Kendall Walton thinks we take when making use of representational artworks. He maintains that we use such works as props for engaging in games of make-believe.[28] The works conjure up worlds that are fictional, but while we are engaged, we treat them as real. Similarly, people who direct communications toward the dead are engaging in a personal ritual in which they treat a fiction as though it were real. This does not entail that they believe that genuine communication with the dead is possible.

We should, however, note the difference between engaging with art as Walton envisions it and engaging in rituals or using aesthetic props in bereavement. Walton maintains that we voluntarily engage in a game of make-believe with the artwork, recognizing a distinction between the world of the artwork and reality. By contrast, bereaved people often have experiences of the deceased person's presence that arise involuntarily. Especially early in the grieving process, bereaved people may be quite unsettled about whether or not they think the person is actually present. Thomas Fuchs observes that they tend to fluctuate between considering their impressions to be "as-if" experiences and taking them to be veridical indicators of the actual situation. This can result in a conflicted sense of reality on a cognitive-affective level. In time, however, the bereaved may shift from considering the deceased as externally present to incorporating the person as an "inner, comforting presence" that is not sought in external reality.[29]

Fuchs sees value in developing various representations of the deceased (some of them aesthetic, for example, "images, statues, gravestones and other memorials" along with narrative forms). By relating to them through an intentional "'as-if' mode," the deceased can be felt to be symbolically "present," but recognized to be externally absent. This can open up an "inner space" that makes possible a renewal of the relationship to the deceased.[30] At that point, the presence of the deceased may be seen as having an "as-if" status somewhat akin to the contents of make-believe that Walton associates with the experience of artworks. Skeptics might interpret their behaviors that seem to presuppose the continued presence of the dead as involving this "as-if" perspective, though in early bereavement consistent perspectives are probably unavailable to skeptics and non-skeptics alike.

A fourth possibility is that skeptics are simply agnostic. Although they are not convinced that the dead can witness our actions, they might be willing to give that possibility the benefit of the doubt. Although this is a kind of "as-if" strategy, it differs from the approach just described because agnostics consider the question of the survival of consciousness as open, whereas skeptics who entertain but disbelieve do not. This agnostic stance seems to be taken by one of the callers making use of the Otsuchi phone booth to contact his wife, son, and parents, all of whom had died in the tsunami. At one point he says, "If this voice reaches you, please listen."[31] This remark acknowledges a lack of full conviction that his loved ones will hear him, and yet the speaker goes on to address a heartfelt message to them.[32]

Thus, it is possible for skeptics to envision the dead as witnesses and communicative targets in ways that are rationally respectable. However, to dwell on the question of rational consistency is to ignore the possible value of regarding the dead in this way. While not proposing that we consider the dead in these terms, Line Ryberg Ingerslev suggests that "being with" the dead in some sense is important to the grieving process. She describes grief as involving ongoing rehearsal of being in the company of the deceased in the person's absence. That might sound oxymoronic, but Ingerslev compares grief to the developmental situation in which children learn to be comfortable being alone by recognizing themselves as being still "carried by an affective relation" with their absent caregivers.[33] Grief involves our learning to be alone in a similar way.

"The rehearsal of being alone in the lived company of the absent other" is Ingerslev's characterization of grief as an inherently "relational activity." "The lived company of the absent other" is a positive way of construing the combination of presence and absence that other theorists of grief tend to emphasize.[34] Awareness of the affective relationship preserves a sense of the deceased as a part of one's present. Grief is thus "a form of togetherness" with the deceased in which one relates to the person in a "form of lived dedication or evocation." In other words, we learn to resume future-directed activity by carrying forward a sense of the ongoing importance of our deceased loved ones in our lives, dedicating ourselves to honoring our relationships to them through the way that we go on. This enables us to live "with the absent other" while being alone.[35] Deceased loved ones can remain our companions, regardless of our views about an afterlife.

Ingerslev does not focus on communicative gestures, but her entire account encourages envisioning the deceased as being "with" us. Nico Frijda, by contrast, emphasizes the value of directing communications toward the dead. He takes it as given that "the dead cannot see and hear us," yet he argues that communicative gestures in commemorative rituals enable us to genuinely relate to them. A commemorative ritual "makes actors construct or reenter an emotional relationship of respecting and caring" for the deceased because these participants actually enter into these emotional attitudes toward the person. In doing so they call to mind the deceased loved ones' "nature as fulfilling their role in the relationships—as one's friend, child or parent, teacher, pupil, or colleague." This involves "evoking or recreating images" of the loved ones' "mode of being, their way of behaving toward you, and their way of viewing the world."[36]

This attentive awareness of the deceased and the relational connection makes the person available as a target of one's own gestures, according to Frijda. This summoning of the dead as recipients of our gestures of respect and gratitude is "nothing magical," though it does involve a genuine kind of presence. "There is a relationship, there is a streaming out to the object, in which one fulfills a relational role: that of parent, or child, or friend, and one need not reflect on the fact that the target is an idea rather than a physical presence."[37] Importantly, in Frijda's account, commemorations make the dead present to us as the persons they were, occupying the same roles in relation to us that they occupied in life. This beneficially enables us to recognize the non-material legacies they have bequeathed to us, such as their "mode of being and way of viewing things," which we are able to assimilate into our own repertoires, and this enriches our own "fund of modes of experiencing."[38]

While Frijda thinks that ritual helps us to internalize the dead in the manner that Fuchs describes, he also sees it as an acknowledgment of the deceased as playing specific roles in our lives that continue to be reciprocal. Although our gestures toward the dead may appear completely one-sided, he contends that there is real interpersonal connection. Our "streaming out" to the deceased person involves our conceiving of ourselves as playing a role in relation to the person, and as we do so we regard the person as having a reciprocal relationship to us. The beloved person was an active participant in the relationship during life, and that is how we still regard the person. In life the person streamed out toward us while playing these roles, and our streaming out as we commemorate responds accordingly. The dead, in fact, continue to perform relational roles toward us by offering us resources for dealing with circumstances that confront us, even though they initiated these offerings through actions performed when they were alive.

COMMUNICATIONS FROM THE DEAD

Frijda's account of our ability to renew reciprocal relationships with the dead involves two-way communication. The dead communicate with us through their legacies, even if they lack any transparent "window" onto the world in which the living continue to operate. In this respect, Frijda's naturalistic description of the dead as active in our world is akin to Ingerslev's when she remarks that we "live in the present absence of others" through finding ourselves in a world in which our "culture, tools, lived understanding of what 'world' means" are inherited from those who have preceded us and whose presence they make manifest. "We can address each other across generative time," she observes, and this is a form of "trans-generational communication."[39]

Such reflections render the idea of communications initiated by the dead as unproblematic. The temporal lag between their actions and our reception of what they communicate is obvious, but this is also true of many forms of creative art made by living artists. Even if we insist that communicative gestures must be intended by their authors, we can consider many creative actions of those who have died as bona fide communications. Many cultural achievements are addressed to the world open-endedly, with the assumption that reception will be gradual. Even in the performing arts, presentations that quickly convey an emotional response in an audience may have gradual perlocutionary effects that performers may intend, and recording technologies are often employed to make performances available to future audiences.

Stokes submits that the dead remain alive in our world through their creative work, not just in cases of outstanding cultural achievements, but also in quotidian productions. He focuses on digital productions through Facebook and other social media platforms. The posts of the dead are communications that emanate from them. Stokes views social media platforms as enabling us to engage with the dead by posting responses to their posts. Here again, there is a temporal lag between their creative activity and our responses, but as Stokes observes, such a lag is familiar from every digital exchange or exchange of letters.

The internet is among a number of relatively recent technological developments that have made it possible to recognize the dead through their works with a hitherto unknown immediacy. Photography, cinema, audio and audiovisual recordings can also give us an impression of seeing and hearing the dead, in action as it were. The dead may not see us, but we often have an impression of having sensory access to them.

According to Walton, photographs of the dead are actually transparent means of seeing them. He asserts that "we see, quite literally, our dead relative themselves when we look at photographs of them."[40] We see them literally, but indirectly, much as we see cells by means of microscopes. We cannot be in their physical presence, but photographs make possible real encounters with deceased loved ones.

The experience of recognizing a person through a photo can have tremendous affective power. Roland Barthes famously reports that when looking through some photographs of his recently deceased mother, he suddenly found one that made him think, "That's her!" He was startled by this recognition, for the picture showed his mother as a child, long before he was born—and yet it was her.[41]

Barthes is quick to acknowledge the photograph's capacity to convey an impression of the person, but he notes that it simultaneously reinforces awareness of the person's death. He sees this awareness as haunting all our encounters with photographs from historically distant times, for any person seen as alive in them is actually already dead. This awareness of death, Barthes claims, is in fact implicit in every photograph, a point earlier made by Susan Sontag.[42] "Whether or not the subject is already dead," claims Barthes, "every photograph is this catastrophe."[43]

If Barthes is right, the photograph reflects the dual significance of every image of the deceased person that appears in the mind of the bereaved. We previously considered this dual aspect of photograph of the dead in connection with Robert Bednar's account of roadside shrines. Each image is full of life, but one sees in it someone who is already dead.[44] As a result of this duality, one might be saddened by an image with manifest content that seems happy. This poignant effect is akin to the irony that Peter Goldie describes as making grief like free indirect discourse in literature. We do not remember experiences with the deceased as they were, he observes, but see them through the filter of recognizing that they are no longer with us. This affective tone overshadows even very happy memories.

However, we can emphasize the happy aspect of the ambiguity associated with photographs of deceased loved ones. As Walton observes, there is a sense in which one sees, not an image, but the actual person brought to life in a photograph or film. We can consider this another way in which the dead communicate with us. But by contrast with many artistic works and cultural products whose address seems wide-ranging, the dead that we see in photographs can seem to actively address us in an especially vivid and personal way (though realistic paintings can sometimes have this effect as well).

Stokes does not shy away from describing encounters with deceased individuals through their internet posts as genuine communications from the dead. "We really are, in some more-than-metaphorical sense, present with those we engage with online," says Stokes, and this has "the startling implication that we are in fact in the presence of the dead, in some more-than-metaphorical way, when we engage with their online traces."[45] While this is remarkable, it is in keeping with the idea that photographs and other media enable us to see the person him- or herself.

Stokes is uneasy, however, about the development of chatbots that use artificial intelligence seemingly to reanimate the deceased person in digital form. His worry is not that this way of encountering the dead is especially spooky. His concern is we do not encounter them at all. Chatbots are made to sound like the deceased because their seemingly "live" responses are constructed on the basis of statements and digitalized messages the person posted, and they look like the deceased because they draw on video images produced while the person was alive. Stokes sees a chatbot simulacrum as substituting a contrived version of the deceased for the person. It may be an advanced form of puppetry, but it is puppetry, nonetheless. Chatbots do not allow the dead to speak, but instead substitute for the singular person of the deceased a comfortingly familiar surrogate. Instead of honoring the dead, such chatbots obliterate them from our memories. Stokes recalls Derrida's admonition that we cannot and should not speak for the dead, even though they cannot speak for themselves, because we cannot avoid obscuring who they were by representing our own versions of them.[46]

Stokes's concern that we will silence the deceased if we aim at too lifelike a virtual image touches on the long-standing problem of how to be sure that one really loves another person and not just an image we carry of him or her. This becomes especially clear in relation to memory, as C. S. Lewis observes when he laments that his sense of the actual person of his deceased wife was being slowly covered over by his projections.[47] The ethical questions regarding how one should think and speak of the deceased are important ones. A starting point for addressing them is to remain cognizant of the distinction between the deceased and our fantasies about the person. Stokes may be right that the effort to domesticate the dead through chatbot surrogates and reinvent them to serve our needs makes it more difficult to maintain this distinction.[48]

But this need not be the effect of all lifelike representations. Stokes himself sees a place for glimpsing the person as a unique individual by way of relating to digital remains. Creative productions involving representations of the deceased may enable us to recognize the person's unique style, and when they give the impression of live communication, they may help us maintain awareness of the person's individual way of operating, much as videos might do.

Anthropologist Jason Throop uses the term "singular particular" to get at the idea of a person's uniqueness. He contrasts the singular particular with the "typified particular," the usual focus within ethnographies. Typified particulars enable anthropologists to give "thick" descriptions of specific cultures, for they specify distinguishing features of the way members of a culture conduct themselves. A singular particular, on the other hand, shines through as the irreplaceable "excess" that distinguishes the specific instance from the generic. Throop maintains that singular particularity is prominently visible in cases of death and mourning.[49] In death, it is the singular particularity of the person that is permanently lost.

Alexander Nehamas, in his discussion of Montaigne's essay on friendship, draws attention to the importance of the singular particular in personal relationships and in loss. He initially marvels that although everything that Montaigne tells us about his intimate friend Étienne de la Boétie "is generic and vague," the essay describes this intense friendship as having "no model other than itself." Montaigne's elaboration on this idea includes what Nehamas terms "the most moving statement about friendship ever made: 'If you press me to tell you why I loved him, I feel that this cannot be expressed except by answering: *Because it was he, because it was I.*'"[50]

If photographs, films, and other recordings of a person give us a special form of access to him or her, it is because they present the person in a way that allows us to recognize this singular particularity. Internet posts offer opportunities for subterfuge, enabling one to adopt an online persona that is out of keeping with the other ways in which one presents oneself to the world. But particularly in the case of someone who is also known apart from social media, a post might serve as well as a photograph as a means for recognizing "That's her!"

Recognition of the singular, particular person in a photo, video, or creative product can occur in a private experience, such as the one that Barthes describes. But it can also occur in collective experiences, as we observed in connection with storytelling. The shared observational detail or anecdote can bring the person before the mind's eye. This seems to be the effect Donald Keefer experienced when his nephew described his grandmother at her funeral: "My grandmother was the sort of person who would never sacrifice good taste for nutrition." Keefer remarks, "It was funny in that Oscar Wilde sort of way; it was touching and true. Most of all, it captured metaphorically what she was all about."[51]

Recently developed media give us new perceptual means for recognizing a deceased person as a singular, particular individual, but other aesthetic phenomena, such as the eulogy just described, can also do this. By facilitating this recognition, they enable us to "see" the dead in imagination. This suggests another way to regard our communicative gestures toward the dead. When we envision them as observing us and address them (internally or externally), we might "see" them as Aritsune's daughter sees her dead husband while gazing into the well. They come into view through our intentional, albeit imaginative activity, but we glimpse the singular particularity of our loved one in a way that preserves a sense of that person's unique way of being in the world.

Matthew Ratcliffe observes, "To *know someone* is, in part, to experience and be affected by that person's distinctive style, by relational possibilities that are unique to her." Although bereavement involves the loss of these relational possibilities, "to retain a sense of that person's style is to be open to new possibilities involving them, new ways of being affected by them."[52] By directing gestures of communication toward the dead, we adopt a stance of openness that makes possible recollections of that person as having a unique style. By attending to the specificity of the person that we have summoned into view, our sense of the deceased is not only accessed, but engaged with afresh. We might notice aspects of the person or the relationship that we had not previously seen in quite the same way.

Our own communicative stance allows the dead to continue to address us. Our engagement in communicative gestures sets up the conditions for envisioning them as the particular persons that we know. If we catch a glimpse of them in this way, there is a sense in which they "present themselves" as being more than our projections. A form of communicative reciprocity is enacted that helps us to keep the relationship alive.

Handling one's relationship with the deceased can be complicated, however, by feelings that one has unfinished business with the dead. Such feelings may arise when the relationship with the person has been dysfunctional, and dealing with these matters, when sufficiently serious, may require therapeutic intervention. In any event, what is needed to address them will be specific to the particular relationship.

However, a sense of unfinished business of a different sort is widespread among the bereaved. Many are afflicted with lingering guilt feelings toward the deceased that strike observers as irrational. I will consider this phenomenon in the following section, once again recommending aesthetic practices as helpful means for dealing with them.

DOING JUSTICE TO THE DEAD

The popularity of the wind telephone suggests that the desire to communicate with the dead can be extremely strong. And as some of the messages spoken into the phone indicate, one reason for this is the common feeling that one has some explaining to do.

Guilt often comes with grief. It can take the form of feeling that one has done something wrong vis-à-vis the deceased. The primary use of the term *survivor guilt* is to refer to feelings of guilt at having survived some catastrophic event in which other people have died, such as the Japanese earthquake and tsunami or the Shoah during World War II. A secondary use is to refer to guilt over having survived a person's death, whether or not it was part of a larger catastrophe. I will be describing survivor guilt in this secondary sense.

The bereaved often feels guilt over having failed to prevent a loved one's death. But why? Third parties are often mystified at the lengths grieving people will go to demonstrate that they are somehow culpable. Some theorists have argued that they insist on their own guilt in an effort to fend off the sense of powerlessness that the loved one's death provoked. If you are to blame, you had some control over the situation. Feeling guilty is awful, but feeling powerless is perhaps even worse.

Another possible source of self-blame may be the feeling that some injustice has been done to the loved one. How often one feels, after a loved one's death, that the person died too soon. It is a short mental move from that view to the feeling that the person has been wronged, and another small step to the sense that there must be a guilty party. One option is to rail against God or the universe. Another is to locate the guilty party in oneself. One's distress is furthered by the fact that one cannot defuse guilt feelings by thoroughly discussing the problem with the deceased, as one might have done if the person were alive. Worst of all, one cannot make it up to the person, or even if one could in principle, one could never do enough.[53]

Feeling guilt toward the deceased is intensified by the fact that every step toward adjusting to the new situation can be interpreted as an act of disloyalty. I recall a widow once describing being taken on a trip by her adult daughters after her husband died and having a very good time. But when she came home, she said, she felt like she had been unfaithful to her husband. Doing anything that might distract attention from the deceased can feel like an act of abandonment. One feels as though one should be mindful of the loss at every moment, so any joy feels like a betrayal. Even attending to practical matters can seem to dishonor the deceased, who should be at the forefront in one's mind. And being numb because of simple exhaustion can itself seem disloyal and uncaring.

In this frame of mind, changing the environment in any way can feel like an act of infidelity. Undoing something that the deceased has done (be it as simple as moving a pair of shoes that the person had removed) seems a violation, as though one were erasing the person more thoroughly by disturbing the effects of his or her actions. Moving the furniture around, however logistically desirable, can seem a slight, replacing the setting as the person had known it with something alien to him or her.

The result is a very real struggle between efforts to normalize the situation and the perceived obligation to devote one's full agency to responding to the loved one's death. Despite the best of efforts, it is both psychologically and logistically impossible to focus all one's energy on the deceased. To do so would be to subordinate one's entire life to vicariously acting on another's behalf. Rerouting the trajectory of one's own life in such an all-encompassing way would not acknowledge any of one's own psychological needs beyond the felt impulse to honor the departed. And one usually has to engage in activities unrelated to the deceased, if only to support oneself.

Guilt feelings in bereavement often strike other people as inappropriate. Meaning well, they might argue that these attitudes are delusional. Or they may point out that guilt is just a side effect of grief (as I am saying here). The bereaved person may grant that people often feel guilty without good reason, but this does nothing to assuage the sense of being in the wrong. The fact that other people find one's emotions irrational only makes one feel more isolated. Guilt feelings can also undercut the impact of others' efforts to be emotionally supportive. The bereaved person may feel that their kindness would evaporate if they knew all the facts, such as the imagined sins of omission that causally contributed to the death. And even if emotional support were still forthcoming, it might be resisted out of a sense that it is undeserved.

Feeling condemned to a guilt-ridden interpretation of events that one cannot explain to others, the bereaved is often further tormented by recurrent mental replays of the events leading to the death. One may seek points at which one's own actions or inaction fit into the causal developments that led to the calamitous result. These repetitive rehearsals of the details of the death often arise spontaneously, particularly at times when one is not concentrating on anything, such as the moments before one falls asleep. The mental tendency to go over and over the details mimics constructive reevaluation in other contexts, which has the goal of helping one to fix a problem. Thinking through situations in which one failed at something can often help identify ways of doing things differently and avoiding similar problems in the future. In the case of bereavement, however, the repair of the situation is impossible. Hence the mental repetition of the events that led to the loss tends to be unproductive and to reinforce the sense of guilt. And if this mental sequence replays at the end of the day, it can contribute to the insomnia to which bereaved people are especially prone.

Further guilt can emerge from self-critical attitudes about the way that one is grieving. Although societies have implicit rules for grieving, whether one is achieving the emotional ideal may be hard to determine. Arlie Hochschild, for example, describes a pair of bereaved parents who were at times uncertain as to whether they were being stoical or insufficiently caring. She also mentions various other ways in which one can fail to realize the societal ideal. These include feeling relief at a death (at best a form of ambivalence), "mistiming" one's feelings (feeling grief prematurely or only after some delay), or being in a place in which expressions of grief would seem improper. People whose grief fails to conform with societal expectations may feel that they have "misexperienced" the funeral. Hochschild concludes, "The ways in which people think they have grieved poorly suggest what a remarkable achievement it is to grieve well."[54]

Convoluted as survivor guilt is, recovery from it is possible, and aesthetic activities undertaken to honor the deceased can help. When memorializing activities involve other people, either as audience or as co-participants, they can also help eliminate the sense of isolation that guilt feelings may have been exacerbated.

Activities undertaken in response to the dedicatory impulse to honor a deceased loved one often take aesthetic form. This is not always the case. Engaging in some charitable activity that was important to the deceased could certainly amount to a dedicatory gesture, but it does not seem to be intrinsically aesthetic. Nevertheless, many activities and gestures undertaken from dedicatory impulses are aesthetic, and aesthetic means are stock-in-trade for such purposes. The very idea of honoring a person suggests that one does so before witnesses and that what one presents is done in a manner that reflects the high value placed on the person. Both presentation and manner are central, and this is enough to see the activity as aesthetic.

Placing a marker on a tomb can follow through on dedicatory impulses, typically in a way that is aesthetically pleasing, and the marker may be an artwork itself. Artistic dedications to deceased loved ones commemorate the person through straightforwardly aesthetic projects. While dedicated works and performances can be innovative, their efficacy as means of honoring a person may be limited if they are not well received, a consideration that may place limits on how nonstandard they are likely to be. However, a functional item not usually considered an artwork (such as a window, a park bench, a brick, or a whole building) can also be installed as a commemoration, and its appearance must be aesthetically acceptable if it is to honor the person. Similarly, dedicating a tree or a garden for memorial purposes is another way of honoring the person through association with something that is or will become aesthetically pleasing.

I have suggested that commemorative works require an audience of witnesses, but this does not imply that they are necessarily public. Dedicatory works can also occur in more intimate locations. A home altar or household shrine, for example, is not in public view. It is nevertheless presentational, assembled with the idea of calling the deceased to mind for anyone who enters the space and beholds it. Thus, their commemorative aim does not differ from that of public memorials, though the number of anticipated witnesses is considerably smaller.

Commemorative aesthetic activities can help the bereaved overcome survivor guilt. Importantly, their focus on the deceased is front and center. To the extent that they are directed toward the deceased as implicit witness, they mitigate the sense that one cannot communicate with the person. Admittedly, they address the person at a distance and without apparent response, yet one at least is not paralyzed by a sense of communicative incapacity.

By undertaking memorial activities, one is also doing something on behalf of the deceased person.[55] Far from letting the person down, one is acting on the person's behalf to ensure his or her place in the minds and hearts of the community. Because they are focused on the person who has died, commemorative aesthetic activities enable one to act as an agent and introduce innovations without the feeling of betrayal that often occurs in connection with other pleasant activities. As Stokes notes, "Organized remembrance, or remembrance formalized into physical structures like statues and plaques, does not merely recall the dead, but presents them as *worthy of recall*."[56]

The many kinds of aesthetic activities that involve the completion of a project or performance (for example, a memorial event or an artwork constructed in the person's honor) also provide determinate goals that can be accomplished. This counters the frustrated feeling that one can do little for the person who has died. One may not be able to do as much as one feels he or she deserves, but one can realize specific projects that honor the person, thereby attaining a sense of relative closure.

Still, guilt may seem intransigent. In the face of the death of a loved one, one may feel that no gesture can really do justice to the person or reflect the magnitude of the loss. The most apposite gestures (aesthetic and otherwise) in response to the death may thus be accompanied by anticipation of inadequacy.

This consideration recommends following conventional forms, for reasons that the ancient Chinese philosopher Xunzi articulates. Writing in the third century BCE, Xunzi was defending aesthetically elaborate funerals against Mozi, who claimed that funerals should be simple and mourning short-lived. Mozi's reasoning was that while paying respects to the dead is in order, this should not divert large amounts of wealth away from providing for the needs of the living. For the same reason, he considered it undesirable for the bereaved to be removed from the workforce for extended lengths of time. Given the prolonged periods of mourning that the Confucians advocated (particularly in the case of a parent), we might sympathize with Mozi's concerns, even if we do not endorse his insistence on minimalistic funerals.[57]

Xunzi, however, contends that Mozi has an insufficiently penetrating grasp of the emotional need of human beings. Regarding mourning, Xunzi argues as follows:

> Everyone is at times visited by sudden feelings of depression and melancholy longing. A loyal minister who has lost his lord or a filial son who has lost a parent, even when he is enjoying himself among congenial company, will be overcome by such feelings. If they come to him and he is greatly moved, but does nothing to give them expression, then his emotions of remembrance and longing will be frustrated and unfulfilled, and he will feel a sense of deficiency in his ritual behavior. Therefore, the former kings established certain forms to be observed on such occasions so that men could fulfill their duty to honor those who deserve honor and show affection for those who command affection.[58]

Xunzi's argument is that everyone who experiences significant loss is flooded with sadness and longing for the person who has died. These emotions need expression. The bereaved person also feels the obligation to do right by the dead. Given the intensity of the emotions involved, the mourner will feel deficient if left on his or her own to determine appropriate expressions of grief. The rituals have been established, therefore, to provide the grieving definite procedures for emotional expression. One of the benefits of having detailed specifications for funerals and mourning practices is that the bereaved who engage in them will not be left with any doubts as to the adequacy of what they do.[59]

Xunzi's arguments apply in contemporary times as well. Rituals and mourning practices that are societally understood as appropriate give mourners some clarity about specific steps they should take to honor the deceased. These are not a magic bullet for ending survivor guilt, but they help us feel that we are doing right by the deceased (while leaving them undone would commonly give rise to guilt feelings).

Dedicatory impulses extending beyond established rituals prompt further commemorative activity, which can assuage the feeling that one is somehow failing the person. The motivation to act on behalf of a deceased loved one is never completely exhausted, so there will always be room for the feeling that one has not done enough. Ideally, though, the focus will shift from self-reproach to dedication of the sort that Ingerslev describes. Recognizing that the project of endeavoring to honor our late loved ones has no natural cessation point, we can pursue this project in all our doings by trying to live in a way that does credit to them.

As I have argued in this chapter, aesthetic practices are useful means for renewing relationships with the dead. By engaging our senses and enabling us to comport ourselves toward deceased loved ones, they help us restore a sense of self-familiarity and maintain fulsome impressions of the dead as particular individuals. They can serve as means for directing communications toward the dead and for recognizing that our relationships still involve a degree of reciprocity. They provide vehicles for commemoration that help surmount survivor guilt by demonstrating that we can simultaneously honor the dead and engage with the living.

Conclusion

In light of the many ways that aesthetic activity can benefit those who are grieving, we can see the wisdom in the long human tendency to respond to loss through aesthetic means. I submit that this tendency did not arise by accident. This book has been an exploration of specific ways that aesthetic activity might constructively contribute to grieving people's efforts to reconstruct their sense of themselves and their way of relating to the rest of the world while sustaining and renewing their relationships with the dead.

I see aesthetic practices as means through which we imaginatively explore possibilities, and such exploration is vital in contexts in which we do not know how to move forward. Jonathan Lear emphasizes the way that mourning stimulates imagination in ways that do not remain immersed in the past but reorient us toward the future. As he describes it, mourning involves our remembering the dead in a way that involves "recreating in memory and imagination what we have lost and reanimating forms of life that might otherwise disappear."[1] By staying mindful of the deceased, we keep being reminded of all the good things they have given us and being motivated to amplify and build on their non-material legacies in a spirit of gratitude. By contrast with negative forms of repetition that manifest an inability to grow and reinforce patterns that yield unhappiness, according to Lear, imaginative confrontation with our loss represents a positive form of repetition. Through mourning, as we maintain our sense of loss and reflect on its significance, "it is we who return transformed by painful loss and active imagination. The return is itself an expression of hope."[2]

I have endeavored to show that aesthetic practices can serve as resources in our attempts to make sense of life after loss. They serve us well in our imaginative efforts to come to grips with the deaths of those who are important to us. They also stimulate our imaginations further, helping us to envision ways of building on the non-material legacies we have inherited from the dead as we proceed into the future.

I will conclude by suggesting that a consideration of aesthetic practices in relation to grief might have implications for thinking about the role of aesthetics in our lives more generally. First, we can consider how the valuable roles played by aesthetic activity in bereavement might apply to other circumstances in which our lives are disrupted. Many scholars have recently reminded us of the many ways in which aesthetic activities can enhance our everyday lives. I have suggested that we should see aesthetic practices as generally valuable in cases in which we are uncertain as to how to go forward, and that we should recognize that such situations are commonplace in our everyday lives, though not on a predictable schedule.

Some of the ways that aesthetic practices facilitate transitions and the reassertion of agency in bereavement might apply to other contexts in which disorientation has occurred. Unexpected circumstances might at any point catch us off guard, creating ruptures between life as we have known it in the past and life ahead. Aesthetic activities are ways of marking continuities amidst what is discontinuous and recognizing that even massive changes do not alienate us from all that we have previously found valuable in our lives.

We have been considering ways that aesthetic practices help us preserve bonds with the deceased despite the radical change that the relationship has undergone. We might consider analogous ways that aesthetic practices can help us navigate in cases of grief over other kinds of loss, such as the loss of a prior home in the case of migration or the loss of a former role through radical changes to one's livelihood or through retirement. For example, people who have migrated often continue previous traditions through means that are artistic (such as continuing to enjoy music from one's previous context), ritual (as when one continues to celebrate holidays from one's homeland), or decorative (for example, cherishing some object that one has transferred from the prior context to the present one). Cherished items and practices that have made the transition from a prior situation underscore the continuity of the present with one's previous life and provide bases for feeling connected with people one no longer sees (or sees regularly).

A second way in which we might extend our reflections on aesthetics in bereavement is by recognizing resources in our aesthetic backgrounds for orienting ourselves and navigating in other challenging situations. We might find previous encounters with artworks especially helpful in this connection. I have been suggesting that by drawing on our previous engagements with art, we can bolster confidence in our coping skills and enhance our ability to communicate about unfamiliar aspects of our experience. I suspect that many people would not automatically think of their previous experiences with art as helping them orient themselves in grief, and this is one reason that I draw attention to some of these connections.

But these experiences can be helpful in connection with other demanding circumstances, too. Werner Stegmaier has developed a philosophical account of how human beings orient themselves in situations in which confusion, uncertainty, and change abound, and yet one is nevertheless required to act.[3] In situations in which prior beliefs and expectations have broken down, he observes, we stabilize ourselves by finding "footholds" that are sustainable enough that we can lean on them provisionally. Along with clues and leads that suggest patterns, footholds are basic to orienting ourselves within reality, particularly when we are faced with uncertainties. I am proposing that experiences with art and other aesthetic activities can help us to find such clues and leads and footholds.

Stegmaier draws attention to features of what is involved orienting ourselves when we have lost our bearings. Both orientation and disorientation are typical aspects of human experience, particularly in a world in which accelerating change has massive impact on our ways of operating. We adjust to change by provisionally orienting ourselves and building on these preliminary orientations, but we keep reinterpreting and adapting as we notice new developments that require response. I have been suggesting that aesthetic experiences and reflections built upon them can help us orienting ourselves in the confusing context of bereavement. It would be worthwhile to analyze further some of the mechanisms we have considered, attending to how they provide sufficient stability to offer provisional footholds while keeping us alert to ways in which orientational revision and readjustment are called for.

A third way in which we might extend our consideration of aesthetic practices to contexts aside from grief and mourning follows from this last comment. Aesthetic practices help us to mediate apparent tensions among our goals when negotiating change. We have observed that the strange interplay of presence and absence in bereavement creates tensions within our thinking about the dead and our ability to relate to them. Aesthetic projects that develop symbolic representations of the deceased or modes of marking a physical or conceptual "place" for them can help reconcile the need to acknowledge the actuality of the death with appreciation of the relationship as an ongoing part of one's life. We find analogous challenges to those faced in bereavement in many other contexts in which we require some predictability in order to function but also find it necessary to contend with considerable change. I think it would be worthwhile to give further thought to the usefulness of aesthetic practices in these other contexts.

In general, aesthetic practices utilize standing forms but incorporate original content. One way in which they contribute positively to our experience is by transcending the merely conventional and injecting customary forms with new life.[4] In rites of passage, for example, individuals engage in well-defined procedures to mark their transition from one social status to another, yet optimally those present experience the ritual not as routine, but as fresh and immediate. The customization of standard rites, such as weddings and funerals, reflects an effort to make scripted procedures come to life in the experiences of those involved. At the same time, the renewal of standard forms and procedures assures participants that their way of marking important events in individuals' lives is endorsed by a whole transgenerational community. Looking at aesthetic practices' capacity to combine tradition and novelty and to link the generations might suggest ways that they can help us deal with the disruptive every day in its full variety.

Fourth, among the things we might notice when looking at our experience through an aesthetic lens is that aesthetic gestures are powerful means for conveying emotional support, respect, and inclusion. Reflection on some of the ways that they are employed in marking a person's death, paying one's respects, and supporting the bereaved can help us recognize their value for interpersonal interactions in other contexts as well. In many such cases, actions speak louder than words, but often the most eloquent actions are symbolic and gestural. Etiquette in general has something of this symbolic and gestural aspect. Individualizing acts prescribed by etiquette, like individualizing rituals, can give a gesture particular force by drawing attention to the individuality of those involved and the specificity of the relationship between them. And here we can face the same challenge that Donald Keefer identified in connection with eulogies. The aim is not to draw attention to the creative prowess revealed in the gesture, but to make the gesture serve the relational aim in the context.

Elsewhere I have argued that using cliché formulations to convey sympathy can be appropriate and heartfelt, though one should consider the probable uptake on the part of the person one aims to console.[5] Simple gestures of a conventional sort can be moving, and often the recipient of these gestures is more attentive to who is making the gesture than to how much creative talent is displayed. Similar considerations apply to polite gestures in other contexts. Preoccupation with niceties in etiquette may sometimes stand in the way of simple politeness, but using socially recognizable formulas can be like using language to convey a message. One needs conventionalized forms to get one's point across, though the means should not distract attention from what is being said or what one is trying to convey.[6]

We might recall Robert Audi's notion of adverbial duties: duties that are only fulfilled when performed in a certain manner, with a certain spirit. While we need not make reference to duty as such to notice the importance of manner in human interactions, Audi's idea is relevant to most of the ways in which we show respect to other people (a basic duty if we want to use such language). Extending small courtesies to others can be decisive for whether they feel included as participants in an exchange. Withholding them can be a slight that injures. Some of these small courtesies are aesthetic, and they are often quasi-theatrical. Shaking hands in non-pandemic conditions is one such example.[7] Another is making slight adjustments in one's physical position and bearing to shift the shape of a conversational huddle in order to draw someone on the margins into the group.

We should not be surprised that aesthetic activity is so important in granting recognition to other people and conveying respect in everyday contexts. Aesthetic activity is central to what it is to be human.[8] Human communities transcend individual lives, and aesthetic means are central to our acknowledgment of the intergenerational character of social life and our affective ties to those who have come before and those who will succeed us. If this does not seem obvious, consider the way in which artworks are often thought to communicate through time, or the way in which we think of ourselves as having access to the very thoughts of a now-dead individual when reading a book or hearing music the person composed. Artworks and aesthetic practices are central means through which the presence of others who have shaped our historical past are made manifest in everyday life.

Lear's contention that mourning is at the root of the civilizational enterprise, which forges intergenerational bonds in continuing societies, resonates with Thomas Laqueur's view that care of the dead is foundational for both community and civilization itself. As we have seen here, much of that care of the dead takes the form of activities with a marked aesthetic aspect. But this is also true of many other ways in which we manifest care for each other. Our consideration of the beneficial roles aesthetics can play in grief can serve as a basis for further exploration of the ways aesthetic practices can help us to care for ourselves and each other in challenging situations. Yuriko Saito has recently drawn attention to aesthetic practices involved in many kinds of caring relationships.[9] I hope that this present work will also illuminate the aesthetic aspects of living well with each other and the power of aesthetic means for confronting some of the challenges we face, both personally and collectively.

Acknowledgments

My thoughts about grief and aesthetics have been influenced by many people, living and dead, to whom I wish to express my gratitude. Foremost among them is my late husband, Robert C. Solomon (1942–2007), who brought many of my ideas into focus through our extended interactions, not to mention his sustaining love and the many ways in which he expanded my repertoire of ways to handle life's challenges. I cannot count the number of conversations on aesthetics that have shaped my thinking, but I have been particularly influenced by my Doktorvater, Karsten Harries. Conversations with Stephen Davies over many years have also shaped the way I consider aesthetic matters. I am grateful to both of them for the many ways they have contributed to my understanding of all things aesthetic and helped my thinking in connection with this project.

As I suspect is true of most people who think seriously about grief, experience brought me to the topic. Those with whom I shared the experience of grieving, to the extent that is possible, helped me put words to my ideas. These include my parents, Kathryn Higgins (1925–2003) and Eugene Higgins (1923–2013), and my siblings, Timothy Higgins, Colleen Cook, Jeanine Felten, Maureen Daily, and James Higgins (1966–2021). These family members also supported me emotionally through challenging experiences. A list of everyone who provided me with moral and practical support in grief would go on for pages, but I want particularly to thank the following individuals for sharing both solace and insight through our extended conversations: Jenene Allison, Sheila Steiner Asher, Purushottama Bilimoria, Douglas Buhrer (1956–2016), Sarah Canright, Steven Feld, Betty Sue Flowers, Henry Frankel (1944–2019), Paula Fulks, Ali Gallagher, Alex S.

Hill (1936–2021), Janice MacRae, Richard McKim, Garret Sokoloff, and Elke Solomon.

Dialogue with numerous colleagues and other interlocutors informed the work that led to this book. Colleagues at the University of Auckland's Philosophy Department invited me to present the first Robert C. Solomon Memorial Lecture, which motivated me to take up this topic. Participants in the Robert C. Solomon Memorial Conference, sponsored by the University of Texas at Austin Philosophy Department in 2008, also offered many observations that influenced this project's development. It took shape during my visit to Katholieke Universiteit Leuven under the auspices of Batja Gomes de Mesquita and her research group, and it solidified during a visit to the University of Vienna, where I was hosted by Matthew Ratcliffe and his research group. Many colleagues at the University of Texas at Austin and the University of Auckland were my interlocutors as the project unfolded, as were members of various audiences for talks I gave about some of the content and my fellow participants in University of Texas at Austin Humanities Institute's Faculty Fellows Seminar on "Health, Well-Being, and Healing" in the fall of 2017. I wish to extend my gratitude to these individuals and institutions. I want to note in particular conversations with the following people that informed this project, although this is only a partial list: Jamaal Abdul-alim, Roger Ames, Ashley Atkins, Thomas Attig, David Beaver, Judith Beck, Amelie Benedikt, Michael Benedikt, Nalini Bhushan, Jeanette Bicknell, John Bishop, Natalie Bograd, G. Lee Bowie, Ray Bradley (1930–1922), Svend Brinkmann, Luke Brunning, Olga Bukhina, Vivian Bullock, Casey Caldwell, Edward Casey, Chan-fai Cheung, Michael Cholbi, Amber Clifford, Jonathan Cohen, Jonathan Cole, Jan Crosthwaite, Laura Cumming, Miloš Čuřík, Vrinda Dalmiya, Stephen Davies, Jozefien De Leersnyder, Padmasiri de Silva, Ronald de Sousa, John Deigh, William Desmond, Christoph Durt, Michael Fanelli, Susan Feagin, Agneta Fischer, Tecumseh Fitch, Arthur Frank, Paula Frankel, Mikkel Krause Frantzen, Cynthia Freeland, Nico Frijda (1927–2015), Thomas Fuchs, Ali Gallagher, Luis-Manuel Garcia, Kay Getzoff, Leeat Granek, Derek Haderlie, Garry Hagberg, Rev. Thomas Hawkins, Catherine Hays, Sara Heinämaa, Peter Hershock, Courtney Hilton, Matthias Hunger, John Hyman, Line Ryberg Ingerslev, Andrew Ingram, Kirsten Jacobson, Alba Jasini, Piotr Karasinski, Donald Keefer, Ward Keeler, Hagi Kenaan, Dennis Klass, Ester Holte Kofod, Carolyn Korsmeyer, Allan Køster, Joel Krueger, Jonathan Lear, Dorothée Legrand, Cynthia Levinson, Sanford Levinson, Paisley Livingston, Oliver Lukitsch, Peter Clement Lund, Rev. Timothy Mabbott, Bernd Magnus (1937–2014), Eva Kit-Wah Man, Clancy Martin, Leslie Martinich, John McDermott (1932–2018), Rev. Walter Meier, Anjolie

Ela Menon, Meredith Michaels, Michelle Montague, Luisa Nardini, Robert Nola (1940–2022), Vasilina Orlova, Graham Parkes, W. Gerrod Parrott, Isabelle Peretz, Anders Petersen, Hope Phillips, Stephen Phillips, Heleen Pott, Ryan Preston-Roedder, Betsy Prioleau, Ljiljana Progovac, Ian Proops, Riley Ratcliffe, Matthew Ratcliffe, Ann Reynolds, Bernard Rimé, Sonja Rinofner-Kreidl, John Robertson (1943–2017), Denis Robinson, Jenefer Robinson, Henry Rosemont (1934–2017), JoAnn Rosemont, Stephanie Ross, Yuriko Saito, Sandra Salstrom, Barbara Sandrisser, Richard Schacht, Philipp Schmidt, Scott Schumann, Johanna Seibt, Harriet Senie, Andrew Sharp, David Sherman, Nancy Sherman, Alfred Thomas Bordado Sköld, Tara Smith, Edith Steffen, Johannes Steizinger, Robert Stolorow, Galen Strawson, Karsten Struhl, Anne Suhr, Marco Susino, John Swanay (1925–1985), Taylor Swan, Christine Swanton, Luca Tateo, Ralph Taylor, Enrico Terrone, C. Jason Throop, Susan Tilbury, Dylan Trigg, Emilio Valadez, Jorge Valadez, Silius Vytis, Brady Wagoner, Tony Walter, Sanford Weimer, Wolfgang Welsch, Robert Wicks, Ditte Alexandra Winther-Lindqvist, Mary Wiseman, Lucia Woodruff, Paul Woodruff, and Nicholas Zangwell.

I am grateful to my editors at the University of Chicago Press and their assistants. Elizabeth Branch Dyson initially expressed interest in this project, and Kyle Wagner brought it to fruition with the help of Kristin Rawlings. I thank them as well as Erin DeWitt, manuscript editor; Nathan Petrie, promotions manager; and Isaac Tobin, book designer. My thanks also go to June Sawyers, who prepared the index. I appreciate the work of the anonymous readers whose suggestions helped me to improve the book. I also wish to thank the College of Liberal Arts at the University of Texas at Austin for two College Research Fellowships that enabled me to concentrate on this project. The Office of the Vice President for Research, Scholarship and Creative Endeavors of the University of Texas at Austin and the Department of Philosophy of the University of Texas at Austin made generous subvention grants to help make the publication of this book possible, and I wish to express my appreciation to them as well.

Portions of chapter 3 were originally published as "Putting the Dead in the Their Place," in *Philosophies of Place: An Intercultural Conversation*, ed. Peter D. Hershock and Roger T. Ames (Honolulu: University of Hawaiʻi Press, 2019).

Finally, I wish to express my gratitude to my partner, Eugene Garver, for his nurturing affection, thoughtful advice, practical assistance, and endless patience.

Notes

CHAPTER ONE

1 Natalie Bauer-Lechner, *Recollections of Gustav Mahler*, ed. Peter Franklin, trans. Dika Newlin (Cambridge: Cambridge University Press, 1980), 50.

2 I should note that I take *aesthetic practices* to include modes of attention and contemplative savoring as well as more ostensibly active creative projects.

3 Arthur C. Danto, *The Abuse of Beauty: Aesthetics and the Concept of Art* (Chicago: Open Court, 2003), 111.

4 Catherine Wilson, "Grief and the Poet," *British Journal of Aesthetics* 53, no. 1 (2013): 91, 89. David Harrington, founding member of the Kronos Quartet, similarly thinks that a lot of music is about loss (personal communication).

5 Rachel Martin, "'Love, Me' Is a Community Poem Crowdsourced from Hundreds of Letters," *Morning Edition*, National Public Radio, July 28, 2022.

6 Barbara E. Thompson and Robert A. Neimeyer, eds., *Grief and the Expressive Arts: Practices for Creating Meaning* (New York: Routledge, 2014), 3.

7 See, for example, Jan Richardson, "What to Say When There Are No Words: Supporting the Bereaved with Respect and Sensitivity," *Wild Grief*, June 3, 2019, https://wildgrief.org/blog/what-to-say-when-there-are-no-words.

8 See, for example, Dominic McIver Lopes, *Being for Beauty: Aesthetic Agency and Value* (New York: Oxford University Press, 2018).

9 Steven Feld, *Bosavi: Rainforest Music from Papua New Guinea* (Smithsonian Folkways Recordings Center for Folklife and Cultural Heritage, in collaboration with the Institute of Papua New Guinea Studies, 2001), SFW40487, tracks 301, 302, and 303.

10 For a discussion of the development of this music, see Steven Feld, *Jazz Cosmopolitanism in Accra: Five Musical Years in Ghana* (Durham, NC: Duke University Press, 2012), 42–49.

11 Feld compares Por-Por processions to the processions involved in New Orleans jazz funerals. Feld, 43, 47, 49. The comparison is also brought out in the documentary film *A Por-Por Funeral for Ashirife*, directed and produced by Feld, with Nii Yemo Nunu as associate director (Montage Video Productions, 2009).

12 Janet McCracken, "Grief and the Mnemonics of Place: A Thank You Note," in

Passion, Death, and Spirituality: The Philosophy of Robert C. Solomon, ed. Kathleen Higgins and David Sherman (Dordrecht: Springer, 2012), 144.

13 "A science of sensitive knowing" is Nicholas Davey's translation of "*scientia cognitionis sensitivae*," Baumgarten's characterization of aesthetics in *Aesthetica*, §1. See Nicholas Davey, "Baumgarten, Alexander G(ottlieb)," in *A Companion to Aesthetics*, ed. Stephen Davies et al., 2nd ed. (Oxford: Wiley-Blackwell, 2009), 162.

14 Stephen K. Levine, "Poesis, Praise and Lament: Celebration, Mourning and the 'Architecture' of Expressive Arts Therapy," in *Grief and the Expressive Arts*, ed. Thompson and Neimeyer, 14. Levine interprets beauty in terms of form within the world striking us "as pleasing and meaningful."

15 Cf. Katya Mandoki, *Everyday Aesthetics: Prosaics, the Play of Culture and Social Identities* (Aldershot, Hampshire: Ashgate, 2007), 61–63. This is in keeping with an approach that Yuriko Saito describes as growing among those who are concerned with aesthetics in everyday life. She notes that some think that for aesthetic experience to occur, sensory perception and reflection must work together in the subject's relating to an object. See Yuriko Saito, "Aesthetics of the Everyday," revised November 18, 2019, in *The Stanford Encyclopedia of Philosophy*, edited by Edward N. Zalta, Spring 2021 ed., https://plato.stanford.edu/archives/spr2021/entries/aesthetics-of-everyday/.

16 See Berys Nigel Gaut, *Art, Emotion and Ethics* (Oxford: Oxford University Press, 2007), 34–35. If *aesthetics* is defined in this manner, beauty need not be primary among its concerns. Much contemporary art shuns beauty. For an analysis of the avoidance of beauty in recent art, see Danto, *The Abuse of Beauty*, 25–37.

17 James Shelley, "The Concept of the Aesthetic," revised February 28, 2022, in *The Stanford Encyclopedia of Philosophy,* edited by Edward N. Zalta, Spring 2022 ed., https://plato.stanford.edu/archives/spr2022/entries/aesthetic-concept/.

18 Shelley.

19 Cf. John Dewey, *Art as Experience* (New York: Perigee, 1934), 63. Dewey describes the distinction between expression and behavior that gives vent to an emotional condition as follows: "To discharge is to get rid of, to dismiss; to express is to stay by, to carry forward in development, to work out to completion" (62). Expression, according to Dewey, requires a medium and effort to shape the trajectory of the experience that someone engaging with the expression will have. I will follow Dewey in taking expression to involve deliberate selection and controlled use of materials with the aim of producing meaning.

20 For discussion of a broad range of aesthetic properties, see Frank Sibley, "Aesthetic Concepts," *Philosophical Review* 68, no. 4 (1959): 421–50; and Alan Goldman, "Aesthetic Qualities and Aesthetic Value," *Journal of Philosophy* 87, no. 1 (1990): 23–37. See also Thomas Leddy, "Everyday Surface Aesthetic Qualities: 'Neat,' 'Messy,' 'Clean,' 'Dirty,'" *Journal of Aesthetics and Art Criticism* 53, no. 3 (1995): 259–68; and Thomas Leddy, "Sparkle and Shine," *British Journal of Aesthetics* 37, no. 3 (1997): 259–73.

21 While artists use compositional devices and conventions to create clearly bounded works, framing can also be a matter of the interpretation on the part of the person contemplating a configuration, typically premised on one's conceptual framework. For an account of the phenomenon of framing, see Erving Goffman, *Frame Analysis: An Essay on the Organization of Experience* (New York: Harper & Row, 1974).

22 This is in keeping with eighteenth-century usage. See Shelley, "The Concept of the Aesthetic."

23 Robert Audi, *The Good and the Right: A Theory of Intuition and Intrinsic Value* (Princeton, NJ: Princeton University Press, 2009), 179–80. Cf. Confucius's comment on the importance of manner in filial piety: "Zixia asked about filial conduct (*xiao* 孝). The Master replied: 'It all lies in showing the proper countenance. As for the young contributing their energies when there is work to be done, and deferring to their elders when there is wine and food to be had—how can merely doing this be considered being filial?'" Roger T. Ames and Henry Rosemont Jr., trans. and eds., *The Analects of Confucius* (New York: Ballantine, 1998), 2.8, 78.

24 Debate ensues over whether grief itself is morally obligatory. See Purushottama Bilimoria, "Of Grief and Mourning: Thinking a Feeling, Back to Robert Solomon," in *Passion, Death, and Spirituality*, ed. Higgins and Sherman, 160–61, 171; Michael Cholbi, *Grief: A Philosophical Guide* (Princeton, NJ: Princeton University Press, 2021), 149–65; Kathleen Higgins, "Love and Death," in *On Emotions: Philosophical Essays*, ed. John Deigh (New York: Oxford University Press, 2013), 161–65; Matthew Ratcliffe, *Grief Worlds: A Study of Emotional Experience* (Cambridge, MA: MIT Press, 2022), 143–46; and Robert C. Solomon, *True to Our Feelings* (New York: Oxford University Press, 2007), 75ff. In *Digital Souls: A Philosophy of Online Death* (London: Bloomsbury, 2021), Patrick Stokes contends that in light of the preciousness of persons, we have "at least some sort of moral obligation to preserve the dead and keep them with us" (106), though this is not specifically a claim that grief is obligatory.

25 For some examples, see Arnold Berleant, *Art as Engagement* (Philadelphia: Temple University Press, 1991); Katya Mandoki, *Prosaica: Introducción a La Estética de lo Cotidiano* (Ciudad de México: Grijalbo, 1994), 43–44; Janet McCracken, *Taste and the Household: The Domestic Aesthetic and Moral Reasoning* (Albany: State University of New York, 2001), 9–28; Yuriko Saito, *Everyday Aesthetics* (New York: Oxford University Press, 2007), 26–27; and Robert Stecker, *Intersections of Value: Art, Nature, and the Everyday* (Oxford: Oxford University Press, 2019), 9.

26 While discussion of the activities of artists was not excluded from the purview of eighteenth-century aesthetics (the topic of artistic genius being a matter of interest to Kant, for example), this topic was not front and center. Debates about aesthetic taste predominated, and these concerned the perceiver and criteria for competence as a judge of aesthetic merit.

27 See, for example, Lopes, *Being for Beauty*; C. Thi Nguyen, *Games: Agency as Art* (New York: Oxford University Press, 2020); and Keren Gorodeisky, "Aesthetic Agency," in *Routledge Handbook for the Philosophy of Agency*, ed. Luca Ferrero (Abingdon, Oxon: Routledge, 2022), 456–66.

28 Tony Walter recognizes this bias when he points out the need for empirical research into the extent to which the bereaved make active use of art practices, whether as consumers or practitioners. See Tony Walter, "How People Who Are Dying or Mourning Engage with the Arts," *Music and Arts in Action* 4, no. 1 (2012): 73–98.

29 Ratcliffe, *Grief Worlds*, 246n9. I think it is quite possible that the translator rendered the title "Mourning and Melancholia" instead of "Grief and Melancholia" simply because of the alliteration.

30 Thomas Attig, *How We Grieve: Relearning the World*, rev. ed (Oxford: Oxford University Press, 2011), 8, xxvii.

31 Attig, 8.

32 Cholbi, *Grief*, 21–22.

33 Cf. Ratcliffe, *Grief Worlds*, 4.

34 Juliet Rosenfeld, *The State of Disbelief: A Story of Death, Love and Forgetting* (London: Short Books, 2020), ch. 1, Kindle.

35 Jonathan Lear, *Imagining the End: Mourning and Ethical Life* (Cambridge, MA: Harvard University Press, 2022), 4.

36 This is roughly the range of cultures that anthropologist Joseph Henrich and psychologists Steven Heine and Ara Norenzayan have termed WEIRD, an anachronym for "Western, educated, industrial, rich, democratic," which does not preclude there being subcultures within WEIRD societies that have different characteristics. See Joseph Henrich, Steven Heine, and Ara Norenzayan, "The Weirdest People in the World?" *Behavioral and Brain Sciences* 33, nos. 2–3 (2010): 61–83.

37 Thomas Fuchs, "Presence in Absence: The Ambiguous Phenomenology of Grief," *Phenomenology and the Cognitive Sciences* 17, no. 1 (2018): 45.

38 Saito, "Aesthetics of the Everyday." Drawing on Gernot Böhme's suggestion that aesthetics should focus on the "atmosphere" of situations, she mentions funerals and weddings as typifying cases in which an atmosphere is deliberately orchestrated. See Gernot Böhme, "Atmosphere as the Fundamental Concept of a New Aesthetics," trans. David Roberts, *Thesis Eleven* 36, no. 1 (1993): 113–26.

39 For example, Thomas Leddy emphasizes the discovery of the extraordinary in the ordinary, as is suggested by the title of his book *The Extraordinary in the Ordinary: The Aesthetics of Everyday Life* (Peterborough, ON: Broadview Press, 2012). By contrast, Arto Haapala and Yuriko Saito, among others, have defended the idea that the ordinary in the ordinary can also be an object of aesthetic attention. See Arto Haapala, "On the Aesthetics of the Everyday: Familiarity, Strangeness and the Meaning of Place," in *The Aesthetics of Everyday Life*, ed. Andrew Light and Jonathan Smith (New York: Columbia University Press, 2005), 39–55; and Yuriko Saito, *Aesthetics of the Familiar: Everyday Life and World Making* (New York: Oxford University Press, 2017).

40 Cf. Kendall L. Walton, "Categories of Art," *Philosophical Review* 79, no. 3 (1970): 334–67.

41 Saito, "Aesthetics of the Everyday."

42 See Attig, *How We Grieve*. Indeed, Attig refers to "sorrow-friendly practices," among which he includes "experiencing or creating works of art" (xxxiii).

43 We might note that a significant debate within everyday aesthetics concerns whether much of anything is ruled out of consideration aside from art, which has until recently dominated aesthetic attention since the nineteenth century. See Saito, "Aesthetics of the Everyday."

44 See, for example, Sallie Tisdale, "How a Common Death Ritual Made It Harder to Mourn the Loss of My Mother," *Time*, March 4, 2019, https://time.com/5542117/death-embalming-preservation-cremation-mourning/. Tisdale comments, "Embalming and the so-called restorative arts are about denial and, as a result, they unwittingly cause us greater pain." For a counterargument, see Kathleen Higgins, "Beauty and the Sense of Life," in *Artistic Visions and the Promise of Beauty:*

Cross-Cultural Perspectives, ed. Kathleen Higgins, Shakti Maira, and Sonia Sikka (Dordrecht: Springer, 2017), 163.

45 Donald Keefer, "Speaking Well of the Dead: On the Aesthetics of Eulogies," *Sophia* 50, no. 2 (2011), 304.

46 Even if the behavior is described as an offense against "good taste," the expression of moral disgust is so clear that the aesthetic connotations of the term may be ignored. Carolyn Korsmeyer draws a connection between responses of aesthetic disgust and recognition of human mortality generally, but she is primarily concerned with disgust as an aesthetic reaction to certain artworks and other objects, not behavior that prompts objections based on disgust. See Carolyn Korsmeyer, *Savoring Disgust* (New York: Oxford University Press, 2011), 122.

47 Judith M. Simpson, "Materials for Mourning: Bereavement Literature and the Afterlife of Clothes," *Critical Studies in Fashion and Beauty* 5, no. 2 (2014): 264. She refers here to Margaret Gibson, *Objects of the Dead* (Melbourne: Melbourne University Press, 2008), 15, 4, 10.

48 For a detailed analysis of the interpersonal character of grief, see Ratcliffe, *Grief Worlds*, 109ff.

49 Lear, *Imagining the End*, 14, 68.

CHAPTER TWO

1 Arthur W. Frank, *The Wounded Storyteller: Body, Illness, and Ethics*, 2nd ed. (Chicago: University of Chicago Press, 2013), 97–114.

2 Thomas W. Laqueur, "The Deep Time of the Dead," *Social Research: An International Quarterly* 78 (2011): 801.

3 I will discuss this thought further in chapter 7. Lest there be any doubt about the relevance of the deceased as audience, we should note the common view across many cultures that performing appropriate rituals vis-à-vis the deceased is a means of persuading the person's spirit not to take vengeance on the living.

4 Jacque Lynn Foltyn, "Sojourn, Transformative: Emotion and Identity in the Dying, Death, and Disposal of an Ex-Spouse," in *Emotion, Identity, and Death: Mortality across Disciplines*, ed. Douglas J. Davies and Chang-Won Park (Surrey: Ashgate, 2012), 91, 94. This degree of aesthetic distance does not move everyone in a positive way. Cf. Arthur C. Danto, *The Transfiguration of the Commonplace: A Philosophy of Art* (Cambridge, MA: Harvard University Press, 1981), 143, observes that Monet was appalled when he realized that he was gazing at the face of his deceased wife as he might when he was painting. He found this attitude out of keeping with his actual grief. My thanks to an anonymous reviewer for directing me to this passage. Of interest for our purposes here, Foltyn describes changes in her aesthetic responses after the loss of her ex-husband made death seem more personal to her than before. She reports being offended by news reports showing brutalized corpse images and by fashion trends featuring "skull style" and "'corpse chic' imagery" (94).

5 Traditional Jewish rituals represent an exception in the sense that adornment of cadavers is seen as objectionable, and the dead are typically buried in a simple shroud. See Maurice Lamm, *The Jewish Way in Death and Mourning*, rev. ed. (New York: Jonathan David Publishers, 2000), 11–12. Lamm suggests that this practice was devised to avoid shaming the poor and preventing competitions among the

wealthy to outdo each other in the ornate display of their loved ones' remains. If he is right, this is the rare exception that does prove the rule, in that concern about competitive aesthetic behavior was the basis for the practice.

6 Stephen Davies, *Adornment: What Self-Decoration Tells Us about Who We Are* (London: Bloomsbury, 2020), 4. See also Stephen Davies, *The Artful Species* (Oxford: Oxford University Press, 2012), 3, 190.

7 *Taking Chance*, directed by Ross Katz (HBO Films, 2009). The film is based on the experience of an actual marine lieutenant colonel, Michael R. Strobi, who accompanied the body of fallen PFC Chance Phelps home to his family. Strobi wrote an essay based on his diary from the trip, which was used as a basis for the film.

8 See *Mo Tzu*, in *Basic Writings of Mo Tzu, Hsün Tzu, and Han Fei Tzu*, trans. Burton Watson (New York: Columbia University Press, 1964), 6:11–12, 76–77.

9 Cf. Judith Butler's analysis that to consider a life ungrievable is to consider it a life that does not count in *Frames of War: When Is Life Grievable*? (London: Verso, 2016).

10 See Thomas W. Laqueur, *The Work of the Dead: A Cultural History of Mortal Remains* (Princeton, NJ: Princeton University Press, 2015), 314–15. See also Thomas Laqueur, "Bodies, Death, and Pauper Funerals," *Representations* 1 (1983): 109–31.

11 Audie Cornish with Martha Mullen, "The Search Is Over: Boston Bombing Suspect Has Been Buried," National Public Radio, May 10, 2013. https://www.npr.org/templates/story/story.php?storyld=182938654.

12 A contemporary example that was widely condemned is the 1993 incident in Mogadishu, Somalia, in which the bodies of dead American soldiers were dragged through the streets after their helicopter was shot down. This incident served as the basis for the Hollywood film *Black Hawk Down* (2001).

13 Cf. *Mencius*, trans. D. C. Lau (Harmondsworth: Penguin, 1970), 1b16, 72–73.

14 See J. K. Rowling, *The Casual Vacancy* (London: Little, Brown, 2012), 157.

15 UK News, "Themed Funerals Becoming a Celebration of Life," *UK News*, May 8, 2017, https://www.expressandstar.com/news/uk-news/2017/05/08/themed-funerals-becoming-a-celebration-of-life/.

16 See, for example, Sam Tetrault, "17 Star Wars Themed Funeral and Memorial Ideas," *Cake* (blog), updated May 13, 2022, https://www.joincake.com/blog/star-wars-funeral/. See also Funeral Guide, "How to Plan a Star Wars Funeral," *Funeral Guide* (blog), August 17, 2016, https://www.funeralguide.co.uk/blog/how-plan-star-wars-funeral.

17 See Clinton Yates, "'Best Funeral Ever': Most Frightening Reality TV Show to Date?" *Washington Post*, January 7, 2013, https://www.washingtonpost.com/blogs/therootdc/post/best-funeral-ever-most-frightening-reality-tv-show-to-date/2013/01/07/8106d82a-58ed-11e2-9fa9-5fbdc9530eb9_blog.html. See also HuffPost Entertainment, "TLC's 'The Best Funeral Ever': Golden Gate Funeral Home Hosts Christmas-Themed Ceremony," *Huffington Post*, January 3, 2013, updated January 23, 2014, https://www.huffingtonpost.com/2013/01/03/tlc-best-funeral-ever-christmas_n_2405019.html.

18 Yates, "'Best Funeral Ever.'" For another description and a video of the funeral, see HuffPost Entertainment, "'Best Funeral Ever': Singer of Chili's 'Baby-Back Ribs' Jingle Gets Barbecue-Themed Funeral Service," *Huffington Post*, January 7,

2013, http://www.huffingtonpost.com/2013/01/07/best-funeral-ever-singer-bbq-theme-video_n_2422725.html.

19 Yates, "'Best Funeral Ever'": "To be clear, I'm not passing judgment on anyone that chooses to make their funeral a big, even if ridiculous event, but those events are private. A television show that effectively trivializes death for the purpose of a party is not the direction that we need to be moving in as a society." Although Yates frames his objection in moralized terms, he clearly takes the aesthetic aspects of the featured funerals to be the means through which death is trivialized.

20 Robert Hertz, "Contribution à une Étude sur la Représentation Collective de la Mort," *Année Sociologiques* 10 (1907): 48–137; English translation as "A Contribution to the Study of the Collective Representation of Death," in *Death and the Right Hand*, trans. Rodney Needham and Claudia Needham (New York: Free Press, 1960), 197–212. Hertz observes that the underlying assumptions behind these practices are that death is not instantaneous and that it is a transition (see 203).

21 Hertz, "A Contribution to the Study of the Collective Representation of Death," 202.

22 Federal Trade Commission, "The FTC Funeral Rule," July 2012, https://www.consumer.ftc.gov/articles/0300-ftc-funeral-rule.

23 John Troyer, *Technologies of the Human Corpse* (Cambridge, MA: MIT Press, 2020), 15.

24 Troyer, 28.

25 Cf. Bethan Bell, "Taken from Life: The Unsettling Art of Death Photography," *BBC News*, June 5, 2016, https://www.bbc.com/news/uk-england-36389581. For a scholarly discussion, see Luca Tateo, "The Cultures of Grief: The Practice of Post-Mortem Photography and Iconic Internalized Voices," *Human Affairs* 28 (2018): 471–82.

26 Troyer, *Technologies of the Human Corpse*, 12.

27 Troyer, 17–18, citing James Farrell, *Inventing the American Way of Death, 1830–1912* (Philadelphia: Temple University Press, 1980), 160–61.

28 See Thomas Laqueur, "Form in Ashes," *Representations* 104, no. 1 (2008): 50–72.

29 Laqueur, 66, 68.

30 Pierre Bourdieu, *Distinction: A Social Critique of the Judgement of Taste*, trans. Richard Nice (Cambridge, MA: Harvard University Press, 1984).

31 Robert Webster, *Does This Mean You'll See Me Naked?: A Funeral Director Reflects on Thirty Years of Serving the Living and the Deceased* (Bloomington, IN: Rooftop Publishing, 2007), 69–71.

32 The fact that several Western museums have featured them in art exhibitions provides testimony to their aesthetic status. These include the Centre Pompidou in Paris, the University of Iowa Museum of Art, the Smithsonian's National Museum of African Art, the Oberlin College Art Museum, the Seattle Art Museum, San Francisco's de Young Museum. Fantasy coffins have also been exhibited in more historically oriented museums, including the British Museum, the National Museum of Funeral History in Houston, and Denmark's Moesgaard Museum. Fantasy coffins have been utilized in commercial art as well. The work of the oldest business specializing in their manufacture is reported to have been featured in a Coca-Cola commercial. See Akinyi Ochieng, "The Fantasy Coffins of Ghana,"

Roads & Kingdoms, January 22, 2016, http://roadsandkingdoms.com/2016/the-fantasy-coffins-of-ghana/.

33 Kinkaraco's website directs some of its marketing to the feminist contingent: "For the first time, four strong women can now easily lower their average weight friend by themselves!" See Kinkaraco Funeral Products, "Shrouds for Green Burial," 2017, https://kinkaraco.com/collections/shrouds-for-green-burial. See also Kinkaraco Funeral Products, "The Kinkara-Kart Processional," 2020, https://kinkaraco.com/products/kinkara-kart. A more recent version of the website links to a site showing that the company received an Eileen Fisher grant for women entrepreneurs. See Women of Green, "Eileen Fisher Award Goes to a Woman of Green," 2015, https://womenofgreen.com/2011/04/26/eileen-fisher-award-goes-to-woman-of-green/. See also Amy S. Choi, "Entrepreneurs Reinvent the Funeral Industry," *Bloomberg Businessweek Magazine*, June 19, 2008, http://www.businessweek.com/stories/2008-06-19/entrepreneurs-reinvent-the-funeral-industry.

34 *Six Feet Under*, season 5, episode 10, "All Alone," directed by Adam Davidson (HBO, aired August 7, 2005), https://www.hbo.com/six-feet-under/season-05/10-all-alone. See "Press Page," Kinkaraco Green Funeral Products, 2020, https://kinkaraco.com/pages/press?_pos=1&_sid=97bca1def&_ss=r.

35 On trademark image products as well as many others, see Choi, "Entrepreneurs Reinvent the Funeral Industry."

36 See Dr. Natural, "Pencils Made from Cremated Humans," April 1, 2007, Next Nature Network, https://nextnature.net/2007/04/pencils-made-from-cremated-humans; Nicole Morley, "Artist Creates Portraits of Dead People Using Their Own Remains," *Metro*, March 1, 2017, https://metro.co.uk/2017/03/01/artist-creates-portraits-of-dead-people-using-their-own-remains-6480545/; James Dunn, "Painter Creates Portraits of Dead People Using Their Own Remains Embedded in Wax," *Daily Mail*, February 28, 2017, https://www.dailymail.co.uk/news/article-4267418/Painter-creates-portraits-dead-people-using-ashes.html. See also Michelle Cromer, *Exit Strategy: Thinking Outside the Box* (New York: Jeremy P. Tarcher, 2006), 35, 84. Cromer describes jewelry being made of the deceased person's hair as well (see 60).

37 George Sanders, "Themed Death: Novelty in the Funeral Industry," *Consumers, Commodities, and Consumption* 10, no. 1 (2008), http://csrn.camden.rutgers.edu/newsletters/10-1/sander.htm. See also Sonya Vatomsky, "Thinking about Having a 'Green' Funeral? Here's What to Know," *New York Times*, March 22, 2018, https://www.nytimes.com/2018/03/22/smarter-living/green-funeral-burial-environment.html?emc=edit_nn_20180323&nl=morning-briefing&nlid=6087934620180323&te=1.

38 See Cromer, *Exit Strategy*, 16, 1, 22.

39 See AngelAire, "An Elegant and Memorable Approach to the Intimate Ceremony of Ash Scattering," 2020, https://angelaire.com. See also Cremation Solutions, "Scattering Release Urn Purchase," 1998–2022, https://www.cremationsolutions.com/scattering-release-urn-purchase.

40 See Cromer, *Exit Strategy*. Cromer also reports on other possibilities, such as a mummification process offered in a southwest Texas cryonic service, which preserve the cadaver by freezing it, ostensibly in the hope that it might be "re-animated" in the future. Here as elsewhere, capitalistic motives encourage the development of creative alternatives.

41 My thanks to Barbara Sandrisser for alerting me to the stylistic efforts that are evident in many obituaries. The documentary *Obit.* gives an impression of the considerations that go into the writing of obituaries. See *Obit.*, directed by Vanessa Gould (Green Fuse Films, 2017), https://www.kanopy.com/product/obit.

42 Tim Bullamore, "The Postmodern Obituary: Why Honesty Matters," in *Emotion, Identity, and Death*, ed. Davies and Park, 7–14.

43 Tony Walter argues that the means of social communication available have an impact on the social presence the dead have within society and the role they play in establishing and legitimating groups and institutions. See Tony Walter, "Communication Media and the Dead: From the Stone Age to Facebook," *Mortality* 20, no. 3 (2015): 215–32.

44 Walter, 226–27. Elaine Kasket suggests that mourners more often visit the deceased person's social media sites than a designated memorial site because they are felt to give more of an impression of the person's spirit. See her "Continuing Bonds in the Age of Social Networking: Facebook as a Modern-Day Medium," *Bereavement Care* 31, no. 2 (2012): 66.

45 Keefer, "Speaking Well of the Dead," 305.

46 See Jacques Derrida, *The Work of Mourning*, ed. Pascale-Anne Brault and Michael Nass (Chicago: University of Chicago Press, 2001), 225. Cf. Stokes, *Digital Souls*, 155–57. I suspect that Keefer would consider some of Derrida's eulogies, which refer to this problem, meta-eulogies, at least in part.

47 We might wonder whether the apparently spontaneous postings on social media sites do not similarly conform to implicit stylistic norms. However, we can expect norms to be evolving in the case of such a new form.

48 Greg Urban, "Ritual Wailing in Amerindian Brazil," *American Anthropologist* 90 (1988): 385–86. The "cry break," famously utilized in Hank Williams's recording of "I'm So Lonesome I Could Cry," is among the icons of crying to which Urban refers. He characterizes it as involving

> a pulse of air initiated by a push from the diaphragm. Pressure from the pulse is built up behind the closed glottis, which is then released with the glottal chords vibrating to produce any of various non-distinct vowels. The vibration is often accompanied by a friction noise, as the air is forced out the mouth and/or nose. In addition, the sound is typically produced with a falling tone. The pulse is then checked through a second closure of the glottis, the entire process lasting a fraction of a second. . . . Cry breaks can be chained together to form a sobbing action.

49 Stokes, *Digital Souls*, 59. He notes that COVID restrictions on the number of people who were allowed to be physically present at funerals motivated the development of new products such as this (see 177). Cf. Michael Arnold, Tamara Kohn, Martin Gibbs, James Meese, and Bjorn Nansen, *Death and Digital Media* (London: Routledge, 2018), 113–14.

50 One might question whether CARL is an aesthetic phenomenon. I classify it as such because it is a medium for engaging in ritual mourning practices with its own aesthetic features, which might be evaluated. See Brandon Southward, "Robotics Firm Inspired to Connect Mourners," *Statesman Journal*, June 5, 2015, https://www.statesmanjournal.com/story/money/business/2015/06/05/robotics-firm-works-connect-mourning-loss-loved-one/28557803/. One can imagine such

setups being more or less aesthetically pleasing. CARL is designed to direct attention to the face of the person on the screen. If CARL's material presence succeeds in being unobtrusive, it has passed one aesthetic test, albeit in a way that deflects attention away from the specific aesthetic features of CARL itself.

51 Paul C. Rosenblatt, "Grief across Cultures: A Review and Research Agenda," in *Handbook of Bereavement Research and Practice: Advances in Theory and Intervention*, ed. Margaret S. Stroebe, Robert O. Hansson, Henk Schut, and Wolfgang Stroebe (Washington, DC: American Psychological Association, 2008), 210.

52 Tony Walter, "A New Model of Grief: Bereavement and Biography," *Mortality* 1, no. 1 (1996): 7–25. I will consider the value of storytelling in bereavement at some length in chapter 5.

53 Bärbel Höttges, "Blogging the Pain: Grief in the Time of the Internet," *Gender Forum* 29, no. 4 (2009): 1–10. Conventional grief narratives would qualify as expression in Dewey's sense, described in 182n19 above.

54 Although not relevant to a consideration of aesthetics in the context of bereavement, we might note that considerations of etiquette also may constrain communication with the dying person. Controversy prevails over whether or not one should acknowledge that the person is dying, but I suspect that many people refrain from acknowledging the impending death because it strikes them as not their place to confront the person with the facts about his or her condition.

55 See John Morley, *Death, Heaven, and the Victorians* (Pittsburgh: University of Pittsburgh Press, 1971), 63–79. My thanks to Betty Sue Flowers for directing my attention to the Victorian rules for mourning attire.

56 That sending condolences is a strongly felt obligation is suggested by Freud. After pointing out his resistance to sending messages of congratulations on birthday, anniversaries, etc., gestures that he considered rather disingenuous, he immediately insists that he does not include condolences in this category: "Condolences on someone's death are an exception to my ambivalent attitude; when I have made up my mind to send them I do so at once." Sigmund Freud, *The Psychopathology of Everyday Life*, trans. Anthea Bell (London: Penguin, 2002), 145.

57 Birgit Koopmann-Holm and Jeanne L. Tsai, "Focusing on the Negative: Cultural Differences in Expressions of Sympathy," *Journal of Personality and Social Psychology* 107, no. 6 (2014): 1092–115. My thanks to Jozefien De Leersnyder for drawing my attention to this study.

58 For a discussion of the use of clichés and well-worn conventions in these contexts, see my "Kitsch in Relation to Loss," in *The Changing Meaning of Kitsch: From Rejection to Acceptance*, ed. Max Ryynänen and Paco Barragán (London: Palgrave Macmillan, 2023), 119–41.

59 Stokes, *Digital Souls*, 83.

60 See Stokes, 15, 24.

61 Stokes, 99. Cf. Heidi Ebert, "Profiles of the Dead: Mourning and Memorial on Facebook," in *Digital Death: Mortality and Beyond in an Online Age*, ed. Christopher M. Moreman and A. David Lewis (Santa Barbara, CA: Praeger, 2014), 23–42.

62 Wilson, "Grief and the Poet," 88–89.

63 Stokes, *Digital Souls*, 56.

64 We will return to the controversy surrounding chatbots in chapter 7.

65 Laqueur, *The Work of the Dead*, 414.

66 Contemporary cemeteries, at least in the United States, often restrict the type of

marker that is allowed, as well as more temporary forms of decoration, such as flowers, if they are allowed at all. These regulations, too, are aesthetic choices, though not choices made by relatives of the deceased.

67 U.S. Department of Veterans Affairs, "National Cemetery Administration: Emblems of Belief," updated February 15, 2023, https://www.cem.va.gov/hmm/emblems.asp. One available emblem is the "Hammer of Thor." It has traditional associations with Norse paganism, which continues to have adherents. Unfortunately, it has recently been appropriated by some white supremacists. See Anti-Defamation League, "Hate Symbol: Thor's Hammer," May 3, 2022, https://www.adl.org/education/references/hate-symbols/thors-hammer.

68 Allison Meier, citing a story on National Public Radio, reports that the idea of the crane was put forward by Air Force and National Guard veteran Linda Campbell, who "wanted an emblem to celebrate her wife Nancy Lynchild" and proposed the bird image as a "beautiful symbol of wisdom and protection and a happy marriage." Allison Meier, "The 65 Symbols on US Military Tombstones," *Hyperallergic*, May 29, 2017, https://hyperallergic.com/381933/the-65-symbols-on-us-military-tombstones/.

69 See Laqueur, *The Work of the Dead*, 50.

70 Karsten Harries, *The Ethical Significance of Architecture* (Cambridge, MA: MIT Press, 1997), 293. See also Howard Colvin, *Architecture and the After-Life* (New Haven, CT: Yale University Press, 1991), 1.

71 The Mausoleum at Halicarnassus is considered one of the Wonders of the Ancient World.

72 My thanks to a member of the audience at a talk I presented at the University of Hawai'i's Uehiro Graduate Philosophy Conference in March 2013, who suggested this way of considering such memorials.

73 Harries, *The Ethical Significance of Architecture*, 264, 266.

74 Harries, 284.

75 Laqueur, *The Work of the Dead*, 286–87.

76 See Jack Santino, "Performative Commemoratives, the Personal and the Public: Spontaneous Shrines, Emergent Ritual, and the Field of Folklore," *Journal of American Folklore* 117, no. 446 (2004): 363–72.

77 Robert Matej Bednar, *Road Scars: Place, Automobility, and Road Trauma* (Lanham, MD: Rowman & Littlefield, 2020), 4–5.

78 My thanks to Ward Keeler for making me aware of this kind of reaction.

79 See Santino, "Performative Commemoratives, the Personal and the Public," 363–72.

80 See Associated Press, "Street Shrines to 9–11 Still Dot N.Y.," *Gainesville Sun*, August 31, 2002, https://www.gainesville.com/story/news/2002/08/31/street-shrines-to-9-11-still-dot-ny/31613697007/.

81 This point was made by Robert Bednar in his talk "Placing Affect," presented in the Department of Anthropology at the University of Texas at Austin, November 5, 2012.

82 My thanks to Jamaal Abdul-alim for drawing my attention to this phenomenon.

83 Jasmine Sanders, "Memorial T-Shirts Create a Little Justice, a Tiny Peace," *New York Times*, November 14, 2017, https://www.nytimes.com/2017/11/14/style/memorial-t-shirts.html.

84 Sanders.

85 See Lizette Larson-Miller, "Roman Catholic, Anglican, and Eastern Orthodox Approaches to Death," in *Death and Religion in a Changing World*, ed. Kathleen Garces-Foley (Abingdon: Routledge, 2006), 114.

86 William Wordsworth, "Preface to the Lyrical Ballads," *Lyrical Ballads, with Other Poems, 1800*, vol. 1, 2nd ed., Project Gutenberg, http://www.gutenberg.org/cache/epub/8905/pg8905-images.html.

87 Wilson, "Grief and the Poet," 80.

88 Many such items survive from the time of the Han dynasty (206 BCE–220 CE).

89 Noël Carroll, "Art and Recollection," in *Art in Three Dimensions* (New York: Oxford University Press, 2010), 164, 165.

90 Wilson, "Grief and the Poet," 80, 88–89.

91 Laqueur, however, points out that death masks "became popular in the late eighteenth century and all the rage in the nineteenth." *The Work of the Dead*, 78.

92 Personal communication, in which Vonnegut mentioned that he considered what his sister would have found funny. See also Kurt Vonnegut, David Hayman, David Michaelis, George Plimpton, and Richard Rhodes, "Kurt Vonnegut, the Art of Fiction, No. 64," *Paris Review* 69 (1977): 89; Kurt Vonnegut, *Slapstick; or, Lonesome No More* (New York: Random House, 2004), 16–17; William Rodney Allen, *Understanding Kurt Vonnegut* (New York: Columbia University Press, 1991), 5; Thomas F. Marvin, *Kurt Vonnegut: A Critical Companion* (Westport, CT: Greenwood, 2002), 8–9.

93 *Tree of Life*, directed by Terrence Malick (Fox Searchlight Pictures, 2011). Other examples include the following: *Waking Life*, directed by Richard Linklater (Thousand Words, 2001); *Kaena: The Prophecy*, directed by Chris Delaporte and Pascal Pinon (Xilam, 2003); and *Open Range*, directed by Kevin Costner (Buena Vista Pictures, 2003).

94 Andrea Bayer, a curator in the European Painting Department at the Metropolitan Museum of Art, has posted a discussion of grief accompanied by images of artworks dealing with the theme. Andrea Bayer, "Connections: Grief," *The Met*, http://www.metmuseum.org/connections/grief#/Feature/.

95 See the painting *Conveying the Child's Coffin* (1879) by Albert Edelfelt (1854–1905), Ateneum Art Museum, Helsinki, Finland.

96 See Danto, *The Abuse of Beauty*, 108–13.

97 Lionel Shriver, *We Need to Talk about Kevin* (New York: Counterpoint, 2003).

98 In this category, Jordan Hoffman lists *Last Tango in Paris*, directed by Bernardo Bertolucci (United Artists, 1972); *Lantana*, directed by Ray Lawrence (Palace Films, 2001); *The Sweet Hereafter*, directed by Atom Egoyan (Alliance Communications, 1997); (somewhat surprisingly) *Enemies: A Love Story*, directed by Paul Mazursky (20th Century Fox, 1989); *Tres Couleurs: Bleu*, directed by Krzysztof Kleslowśki (MK2 Diffusion/Rialto Film, 1993); *Truly, Madly, Deeply*, directed by Anthony Minghella (Samuel Goldwyn, 1991); *Solaris*, directed by Andrei Tarkovsky (Mosfilm, 1972); and *Ponette*, directed by Jacques Doillon (BAC Films, 1996). See Jordan Hoffman, "The Best Movies about Grief You Probably Haven't Seen," *Slashfilm*, May 25, 2012, http://www.slashfilm.com/movies-grief/.

99 See Martha Nussbaum, *Upheavals of Thought: The Intelligence of Emotions* (Cambridge: Cambridge University Press, 2001), 281. For Nussbaum's thoughtful extended discussion of *Kindertotenlieder* as emotionally expressive, see 279–93.

100 "Taps" originated as a variant of the earlier "Lights Out" military bugle call,

adapted during the Civil War by Union General Daniel Butterfield. I will discuss the use of "Danny Boy" in funeral contexts in chapter 7.

101 An important example is the recently established National Memorial for Peace and Justice in Montgomery, Alabama, which commemorates African American victims of lynching in the United States.

102 Added at the beginning of the list of names are the words "In honor of the men and women of the armed forces of the United States who served in the Vietnam War. The names of those who gave their lives and those who remain missing are inscribed in the order they were taken from us." At the end of the list the following words were inserted: "Our nation honors the courage, sacrifice and devotion to duty and country of its Vietnam veterans. This memorial was built with private contributions from the American people."

103 Kirk Savage, *Monument Wars: Washington, D.C., the National Mall, and the Transformation of the Memorial Landscape* (Los Angeles: University of California Press, 2009), 277. For further discussion of this and other controversies about public memorials, see Kathleen Higgins, "Collective Memorials in the Face of Loss: The Multiple Roles of the Aesthetic," in *Aesthetics in Dialogue: Applying Philosophy of Art in a Global World*, ed. Zoltán Somhegyi and Max Ryynänen (Berlin: Peter Lang, 2020), 15–28.

104 Cf. Susan Feagin and Carolyn Korsmeyer, "More than Bare Bones: The Artistry and Ethics of Ossuaries," in *Philosophical Perspectives on Ruins, Monuments, and Memorials*, ed. Jeanette Bicknell, Jennifer Judkins, and Caroline Korsmeyer (New York: Routledge, 2020), 69–70.

105 The use of bones as artistic materials is not unique to Sedlec. Feagin and Korsmeyer point out that the Capuchin Cemetery in Rome similarly utilizes bones and skulls to make "decorative patterns and architectural structures" ("More than Bare Bones," 67–68). They cite Paul Koudounaris's estimate that there are approximately seventy decorative ossuaries across four continents. See Paul Koudounaris, *The Empire of Death: A Cultural History of Ossuaries and Charnel Houses* (New York: Thames & Hudson, 2011), 209–11.

106 Denise Inge, *A Tour of Bones: Facing Fear and Looking for Life* (London: Bloomsbury, 2014), 67. For discussion of this type of reaction, see Feagin and Korsmeyer, "More than Bare Bones," 71–72, 74–75.

107 Inge, *A Tour of Bones*, 69–70.

108 Hence the need for works such as Ratcliffe's *Grief Worlds*, which elaborates on the ways in which the many manifestations of grief are all aspects of a unified process.

CHAPTER THREE

1 Cholbi, *Grief*, 3. Cf. Solomon, *True to Our Feelings*, 73–75.

2 Cf. Solomon, *True to Our Feelings*, 75–76.

3 Dewey, *Art as Experience*, 77. We should bear in mind that order itself is a matter of aesthetic judgment.

4 See Attig, *How We Grieve*, xxvii.

5 Cf. Cholbi, *Grief*, 75. While Ratcliffe sees grief as a process, he emphasizes its emotional character when he suggests that we would have a better understanding of emotion in general if we took grief as an exemplary case. See *Grief Worlds*, 6.

6 This paradigm in psychology is reinforced by the fact emotions are commonly

studied in laboratory settings and fMRI machines are often used to link them with signature brain states. Cf. Solomon, *True to Our Feelings*, 5–6.

7 The account of Peter Goldie and the 2007 account of Robert C. Solomon are exceptions. See Peter Goldie, "Grief: A Narrative Account," *Ratio* 24, no. 2 (2011): 119–37; Peter Goldie, *The Mess Inside: Narrative, Emotion, and the Mind* (Oxford: Oxford University Press, 2012), 56–75; and Solomon, *True to Our Feelings*, 6, 72–78, 135.

8 For defenses of the affect program view, see Paul Ekman, *Emotions in the Human Face* (New York: Pergamon Press, 1972); and Paul E. Griffiths, *What Emotions Really Are: The Problem of Psychological Categories* (Chicago: University of Chicago Press, 1997).

9 Magda Arnold considered emotions to be evolutionary developments that aid our chances of survival, and although she considers appraisals that one should maintain a state of affairs, her emphasis on action readiness in emotion is certainly compatible with the expectation that most emotions will be relatively short-lived. See Magda B. Arnold, *Emotion and Personality*, 2 vols. (New York: Columbia University Press, 1960).

10 See Donald Gustafson, "Grief," *Noûs* 23, no. 4 (1989): 457–79. For various responses, see Michael Cholbi, "Grief's Rationality, Backward and Forward," *Philosophy and Phenomenological Research* 94, no. 2 (2017): 255–72; Carolyn Price, "The Rationality of Grief," *Inquiry* 53, no. 1 (2010): 20–40; and Sonja Rinofner-Kreidl, "Grief: Loss and Self-Loss," in *Emotional Experiences: Ethical and Social Significance*, ed. John Drummond (London: Rowman & Littlefield, 2018), 91–120.

11 Max Scheler, *The Nature of Sympathy*, trans. Peter Heath (London: Routledge Kegan Paul, 1954), 12–13.

12 Michael Kelly rejects the idea that grief is a species of sorrow on the ground that grief is not, as many assume, oriented toward the past. See Michael R. Kelly, "Grief: Putting the Past Before Us," *Quaestiones Disputatae* 7, no. 1 (2016): 156–77. Donald Gustafson also distinguishes grief, which he claims is irrational, from sorrow, which he thinks is not. See Gustafson, "Grief."

13 Cf. Ratcliffe, *Grief Worlds*, 248.

14 Cf. Ratcliffe, 6–7.

15 Ludwig Wittgenstein, *Philosophical Investigations*, trans. G. E. M. Anscombe (Oxford: Blackwell, 1953).

16 Other philosophers, too, analyze grief as an ongoing process. For example, see Ratcliffe, *Grief Worlds*, 13; Rinofner-Kreidl, "Grief," 93; Goldie, "Grief," 119–37; and Solomon, *True to Our Feelings*, 6.

17 Rinofner-Kreidl, "Grief," 115n13. See also Cholbi, *Grief*, 17; and Price, "The Rationality of Grief," 30. Price, however, seems to see the other emotions involved as variant forms of sadness.

18 Nina R. Jakoby, "Grief as a Social Emotion: Theoretical Perspectives," *Death Studies* 36 (2012): 683. On the place of anger and hatred, see also John Bowlby, "Processes of Mourning," *International Journal of Psychoanalysis* 42 (1961): 321. With respect to the diverse emotions involved in grief, including joy, cf. Michael Cholbi, "Finding the Good in Grief: What Augustine Knew That Meursault Could Not," *Journal of the American Philosophical Association* 3, no. 1 (2017): 100.

19 Attig emphasizes the importance of these more "positive" emotions, which come increasingly to the foreground as one relearns the world. See Attig, *How We*

Grieve, liii. See Kelly's discussion of regret in grief ("Grief," 172). On gratitude, see Robert C. Solomon, *Spirituality for the Skeptic* (New York: Oxford University Press, 2002), 105, 86.

20 Cf. Cholbi, *Grief*, 41; and Allan Køster, "Bereavement and the Meaning of Profound Feelings of Emptiness," in *Time and Body: Phenomenological and Psychopathological Approaches*, ed. Christian Tewes and Giovanni Stanghellini (Cambridge: Cambridge University Press, 2020), 125. Køster describes grief as an "affective register" that modifies one's entire perspective on the world.

21 Cf. Ratcliffe, *Grief Worlds*, 6.

22 William Lyons, *Emotion* (Cambridge: Cambridge University Press, 1985), 96, 43.

23 Wilson, "Grief and the Poet," 78.

24 Robert C. Solomon, *In Defense of Sentimentality* (New York: Oxford University Press, 2004), 14.

25 This term was coined by Magda Arnold. See her *Emotion and Personality*.

26 Nico H. Frijda, "Emotions Are Functional, Most of the Time," in *The Nature of Emotion: Fundamental Questions*, ed. Paul Ekman and Richard J. Davidson (Oxford: Oxford University Press, 1994), 117, 121.

27 See James R. Averill, "Grief: Its Nature and Significance," *Psychological Bulletin* 70, no. 6, pt. 1 (1968): 721–48.

28 See Solomon, *True to Our Feelings*, 76. Cf. Robert C. Solomon, *The Passions: Emotions and the Meaning of Life*, rev. ed. (Indianapolis: Hackett, 1993), 172.

29 Solomon, *True to Our Feelings*, 74. See also Solomon, *In Defense of Sentimentality*, 90.

30 Solomon, *True to Our Feelings*, 77. Solomon credits Janet McCracken with this insight about dedicatory activities. See Janet McCracken, "Falsely, Sanely, Shallowly: Reflections on the Special Character of Grief," *International Journal of Applied Philosophy* 19, no. 1 (2005): 139–56.

31 Thomas Attig, "Meanings of Death Seen through the Lens of Grieving," *Death Studies* 28, no. 4 (2004): 354. See also Attig, *How We Grieve*, xxxi.

32 See Elisabeth Kübler-Ross and David Kessler, *On Grief and Grieving: Finding the Meaning of Grief through the Five Stages* (New York: Scribner, 2005).

33 John Bowlby and Colin Murray Parkes, "Separation and Loss within the Family," in *The Child in His Family*, ed. Elwyn James Anthony (New York: Wiley, 1970), 197–216. Bowlby originally had a model of three phases: the "urge to recover the lost object," disorganization, and reorganization. See Bowlby, "Processes of Mourning," 333–38.

34 Kübler-Ross and Kessler, *On Grief and Grieving*, 7. See also: "There is no correct way or time to grieve" (xi). Attig acknowledges such qualifications by many authors who have stages accounts of grief. See *How We Grieve*, 43.

35 Bowlby, "Processes of Mourning," 331.

36 See Colin Murray Parkes and Holly G. Prigerson, *Bereavement: Studies of Grief in Adult Life*, 4th ed. (London: Routledge, 2010), 7.

37 See Paul K. Maciejewski, Baohui Zhang, Susan D. Block, and Holly G. Prigerson, "An Empirical Examination of the Stage Theory of Grief," *Journal of the American Medical Association* 297, no. 7 (February 21, 2007): 716–23.

38 See Camille B. Wortman and Roxane Cohen Silver, "The Myths of Coping with Loss," *Journal of Consulting and Clinical Psychology* 57, no. 3 (1989): 349–57.

39 See Wortman and Silver, 355. They note, for example, that those whose expres-

sions of grief exceed what outsiders consider normal commonly feel motivated to conceal what they are privately experiencing.

40 See Wortman and Silver: "Almost every stage model of coping with loss postulates a final stage of adaptation" (352).

41 Attig, "Meanings of Death Seen through the Lens of Grieving," 345. See also Attig, *How We Grieve,* 44–47.

42 Price, "The Rationality of Grief," 30.

43 Berislav Marušić, "Do Reasons Expire? An Essay on Grief," *Philosophers' Imprint* 18, no. 25 (2018): 1–25.

44 Goldie, *The Mess Inside*, 66–67.

45 Cholbi, *Grief*, 181. Cholbi does note, however, that grief can flare up again after it appeared to be resolved (75). And he points out that it can have a fuzzy ending (42).

46 Sigmund Freud, "Mourning and Melancholia" (1917), in *General Psychological Theory: Papers on Metapsychology* (New York: Macmillan, 1963), 164–65.

47 American Psychiatric Association, "Prolonged Grief Disorder," 2022, https://www.psychiatry.org/File%20Library/Psychiatrists/Practice/DSM/DSM-5-TR/APA-DSM5TR-ProlongedGriefDisorder.pdf.

48 P. Appelbaum, "Prolonged Grief Disorder," American Psychiatric Association, May 2022, https://psychiatry.org/patients-families/prolonged-grief-disorder. For further discussion of prolonged grief disorder from a medical perspective, see Kristin L. Szuhany, Matteo Malgaroli, Carly D. Miron, and Naomi M. Simon, "Prolonged Grief Disorder: Course, Diagnosis, Assessment, and Treatment," *Focus* 19, no. 2 (2021): 161–72.

49 Whether major depression itself should be pathologized is also controversial. See Ann Cvetkovich's case against the medicalization of depression in *Depression: A Public Feeling* (Durham, NC: Duke University Press, 2012), 85–114.

50 Appelbaum, "Prolonged Grief Disorder."

51 Paul A. Boelen, Maarten C. Elsma, Geert E. Smid, and Lonneke I. M. Lenferink express hesitancy about the one-year threshold in the new diagnosis category as requiring the lapse of more time than is necessary since "people following chronic grief trajectories mostly show signs of elevated grief before the first anniversary of the death." They argue that predictors of grief that will not abate on their own are evident by six months, and their opinion is that the threshold should be changed accordingly so that severe grief in the second half of the first year of bereavement can be treated. See their "Prolonged Grief Disorder in Section II of DSM-5: A Commentary," *European Journal of Psychotraumatology* 11, no. 1 (2020), https://doi.org/10.1080/20008198.2020.1771008.

52 American Psychiatric Association, "Highlights of Changes from DSM-IV-TR to DSM-5," 2013, https://www.psychiatry.org/File%20Library/Psychiatrists/Practice/DSM/APA_DSM_Changes_from_DSM-IV-TR_-to_DSM-5.pdf. For an alternative perspective, see Stephen Wilkinson, "Is 'Normal Grief' a Mental Disorder?" *Philosophical Quarterly* 50, no. 200 (2000): 289–304. Wilkinson argues that prima facie "normal grief" is a mental disorder, and thus any distinction drawn between pathological from nonpathological grief, such as that attempted by the *DSM*, will be arbitrary.

53 It also represents an improvement over an earlier *DSM* treatment of what is called "complicated grief," i.e., grief involving pathological features.

54 Cholbi, *Grief*, 183.

55 Cf. Cholbi's discussion of the "looping effects" of grief being medicalized and the probable impact on the way the grieving person is seen by herself and others (*Grief*, 177–79).

56 Cholbi, 95, 106.

57 Ratcliffe, *Grief Worlds*, 205; see also 206–8.

58 Lear, *Imagining the End*, 38.

59 Cf. Dewey, *Art as Experience*.

60 Nico H. Frijda, *The Laws of Emotion* (Mahwah, NJ: Lawrence Erlbaum, 2006), 293.

61 See McCracken, "Falsely, Sanely, Shallowly." McCracken's suggestion strikes me as right, assuming a generally positive relationship with the person. We might quibble over whether the expression "loved one" itself implies this. Obviously, ambivalent feelings can be directed toward someone with whom one has a close relationship, and in some cases ambivalence or recent strains in the relationship may hinder or block motivations to honor a deceased person.

62 Cf. Rinofner-Kreidl, "Grief," 109: "Authentic grief does not endorse closure."

63 Brian Carovillano, "Diocese Says 'Danny Boy' Isn't Appropriate at Mass," Providence, Rhode Island (AP), *Standing Stones*, October 24, 2001, http://www.standingstones.com/danny3.html#mass.

64 George A. Bonanno, *The Other Side of Sadness: What the New Science of Bereavement Tells Us about Life after Loss* (New York: Basic Books, 2009), 40.

65 I think that the alleged need for a funeral to provide closure usually amounts to a need for emotional punctuation and a felt obligation toward the deceased. We feel we owe dead loved ones a proper funeral, even if we cannot do much else on their behalf.

66 Frijda, *The Laws of Emotion*, 293.

67 Fr. Healey, I think, recognizes the value of the emotional punctuation such points of cadence involved, but he misses the expressive needs of those for whom the performance of "Danny Boy" is itself an important ritual with an emotional arc, and that the crying it provokes is its own kind of punctuation.

68 Dennis Klass, Phyllis R. Silverman, and Steven L. Nickman, eds., *Continuing Bonds: New Understandings of Grief* (Washington, DC: Taylor & Francis, 1996).

69 See Attig, *How We Grieve*, 178.

70 Attig, "Meanings of Death Seen through the Lens of Grieving," 355. See also Attig, *How We Grieve*, xxxiii, xxxvii, l.

71 Cholbi, *Grief*, 95. Indeed Paul C. Rosenblatt contends that although continuous grief usually passes after a few weeks, "strong feelings of grief for major losses will recur over a lifetime." See his "Grief That Will Not End," in *Continuing Bonds*, ed. Klass et al., 45.

72 Dennis Klass, "Prologue: A Personal History," in *Continuing Bonds in Bereavement: New Directions in Research and Practice*, ed. Dennis Klass and Edith Maria Steffen (New York: Routledge, 2018), xiii.

73 See Simon Shimshon Rubin, Ruth Malkinson, and Eliezer Witztum, "The Two-Track Model of Bereavement and Continuing Bonds," in *Continuing Bonds in Bereavement*, ed. Klass and Steffen, 17–30. See also Simon Shimshon Rubin, "The Wounded Family: Bereaved Parents and the Impact of Adult Child Loss," in *Continuing Bonds*, ed. Klass et al., 217–34.

74 Phyllis S. Kominsky, "Working with Continuing Bonds from an Attachment Theoretical Perspective," in *Continuing Bonds in Bereavement,* ed. Klass and Steffen, 113.

75 Margaret S. Stroebe and Henk Schut, "The Dual Process Model of Coping with Bereavement: Rationale and Description," *Death Studies* 23 (1999): 197–224.

76 Margaret Stroebe, Henk Schut, and Kathrin Boerner, "Continuing Bonds in Adaptation to Bereavement: Toward Theoretical Integration," *Clinical Psychology Review* 30 (2010): 259–68. See Kathrin Boerner and Jutta Heckhausen, "To Have and Have Not: Adaptive Bereavement by Transforming Mental Ties to the Deceased," *Death Studies* 27, no. 3 (2003): 199–226.

77 See Nigel P. Field, "Unresolved Grief and Continuing Bonds: An Attachment Perspective," *Death Studies* 30, no. 8 (2006): 750–51. Field cautions, however, that while the long-term use of externalized forms that situate the deceased in a particular time and place may be symptoms of unresolved grief, there is no invariant correlation. Cf. Ratcliffe, *Grief Worlds,* 142.

78 See Fuchs, "Presence in Absence," 57–59.

79 Cf. Klass and Steffen, "Introduction," in *Continuing Bonds in Bereavement,* ed. Klass and Steffen, 9.

80 Julie Beischel, Chad Mosher, and Mark Boccuzzi, "The Potential Therapeutic Efficacy of Assisted After-Death Communication," in *Continuing Bonds in Bereavement,* ed. Klass and Steffen, 176, 178.

81 Donald Woods Winnicott, "Transitional Objects and Transitional Phenomena," in *Playing and Reality* (New York: Routledge, 2002), 18.

82 Ratcliffe, *Grief Worlds,* 128.

83 Jack Hunter, "Ontological Flooding and Continuing Bonds," in *Continuing Bonds in Bereavement,* ed. Klass and Steffen, 191, 196.

84 Sandra M. Dannenbaum and Richard T. Kinnier, "Imaginal Relations with the Dead," *Journal of Humanistic Psychology* 49, no. 1 (2009): 102.

85 Hubert J. M. Hermans and Harry J. G. Kempen, eds., *The Dialogical Self: Meaning as Movement* (San Diego, CA: Academic Press, 1993).

86 See Hubert J. M. Hermans and Giancarlo Dimaggio, "The Dialogical Self in Psychotherapy: Introduction," in *The Dialogical Self,* ed. Hermans and Kempen, 3.

87 Considering the Joyce estate's rather extreme policies regarding citation, I will simply urge readers to consult the final line of book. See James Joyce, *A Portrait of the Artist as a Young Man* (New York: Viking, 1964), 253.

88 Cf. Attig, "Meanings of Death Seen through the Lens of Grieving, 350: "We are wrong to presume (claim to know when we do not) that whatever posture we assume in the world is solid and permanent. Bereavement reminds us that even the most viable posture is only tentative, and precariously so." On the other hand, one might at times also feel as though death must be "safer," somehow, if loved ones have already gone through it. Cf. Kathleen Higgins, "Death and the Skeleton," in *Death and Philosophy,* ed. J. E. Malpas and Robert C. Solomon (London: Routledge, 1998), 44–45.

89 Cf. Kelly, "Grief," 171.

90 Guy Newland, *A Buddhist Grief Observed* (Somerville, MA: Wisdom Publications, 2016), 2.

91 Certain sentences and passages in what follows also appear in my "Putting the Dead in Their Place," in *Philosophies of Place: An Intercultural Conversation,* ed.

Peter D. Hershock and Roger T. Ames (Honolulu: University of Hawai'i Press, 2019), 318–27.

92 Matthew Ratcliffe, "Relating to the Dead: Social Cognition and the Phenomenology of Grief," in *Phenomenology of Sociality: Discovering the 'We,'* ed. Thomas Szanto and Dermot Moran (London: Routledge, 2016), 207.

93 Cf. Denise Riley, *Time Lived, Without Its Flow* (London: Picador, 2019), 33.

94 Cf. Rosenfeld, *The State of Disbelief*, ch. 1, Kindle.

95 Cf. Fuchs, "Presence in Absence," 53.

96 Cf. Thomas D. Eliot, "Identification in Bereavement," *Midwest Sociologist* 16, no. 2 (1954): 7. See also Simpson, "Materials for Mourning," 258–59.

97 Fuchs, "Presence in Absence," 44.

98 C. S. Lewis, *A Grief Observed* (New York: HarperCollins, 1961), 44–45.

99 Fuchs, "Presence in Absence," 52. Cf. Ratcliffe, "Relating to the Dead," 209. Ratcliffe considers bereavement "illusions" or "hallucinations" at length in *Grief Worlds*, 109–32.

100 Jean-Paul Sartre, *Being and Nothingness: An Essay on Phenomenological Ontology*, trans. Hazel Barnes (New York: Simon and Schuster, 1956), 40, 42. See also Frijda, *The Laws of Emotion*, 283–303; and Ratcliffe, "Relating to the Dead," 207–8.

101 Augustine, *Confessions*, trans. Frank Sheed (Indianapolis: Hackett, 1993), 59.

102 C. S. Lewis points out that we think of the dead in general (whether or not conceiving of them as ghosts) as able to see us more clearly than before. See Lewis, *A Grief Observed*, 71.

103 Riley, *Time Lived, Without Its Flow*, 14.

104 Ratcliffe, *Grief Worlds*, 101. He sees all the permutations of temporal disturbances as stemming from grief's disruptions of one's life structure, which involves "organized values, commitments, projects, and pastimes" that guide pursuits sometimes far into the future and remained bound up with experiences in the past (100).

105 Cf. Fuchs, "Presence in Absence," 50.

106 Cf. Julian Barnes, *Levels of Life* (New York: Alfred A. Knopf, 2013), 107.

107 Fuchs, "Presence in Absence," 50. See also Thomas Fuchs, "Temporality and Psychopathology," *Phenomenology and the Cognitive Sciences* 12, no. 1 (2013): 75–104.

108 This is how Kurt Vonnegut's character Billy characterizes his situation in *Slaughterhouse-Five; or, The Children's Crusade* (New York: Delacorte Press, 1969).

109 Cf. Attig, "Meanings of Death Seen through the Lens of Grieving," 347. See also Michael Kelly's account of grief as "putting the past before us as future," such that our expectation of not seeing the deceased is "always already fulfilled," in "Grief," 173–76.

110 See Attig, "Meanings of Death Seen through the Lens of Grieving," 343. I still sometimes catch myself making a mental note when I hear of something that would have interested my late husband ("Remember to tell Bob!") even though he has been dead for well over a decade.

111 Margaret Stroebe and Henk Schut suggest that dealing adaptively with bereavement involves an oscillation between strategies geared to "addressing the loss" and those aimed at coping with secondary stresses that result from the changed situation. See their "The Dual Process Model of Coping with Bereavement." Attig is skeptical of this notion of oscillation on the grounds that the loss is perceived in

such global terms that the distinction made in this dual-process analysis is untenable. See Attig, *How We Grieve*, xlv–xlvi.

112 Fuchs notes the high incidence of suicidal ideation and suicide itself, citing numerous studies. Fuchs, "Presence in Absence," 52, 52n8.

113 See Attig, "Meanings of Death Seen through the Lens of Grieving," 348. Cf. Bilimoria, "Of Grief and Mourning," 168.

114 Ratcliffe, "Relating to the Dead," 210.

115 Cf. Newland, *A Buddhist Grief Observed*, 11: "My ordinary sense (or ordinary illusion) of my self as a real person did not operate."

116 Ratcliffe, "Relating to the Dead," 210; Riley, *Time Lived, Without Its Flow*, 27.

117 Granted, close relatives may be the people that one does *not* tell about certain things. But this supports the idea that one thinks of them as people one reports to—one simply makes a point of not reporting on some matters.

118 Cf. Ratcliffe, "Relating to the Dead," 205–6; Barnes, *Levels of Life*, 80.

119 Cf. Helen Humphreys, *True Story: The Life and Death of My Brother* (London: Serpent's Tail, 2013), 58. Cholbi defines grief as an identity crisis. See Cholbi, *Grief*, 18, 139.

120 Fuchs, "Presence in Absence," 45.

121 Newland, *A Buddhist Grief Observed*, 10.

122 Fuchs, "Presence in Absence," 46.

123 Barnes, *Levels of Life*, 84, 95.

124 Cf. Lewis, *A Grief Observed*, 11. Lewis describes himself as feeling that his body has become "like an empty house." For an analysis of this phenomenon, see Ratcliffe, *Grief Worlds*, 56–68.

125 See Fuchs, "Presence in Absence," 46–47.

126 Ratcliffe, *Grief Worlds*, 71.

127 See Allan Køster, "The Felt Sense of the Other: Contours of a Sensorium," *Phenomenology and the Cognitive Sciences* 20, no. 1 (2021): 57–73, esp. 68–72. See also Køster, "Bereavement and the Meaning of Profound Feelings of Emptiness," 125–43, esp. 130–32. The film *Departures*, which portrays the experience of a cellist turned mortician, shows him successfully aiming to make cadavers seem lifelike, with the effect that their loved ones feel that this enables them to say goodbye to the deceased. Yōjirō Takita, dir., *Departures*, produced by Tokyo Broadcasting System, distributed by Shochiku, 2008. This representation of attitudes among the bereaved accords with Køster's account. See also Jakoby, "Grief as a Social Emotion," 688.

128 Joseph Luzzi, *Through a Dark Wood: A Memoir* (New York: HarperCollins, 2015), 37.

129 Køster, "The Felt Sense of the Other," 69. See also Allan Køster, "Longing for Concreteness: How Body Memory Matters to Continuing Bonds," *Mortality* 25, no. 4 (2020): 389–401.

130 Freud, "Mourning and Melancholia," 255.

131 Marcel Proust, *The Sweet Cheat Gone*, trans. C. K. Scott Moncrieff, in *Remembrance of Things Past*, 2 vols. (New York: Random House, 1932), 2:725–26.

132 Luzzi, *Through a Dark Wood*, 28.

133 Cf. Erich Lindemann, "Symptomatology and Management of Acute Grief," *American Journal of Psychiatry* 101, no. 2 (1944): 141–48.

134 Fuchs, "Presence in Absence," 48.

135 Cf. Renato Rosaldo, "Introduction: Grief and a Headhunter's Rage," in *Culture and Truth: The Remaking of Social Analysis* (Boston: Beacon Press, 1993), 1–21.

136 Stokes, *Digital Souls*, 23.

137 See J. W. Pennebaker and J. D. Seagal, "Forming a Story: The Health Benefits of Narrative," *Journal of Clinical Psychology* 55, no. 10 (1999): 1243–54; James W. Pennebaker and Robin C. O'Heeron, "Confiding in Others and Illness Rate among Spouses of Suicide and Accidental-Death Victims," *Journal of Abnormal Psychology* 93, no. 4 (1984): 473–76; Bernard Rimé et al., "Social Sharing of Emotion: New Evidence and New Questions," *European Review of Social Psychology* 9, no. 1 (1992): 145–89; and Bernard Rimé, "Emotion Elicits the Social Sharing of Emotion," *Emotion Review* 1, no. 1 (2009): 60–85. That there is a need for expression is supported by studies showing that writing about upsetting emotional experiences yields benefits to both mental and physical health. This is indicated by fewer visits to a health clinic for illness, fewer self-reported symptoms of illness, and better immune functioning. Rimé, "Emotion Elicits the Social Sharing of Emotion," 77.

138 See Rimé et al., "Social Sharing of Emotion," 145–89. For additional discussion of this "ceiling effect," see Rimé, "Emotion Elicits the Social Sharing of Emotion," 67, 71.

139 The social constraints placed on further repetitions of the story by those in whom one might continue to confide may be one of the motivations for indirect emotion sharing through artistic means.

140 Depending on the relationship, the change in the bereaved person's social status may be legally recognized, as it is in the case of widows and orphans. Or it may simply be part of the social atmosphere among those who are aware of the loss and the relationship to the deceased.

141 See Colin Murray Parkes, *Bereavement: Studies of Grief in Adult Life*, 3rd ed. (London: Routledge, 1996), 5.

142 On the impact of others' responses to one's manifestations of grieving, see Ratcliffe, "Relating to the Dead," 207–8; and Rinofner-Kreidl, "Grief,"104.

143 Newland, *A Buddhist Grief Observed*, 5.

144 Rinofner-Kreidl, "Grief," 104.

145 Attig, *How We Grieve*, xxxixff.; Kelly, "Grief," 177.

CHAPTER FOUR

1 Cf. Riva Berleant, who mentions the "added frisson in handling and appreciating" the tactile qualities of tools, noting, "I, for example, enjoy seeing and using my cooking pots and garden tools." Riva Berleant, "Paleolithic Flints: Is an Aesthetics of Stone Tools Possible?" *Contemporary Aesthetics* 5 (2007), http://www.contempaesthetics.org/newvolume/pages/article.php?articleID=488.

2 This may be one of the explanations for the apparent aptness of beauty for healing sorrow that Danto indicated. Along similar lines, see Friedrich Nietzsche, *Thus Spoke Zarathustra*, trans. Walter Kaufmann (New York: Penguin, 1966), IV:13, 293. After noting that "many a pot breaks," Nietzsche's character Zarathustra summarizes the point quite nicely when he urges, "Place little good perfect things around you. . . . What is perfect teaches hope."

3 Immanuel Kant, *Critique of Judgment*, trans. Werner S. Pluhar (Indianapolis:

Hackett, 1987), §23, 98. For further discussion of this theme, see Higgins, "Beauty and the Sense of Life," 151–65.

4 Cf. Emily Brady and Arto Haapala, "Melancholy as an Aesthetic Emotion," *Contemporary Aesthetics* 1 (2003), https://www.contempaesthetics.org/newvolume/pages/article.php?articleID=214&searchstr=melancholy. Brady and Haapala see solitude as "the characteristic backdrop for melancholy," which they consider an aesthetic emotion because it conjoins feelings of pleasure and displeasure along the lines of the Kantian sublime and draw on a range of emotions that it brings into reflective harmony.

5 Martin Heidegger, *Being and Time*, trans. John Macquarrie and Edward Robinson (New York: Harper & Row, 1962), H. 73, p. 102.

6 Attig, "Meanings of Death Seen through the Lens of Grieving," 352.

7 Sonali Deraniyagala, *Wave* (New York: Random House, 2013), 189.

8 Goldie, *The Mess Inside*, 56; see also 65. This kind of remembering, according to Goldie, is characterized by the psychological equivalent of narrative uses of free indirect discourse, in which one encounters a perspective that is not that of anyone inside the story. He thinks that this psychological counterpart to free indirect discourse characterizes autobiographical memory in general.

9 Ratcliffe, *Grief Worlds*, 55.

10 Meyer Schapiro, "The Still Life as a Personal Object: A Note on Heidegger and Van Gogh," in *The Art of Art History: A Critical Anthology*, ed. Donald Preziosi (New York: Oxford University Press, 2009), 296–300.

11 Jakoby, "Grief as a Social Emotion," 689. Cf. Simpson, "Materials for Mourning," 263. See also Kirsten Jacobson, "The Temporality of Intimacy: Promise, World, and Death," *Emotion, Space, and Society* 13 (2014): 107. Stokes considers digital remains in a similar light. See Stokes, *Digital Souls*, 55.

12 Simpson, "Materials for Mourning," 256.

13 Simpson, 260, citing Gibson, *Objects of the Dead*, 120.

14 Carolyn Korsmeyer, "The Triumph of Time: Romanticism Redux," in "Symposium: The Aesthetics of Ruin and Absence," special issue, *Journal of Aesthetics and Art Criticism* 72, no. 4 (2014): 429–30. See also her *Things: In Touch with the Past* (New York: Oxford University Press, 2019).

15 Leon Rosenstein, "The Aesthetic of the Antique," *Journal of Aesthetics and Art Criticism* 45, no. 4 (1987): 399. Appreciation of an object's having undergone deterioration through time is also evident in the Japanese aesthetic concept *mono no aware* ("the pathos of things," or "pleasing melancholy"), which refers to aestheticized sadness regarding the transience of things. See Yuriko Saito, "Letting Objects Speak: Beauty in the Japanese Artistic Tradition," in *Artistic Visions and the Promise of Beauty*, ed. Higgins, Maira, and Sikka, 196.

16 Octavio Paz, "Use and Contemplation," in *In Praise of Hands: Contemporary Crafts of the World*, trans. Helen R. Lane (New York: World Crafts Council, 1974), 24.

17 Cf. Kathleen Higgins, "Music's Role in Relation to Phenomenological Aspects of Grief," in "Understanding Grief: Intentionality, Regulation, and Interpretation," special issue, *Journal of Consciousness Studies* 29, nos. 9–10 (2022): 128–49.

18 Charles O. Nussbaum, *The Musical Representation: Meaning, Ontology, and Emotion* (Cambridge, MA: MIT Press, 2007), 211–13.

19 For a few examples on the internet, see Sarah Burke, "The Surreal, Awkward Parts of Grief That No One Talks About," *Vice*, January 23, 2018, https://www.vice

.com/en/article/vbykpj/we-need-to-talk-about-death-modern-loss; Sunflower Cosmos, "My Dad Died and It's Been Shocking and Surreal," *Grief in Common*, May 15, 2021, https://www.griefincommon.com/connect/threads/my-dad-died-and-its-been-shocking-and-surreal.2642/; and Melissa Gould, "Life after Death: A Surreal Reality," *HuffPost* blog, updated April 19, 2015, https://www.huffpost.com/entry/life-after-death-a-surreal-reality_b_6685418.

20 See, for example, comment A19 from Respondent 73 in Becky Millar, Matthew Ratcliffe, Louise Richardson, and Emily Hughes, *Experiences of Grief: A Phenomenological Survey* (Colchester, Essex: UK Data Service, 2020), DOI: 10.5255/UKDA-SN-856067. Cf. Arthur Dobrin, "Grief Feels Like You're Going Crazy," *Psychology Today* blog, July 26, 2011, https://www.psychologytoday.com/us/blog/am-i-right/201107/grief-feels-youre-going-crazy; and Alan D. Wolfelt, "You're Not Going Crazy—You're Grieving," Center for Loss & Life Transition, December 14, 2016, https://www.centerforloss.com/2016/12/youre-not-going-crazy-youre-grieving/.

21 *Back to the Future,* directed by Robert Zemeckis (Universal Pictures, 1985).

22 Cf. Noël Carroll, *The Philosophy of Horror; or, Paradoxes of the Heart* (London: Routledge, 1990), 80. Carroll distinguishes between endorsing a proposition as a belief and merely entertaining it: "To have a belief is to entertain a proposition assertively; to have a thought is to entertain it nonassertively."

23 Paul Thom considers six different ways in which one's attention moves while attending to a performed work of art. See his *For an Audience: A Philosophy of the Performing Arts* (Philadelphia: Temple University Press, 1993), 205–6.

24 Cf. Kathleen Higgins, *The Music of Our Lives*, 2nd ed. (Lanham, MD: Lexington, 2011), 163–65.

25 David Chase, creator, *The Sopranos*, 6 seasons, aired January 10, 1999–June 10, 2007, on HBO, https://www.hbo.com/the-sopranos. Cf. Noël Carroll, "Sympathy for the Devil," in *"The Sopranos" and Philosophy: I Kill Therefore I Am*, ed. Richard Greene and Peter Vernezze (New York: Open Court, 2004), 121–36.

26 The death of James Gandolfini, the actor who played Tony Soprano, ensured that the sixth season of *The Sopranos* would be the final one, but the final episode did not bring themes in the story to such a definitive end that a seventh season was out of the question had Gandolfini lived. Given developments in "deepfake" technology, perhaps we can imagine a seventh season being made anyway.

27 Line Ryberg Ingerslev, "Ongoing: On Grief's Open-Ended Rehearsal," *Continental Philosophy Review* 51, no. 3 (2018): 350. Too much self-confidence might also preempt the self-knowledge available in grief that Cholbi sees as grief's positive potential. Since this is the theme of his entire book, see Cholbi, *Grief*, especially 82–86.

28 See Mircea Eliade, *Myth and Reality* (1963), trans. Willard R. Trask (New York: Harper & Row, 1981), 19. We shall return to this idea in chapter 7.

29 Arthur Schopenhauer, *The World as Will and Representation*, trans. E. F. J. Payne, 2 vols. (New York: Dover, 1969), I:179, 209.

30 Nico H. Frijda and Louise Sundararajan, "Emotion Refinement: A Theory Inspired by Chinese Poetics," *Perspectives on Psychological Science* 2, no. 3 (2007): 229.

31 John Le Carré, *The Constant Gardener* (New York: Pocket Books, 2001); and *The Constant Gardener*, directed by Fernando Meirelles (Universal Studios, 2005). The screenplay of the latter was by Jeffrey Caine, based on Le Carré's novel.

32 Cf. Luzzi, *Through a Dark Wood*, 25.

33 Amy Tan, *The Hundred Secret Senses* (New York: G. P. Putnam's Sons, 1995), 345–50.

34 Arthur W. Frank, "*Philoctetes* and the Good Companion Story," *Enthymema* 16 (2016): 120.

35 See Cheryl Mattingly, *The Paradox of Hope: Journeys through a Clinical Borderland* (Berkeley: University of California Press, 2010), xiii, 175.

36 Frank, "*Philoctetes* and the Good Companion Story," 121.

37 Lear, *Imagining the End*, 45, 47.

38 Lear, 55.

39 Luzzi is Professor of Italian Studies and Comparative Literature.

40 Luzzi, *Through a Dark Wood*, 1.

41 Luzzi, 10.

42 Luzzi, 4–5.

43 Laura Cumming, *The Vanishing Velázquez: A Nineteenth-Century Bookseller's Obsession with a Lost Masterpiece* (New York: Scribner, 2016), 2.

44 Cumming, 4.

45 Cumming, 268.

46 Frank, "*Philoctetes* and the Good Companion Story," 121n.

47 Alexander Nehamas, *On Friendship* (New York: Basic Books, 2016), 144.

48 See Newland, *A Buddhist Grief Observed*, 78–79.

49 Peter D. Hershock, *Liberating Intimacy: Enlightenment and Social Virtuosity in Ch'an Buddhism* (Albany: State University of New York Press, 1996), 14–16.

50 Hershock, 14–16.

51 Hershock, 16.

CHAPTER FIVE

1 Urban, "Ritual Wailing in Amerindian Brazil," 386.

2 Urban, 392.

3 Steven Feld, "Wept Thoughts: The Voicing of Kaluli Memories," *Oral Tradition* 5, nos. 2–3 (1990): 252.

4 Feld, 246. Urban acknowledges this function, but he does not see it as primary. See Urban, "Ritual Wailing in Amerindian Brazil," 392.

5 G. W. F. Hegel, *Introductory Lectures on Aesthetics*, trans. Bernard Bosanquet, ed. Michael Inwood (Harmondsworth: Penguin, 1993), 54–55.

6 Kendall Walton, "*Thoughtwriting*—in Poetry and Music," *New Literary History* 42, no. 3 (2011): 455–76.

7 Anna Christina Ribeiro, "Heavenly Hurt," in *Suffering Art Gladly: The Paradox of Negative Emotion in Art*, ed. Jerrold Levinson (New York: Palgrave Macmillan, 2014), 200.

8 In this connection, see Michael Spitzer, *A History of Emotion in Western Music: A Thousand Years from Chant to Pop* (Oxford: Oxford University Press, 2020), 80, 82. Spitzer suggests that composers in the Western classical tradition have frequently employed certain standard sequences of expressed emotions to convey grief. One of these is to oscillate between sadness and tenderness. Another is a cycle of love-sadness-grief-anger. One might well find these recurrent sequences illuminating with respect to the way that one emotional state gives way to another

in grief, particularly with the respect to the way that envisioning the object in one light might set up another emotional response (for example, tender love feelings toward the deceased setting up a new bout of sadness). Cf. Robert Hatten, *A Theory of Virtual Agency for Western Art Music* (Bloomington: University of Indiana Press, 2018), 25, 197.

9 Ribeiro, "Heavenly Hurt," 197.

10 Ribeiro, 199.

11 For a more extended discussion, see Kathleen Marie Higgins, *The Music between Us: Is Music a Universal Language?* (Chicago: University of Chicago Press, 2012), 53–54.

12 My thanks to Ann Reynolds for suggesting the relevance of pilgrimage sites to the idea of aesthetic accumulation.

13 Theresa Machemer, "You Can Now Explore All 48,000 Panels of the AIDS Memorial Quilt Online," *Smithsonian Magazine*, July 21, 2020, https://www.smithsonianmag.com/smart-news/aids-memorial-quilt-now-online-180975370/.

14 Cf. Judith Butler on the topic of grievability. She analyzes the tendency to view some people as undeserving of grief (particularly by virtue of their being identified as a member of a stigmatized group) as a mode of dehumanization. See, in particular, her "Violence, Mourning, Politics," in *Precarious Life: The Powers of Mourning and Violence* (New York: Verso, 2004), 19–49. See also her *Frames of War*, esp. 38–43. She explicitly mentions the NAMES Project in this connection on page 39 of the latter work.

15 See American Foundation for Suicide Prevention, "Digital Memory Quilt," 2020, https://afsp.org/quilt/. See also Survivors of Suicide Loss, "Create a Virtual Quilt Square to Honor a Loved One Lost to Suicide," https://www.soslsd.org/memorial-quilt-donate/. In the latter case, fundraising also seems to be a goal of the quilt project, in that those who wish to memorialize a loved one are asked to make a financial donation.

16 See Walter, "Communication Media and the Dead." See also Carla J. Sofka, "Social Support 'Internetworks,' Caskets for Sale, and More: Thanatology and the Information Superhighway," *Death Studies* 21, no. 6 (1997): 553–74. However, as already noted in chapter 2, the accumulation of postings can have the ironic effect of making those of the deceased less visible.

17 The absence of comments on a legacy site, however, is emotionally affecting in a different way. I was intensely saddened to see an obituary site for a former schoolmate that listed only the dates of his birth and his death. Returning to it just again and scrolling down, I was relieved to see that one person had posted a one-sentence message that it had been a pleasure to know him. But the absence of any outpouring of messages seems almost a mark of disparagement. We have already noted Stokes's concern that appropriating the deceased person's own social media site as a memorial space can backfire as a means of keeping the dead person in memory. This may be reason to prefer sites that are designed for memorial purposes. The appropriation of a person's own site, however, is somewhat akin to the production of spontaneous memorials. Both allow grieving people to respond more immediately to loss than is the case when formal arrangements are made. They also share the problem that lack of planning may give rise to unforeseen consequences.

18 The impossibility during some stages of the COVID-19 pandemic of in-person

funerals prevented or limited this sense of collective connection, and many felt that its absence added to the difficulties they were experiencing in dealing with grief. Cf. Louise Richardson, Matthew Ratcliffe, Becky Millar, and Ellie Byrne, "The COVID-19 Pandemic and the Bounds of Grief," *Think* 20, no. 57 (2021): 89–90.

19 Bernard Rimé defines social sharing as "a description of the emotional event in a socially-shared language by the person who experienced it to another." Rimé, "Emotion Elicits the Social Sharing of Emotion," 66.

20 One might consider this a version of what Arthur Frank calls a "chaos narrative," in which events are presented as "without sequence or discernable causality." Frank considers such stories "anxiety-provoking," because they remind us of "how easily any of us could be sucked under." Frank, *The Wounded Storyteller*, 97.

21 Anna Deavere Smith, *Twilight: Los Angeles, 1992: On the Road: A Search for American Character* (New York: Anchor Books, 1994).

22 See Jerome Bruner, *Acts of Meaning* (Cambridge, MA: Harvard University Press, 1990), 47–50. See also Rimé, "Emotion Elicits the Social Sharing of Emotion," 63.

23 See Lorraine Hedtke and John Winslade, *The Crafting of Grief: Constructing Aesthetic Responses to Loss* (New York: Routledge, 2017).

24 We might note that concern to shape the presented narrative with an eye to impact on the audience is an aesthetic activity, even though the editing process may in large part be subliminal and may limit the extent to which the story told feels emotionally unburdening.

25 Rimé, "Emotion Elicits the Social Sharing of Emotion," 75. Cf. Emmanuelle Zech, Bernard Rimé, and James W. Pennebaker, "The Effects of Emotional Disclosure during Bereavement," in *The Scope of Social Psychology: Theory and Applications*, ed. Miles Hewstone, Henk A. W. Schut, John B. F. de Wit, Kees Van Den Bos, and Margaret S. Stroebe (London: Psychology Press, 2007), 278.

26 Rimé, "Emotion Elicits the Social Sharing of Emotion," 76.

27 Wolfgang Stroebe, Henk Schut, and Margaret S. Stroebe, "Grief Work, Disclosure, and Counseling: Do They Help the Bereaved?" *Clinical Psychology Review* 25 (2005): 395. See also Margaret S. Stroebe, Henk Schut, and Wolfgang Stroebe, "Who Benefits from Disclosure? Exploration of Attachment Style Differences in the Effects of Expressing Emotions," *Clinical Psychology Review* 26, no. 4 (2005): 66–85.

28 For further discussion of the effect that the death of a beloved person has on one's impression of the larger social matrix in which one is ensconced, see Higgins, "Love and Death," 159–69.

29 Donald Baxter claims that we can learn something similar from grief, that our egos aren't as separate as we often think. He thinks this realization can stem from the bereaved person's discovery of how interpenetrated his or her own sense of identity is with that of the deceased. Donald L. M. Baxter, "Altruism, Grief, and Identity," *Philosophy and Phenomenological Research* 70, no. 2 (2005): 381.

30 Walter, "A New Model of Grief," 7–25. See also Nigel P. Field, "Whether to Relinquish or Maintain a Bond with the Deceased," in *Handbook of Bereavement Research and Practice*, ed. Stroebe et al., 113.

31 Elaine Kasket describes online mourning as being especially conducive to the creation of a collaborative durable biography of the deceased. See her "Continuing Bonds in the Age of Social Networking," 67.

32 See Higgins, "Love and Death," 174–75.

33 Stokes, *Digital Souls*, is concerned about this problem, which he sees as especially worrisome in connection with the development of chatbots that use artificial intelligence to conjure up seeming virtual images of the deceased that draw on things the person really said but extrapolate, as we will consider in chapter 7.

34 Milan Kundera, *Immortality*, trans. Peter Kussi (New York: Grove Weidenfeld, 1991), 48.

35 Kundera, 73.

36 Cf. Fuchs, "Presence in Absence," 58–59: "Telling the story of one's relation with the lost loved one is a way of coping with the loss by raising and integrating it into an intersubjective sphere—the sphere of the symbolic." He sees this also on the cultural sphere, accomplished through stories about ancestors and primordial founders, noting the gospel accounts as serving this function. Cf. Hedtke and Winslade, *The Crafting of Grief*, 17. They contend that the narratives of grieving people draw from the many texts that surround us, which serve as "cultural repositories" that suggest possible patterns for crafting our individual stories.

37 Paul Ricoeur, *Time and Narrative*, trans. Kathleen McLaughlin and David Pellauer, 3 vols. (Chicago: University of Chicago Press, 1984), 1:65.

38 Arnar Árnason, "Biography, Bereavement, Story," *Mortality* 5, no. 2 (2000): 201.

39 Cf. Friedrich Nietzsche, *Beyond Good and Evil: Prelude to the Philosophy of the Future*, trans. Walter Kaufmann (New York: Random House, 1967), §148, 89–90; §261, 209.

40 This may be especially helpful in preempting or disrupting guilt-ridden ways of thinking about one's relationship to the deceased, a matter I will discuss further in chapter 7.

41 See Galen Strawson, "Against Narrativity," *Ratio* 17, no. 4 (2004): 428–52.

42 Strawson, 447.

43 Higgins, "Love and Death."

44 Cf. Rita Charon, *Narrative Medicine: Honoring the Stories of Illness* (New York: Oxford University Press, 2006). Charon, founder of the field of narrative medicine, uses literature to help her students to attend more to their patients' concerns and the subtleties of what they are communicating. The fact that she makes extensive use of works by Henry James indicates that she sees nuanced attentiveness to narrative detail as having the potential to enable new insight into what patients need.

45 Cf. Higgins, "Love and Death," 173–78.

CHAPTER SIX

1 Murray Smith, "Empathy, Expansionism, and the Extended Mind," in *Empathy: Philosophical and Psychological Perspectives*, ed. Amy Coplan and Peter Goldie (Oxford: Oxford University Press, 2011), 100.

2 Amy Coplan, "Understanding Empathy: Its Features and Effects," in *Empathy*, ed. Coplan and Goldie, 5.

3 Steven Darwall, "Empathy, Sympathy, Care," *Philosophical Studies* 89, nos. 2–3 (1998): 261. Cf. Nancy Eisenberg and Janet Strayer, "Critical Issues in the Study of Empathy," in *Empathy and Its Development*, ed. Nancy Eisenberg and Janet Strayer (Cambridge: Cambridge University Press, 1987), 5; Graham McFee, "Empathy: Interpersonal vs. Artistic?" in *Empathy*, ed. Coplan and Goldie, 190, 193; and Smith, "Empathy, Expansionism, and the Extended Mind," 101.

4 S. D. Preston and F. B. de Waal, "Empathy: Its Ultimate and Proximate Bases," *Behavioral and Brain Sciences* 25, no. 1 (February 2002): 1–20.

5 Rimé observes that even in ordinary circumstances, "simple approaches and simplistic interventions usually prevail because non-victims dramatically underestimate a victim's situation. . . . Most laypersons are unable to take into account the complex consequences negative emotional experiences entail." Rimé, "Emotion Elicits the Social Sharing of Emotion," 76.

6 Jonathan Vanderhoek argues what we experience does not need to be identical to the other person's state to count as empathy. It needs only to be "an echo" of it or what Adam Smith calls an "enlivened" representation. See Jonathan Vanderhoek, "The Indispensability of Empathy: The Role of Empathy in Making Moral Judgments," (PhD diss., University of Texas at Austin, 2016), 12, 32, 43. See also Adam Smith, *The Theory of Moral Sentiments* (1790), ed. K. Haakonssen (Cambridge: Cambridge University Press, 2002), I.i.2.2.

7 McFee, "Empathy," 191.

8 *2001: A Space Odyssey,* directed by Stanley Kubrick (Stanley Kubrick Productions, 1968).

9 Cf. Wilson, "Grief and the Poet."

10 Cf. XIV, where Aristotle contends that emotion is aroused simply by hearing a summary of a well-constructed tragic plot, which touches on universal human themes. Aristotle, *De Poetica (Poetics)*, trans. Ingram Bywater, in *The Basic Works of Aristotle*, ed. Richard McKeon (New York: Random House, 1941), XIV, l.5, 1468.

11 Jeanette Bicknell, "Architectural Ghosts," in "Symposium: The Aesthetics of Ruin and Absence," special issue, *Journal of Aesthetics and Art Criticism* 72, no. 4 (2014): 435.

12 See Michael Benedikt, "One, Two, Three, . . . Louis, I., Kahn," in *Louis Kahn: The Importance of a Drawing*, ed. Michael Merrill (Baden: Lars Müller, 2021), 327–52. Benedikt indicates the source of the photo as follows: "The photo appears in Aldo van Eyck, 'Building in the Southern Oases,' *Forum* (Holland), 1953. See also Robert McCarter, *Aldo van Eyck* (New Haven, Yale University Press, 2015), 36–38."

13 Scott C. Schumann, "The Presence of Absence in Stravinsky's *Élégie*," unpublished manuscript presented at West Coast Conference of Music Theory and Analysis, 2011.

14 Laqueur, *The Work of the Dead*, 65.

15 Laqueur, 76–78.

16 Laqueur, 78; citing Terry Castle, *The Female Thermometer: Eighteenth-Century Culture and the Invention of the Uncanny* (New York: Oxford University Press, 1995), 8.

17 I will not, however, insist that experiences of being haunted can be reduced without remainder to psychic projections.

18 TVTropes, "Our Ghosts Are Different," https://tvtropes.org/pmwiki/pmwiki.php/Main/OurGhostsAreDifferent.

19 Randolph Neese takes it as a given that searching behavior "gives rise to belief in ghosts." See Randolph M. Neese, "An Evolutionary Framework for Understanding Grief," in *Spousal Bereavement in Late Life*, ed. Deborah Carr, Randolph M. Neese, and Camille B. Wortman (New York: Springer, 2005), 210.

20 A. O. Scott, "Review: 'A Ghost Story' Has a Sensitive Specter with Time on His

Hands," *New York Times*, July 5, 2017, https://www.nytimes.com/2017/07/05/movies/review-a-ghost-story.html.

21 Cf. Ross Poole, "Two Ghosts and an Angel: Memory and Forgetting in *Hamlet*, *Beloved*, and *The Book of Laughter and Forgetting*," *Constellations* 16, no. 1 (2009): 125–49.

22 Alan Ball, director and writer, *Six Feet Under*, pilot episode, aired June 3, 2001, on HBO.

23 This is among the motives considered by Michiko Iwasaka and Barre Tolken, *Ghosts and the Japanese: Cultural Experience in Japanese Death Legends* (Logan: Utah State University Press, 1994), 16.

24 *The Sixth Sense*, directed by M. Night Shyamalan (Buena Vista Pictures, 1999).

25 *High Plains Drifter*, directed by Clint Eastwood (Universal Pictures, 1973).

26 Cf. Wilson, "Grief and the Poet," 88. Wilson observes that bereaved people "may be drawn to literature that reawakens their emotional experience of simultaneous absence-and-presence."

27 My thanks to Garret D. Sokoloff for first directing me to this play and for years of ongoing conversation about it.

28 Zeami, *Izutsu*, in *Masterworks of the Nō Theater*, trans. and ed. Kenneth Yasuda (Bloomington: Indiana University Press, 1989), 225.

29 The impression of being something of a ghost yourself in bereavement is exacerbated if others are accustomed to seeing you with the deceased and encounter you in a manner that suggests that they are seeing a ghost. This is not an uncommon tendency, for seeing a surviving next of kin often leads third parties to think of the deceased, whose ambiguous presence and absence they may already be experiencing.

30 Zeami, *Izutsu*, 210.

31 For an interpretation of the in-betweenness of the experience of absence in grief that emphasizes compatibilities among seemingly inconsistent aspects of the experience, see Louise Richardson, "Absence Experience in Grief," *European Journal of Philosophy* (2022): 1–16, https://doi.org/10.1111.ejpo.12778.

32 *Solaris*, directed by Andrei Tarkovsky (Mosfilm, 1972).

33 Chris Barsanti, "Love Is a Ghost in 'Solaris,'" *Eyes Wide Open*, July 3, 2017, https://medium.com/eyes-wide-open/love-is-a-ghost-in-solaris-4d0f77632367.

34 Phillip Lopate, "*Solaris*: Inner Space," *The Criterion Collection*, 2002; reposted May 24, 2011, https://www.criterion.com/current/posts/239-solaris-inner-space.

35 Joey Armstrong, "Grief as a Dream: Andrei Tarkovsky's *Solaris*," *The Stake*, October 24, 2016, http://thestake.org/2016/10/24/grief-as-a-dream-andrei-tarkovskys-solaris/.

36 Armstrong, "Grief as a Dream."

37 Lopate, "*Solaris*."

38 My thanks to W. Gerrod Parrott for drawing my attention to the way that the camera angle creates a distorted sense of space, reminiscent of the physical disorientation that is common in grief.

39 Cf. Lewis, *A Grief Observed*, 18: "Slowly, quietly, like snowflakes—like the small flakes that come when it is going to snow all night—little flakes of me, my impressions, my selections, are settling down on the image of her. The real shape will be quite hidden in the end. Ten minutes—ten seconds—of the real H. would correct this. And yet, even if those ten seconds were allowed, one second later the little

flakes would begin to fall again. The rough, sharp, cleansing tang of her otherness is gone."

40 Lopate, "*Solaris*."

CHAPTER SEVEN

1 James Joyce, *Dubliners* (New York: Random House, 1967).

2 Cf. Hedtke and Winslade, *The Crafting of Grief*, 201.

3 See Køster, "The Felt Sense of the Other."

4 Køster, "Longing for Concreteness," 5, 2.

5 Cf. John Bowlby, *Attachment and Loss*, vol. 3: *Loss: Sadness and Depression* (London: Pimlico, 1980), 232; and Alfred Bordado Sköld, "Relationality and Finitude: A Social Ontology of Grief" (PhD diss., Aalborg University, 2021), 11.

6 Robert Matej Bednar points out that many people leave notes directly addressing the deceased at roadside shrines, typically using present or future tenses. See his "Materialising Memory: The Public Lives of Roadside Crash Shrines," *Memory Connection* 1, no. 1 (2011): 23, http://www.memoryconnection.org/article/materialising-memory-the-public-lives-of-roadside-crash-shrines-2/.

7 Dannenbaum and Kinnier, "Imaginal Relations with the Dead," 100–113.

8 Afterward, the client may be asked to sit in the chair and assume the role of the person addressed, responding to what has just been said, and this back-and-forth may be repeated. But often the client simply speaks to the absent person.

9 Dannenbaum and Kinnier, "Imaginal Relations with the Dead," 107. I should add that the therapists cautioned that these techniques are not appropriate for everyone, noting that clients who have difficulty with "reality boundaries" are not good candidates for this practice. (I will have more to say about photographs presently.)

10 Nancy Gershman and Barbara E. Thompson, *Prescriptive Memories in Grief and Loss: The Art of Dreamscaping* (New York: Routledge, 2019).

11 See Jordan S. Potash and Rainbow T. H. Ho, "Expressive Therapies for Bereavement: The State of the Arts," in *Grief and the Expressive Arts: Practices for Creating Meaning*, ed. Barbara E. Thompson and Robert A. Neimeyer (New York: Routledge, 2014), 29. See also Hedtke and Winslade, *The Crafting of Grief*, 36: "An aesthetic approach supports the intentional remembering of the deceased, and the fostering of relational connections, both in life and in death."

12 Diana C. Sands, "Restoring Hope Following Suicide," in *Grief and the Expressive Arts*, ed. Thompson and Neimeyer, 220.

13 Shanee Stepakoff, "Graphopoetic Process," in *Grief and the Expressive Arts*, ed. Thompson and Neimeyer, 67.

14 Yu-Chan Li and Cypress Chang, "The Grief Healing Garden," in *Grief and the Expressive Arts*, ed. Thompson and Neimeyer, 250.

15 Li and Chang "The Grief Healing Garden," 252.

16 Miki Meek, "Really Long Distance," *This American Life*, 597: "One Last Thing Before I Go," September 23, 2016, https://www.thisamericanlife.org/597/one-last-thing-before-i-go. Excerpts recorded by NHK Sendai in connection with their documentary *The Phone of the Wind: Whispers to Lost Families*. The documentary in English translation is available as *The Phone of the Wind: Whispers to Lost Fami-*

lies, directed by Ryo Urabe and Tomohiko Yokoyama (NHK, 2016), https://www.youtube.com/watch?v=ke-H5EEqvRs.

17 Cf. Stokes, *Digital Souls*, 22. Stokes suggests that the affordance of the phone may enable people to unburden themselves, perhaps speaking more candidly than they would speak to a living person.

18 For an interesting editorial discussion of some of the elaborate paper items that are currently being burned on behalf of deceased loved ones in Hong Kong, see Nury Vittachi, "You Are What You Burn," *New York Times*, April 27, 2015, https://www.nytimes.com/2015/04/28/opinion/hong-kong-you-are-what-you-burn.html. See also Qin Xie, "Laptops, Mansions and Helicopters: The Weirdest Paper Offerings Chinese People Burn for the Deceased to Ensure Them a Happy Afterlife," *Daily Mail Online*, April 1, 2016, http://www.dailymail.co.uk/news/peoplesdaily/article-3515806/Laptops-mansions-helicopters-weirdest-paper-offerings-Chinese-people-burn-deceased-ensure-happy-afterlife.html.

19 See Friedrich Nietzsche, *The Gay Science*, trans. Walter Kaufmann (New York: Random House, 1974) §84, 139. A similar view of the origins of music as a means of communicating with the supernatural was defended by Siegfried Nadel, "The Origins of Music," *Music Quarterly* 16 (1930): 531–46, esp. 538–44. Bruno Nettl notes the pervasiveness of the myth that this desire was the original motive that led to the origination of music. See Bruno Nettl, *The Study of Ethnomusicology: Twenty-Nine Issues* (Urbana: University of Illinois Press, 1983), 165.

20 Johannes Steizinger has suggested to me that the wind telephone is particularly evocative, in that both the phone booth and the outmoded telephone are archaic, and thus they position one as gesturally traveling into a place outside of present time, a location in which one can envision the dead as still existing. Personal communication with Johannes Steizinger.

21 Stokes, *Digital Souls*, 77. He appeals to Kasket's report in "All the Ghosts in the Machine" (54) that 77% of visitors in the late 2010s were doing so, up from about 30% in the early 2000s.

22 Cf. Hedtke and Winslade, *The Crafting of Grief*, 51, who point out that several studies conducted after the introduction of the idea of continuing bonds were aimed at assessing whether efforts to maintain a relationship with the deceased might "add to the risk of complicated grief."

23 See Eliade, *Myth and Reality*, 19.

24 This seems to be the viewpoint of Anne Roiphe. See her *Epilogue: A Memoir* (New York: HarperCollins, 2009).

25 See David Farrell Krell and Donald L. Bates, *The Good European: Nietzsche's Work Sites in Word and Image* (Chicago: University of Chicago Press, 1997), 15.

26 G. W. F. Hegel, *Phenomenology of Spirit*, trans. by A. V. Miller (New York: Oxford University Press, 1977), 270–71. See McCracken's comment on this passage in "Grief and the Mnemonics of Place," 143–44.

27 Hans Georg Gadamer, *Reason in the Age of Science*, trans. Frederick G. Lawrence (Cambridge, MA: MIT Press, 1981), 75.

28 See Kendall L. Walton, *Mimesis as Make-Believe: On the Foundations of the Representational Arts* (Cambridge, MA: Harvard University Press, 1990).

29 Fuchs, "Presence in Absence," 58.

30 Fuchs, 58, 60.

31 Meek, "Really Long Distance."

32 Dannenbaum and Kinnier report that of the elders they interviewed who acknowledged that they engaged in imaginal conversations with the dead, "most . . . seemed willing to remain open to the possibility that the souls of their loved ones did exist and that the conversation might be real." Dannenbaum and Kinnier saw this attitude even among some who were skeptical. About half, they claim, "believed that they had actually contacted a deceased loved one." Dannenbaum and Kinnier, "Imaginal Relations with the Dead," 108.

33 Ingerslev, "Ongoing," 356.

34 Ingerslev, 345, 356.

35 Ingerslev, 356.

36 Frijda, *The Laws of Emotion*, 299. Cf. Field's reference to the way in which the deceased can provide the living with "an image of his or her comforting presence when under duress" and "an important reference point when making important autonomy-promoting decisions" ("Whether to Relinquish or Maintain a Bond with the Deceased," 120–21). Cf. Dannenbaum and Kinnier, "Imaginal Relations with the Dead," 102.

37 Frijda, *The Laws of Emotion*, 298.

38 Frijda, 297, 299.

39 Ingerslev, "Ongoing," 355–56.

40 Kendall L. Walton, "Transparent Pictures: On the Nature of Photographic Realism," *Critical Inquiry* 11, no. 2 (1984): 251–52.

41 Roland Barthes, *Camera Lucida: Reflections on Photography*, trans. Richard Howard (New York: Hill and Wang, 1981), 67–70.

42 See Susan Sontag, *On Photography* (New York: Dell, 1973), 15.

43 Barthes, *Camera Lucida*, 96.

44 This is the same ambiguity that Cumming (*The Vanishing Velázquez*) sees in *Las Meninas*, though she emphasizes the positive aspect, as we considered in chapter 4.

45 Stokes, *Digital Souls*, 55.

46 Ratcliffe (*Grief Worlds*, 130) draws attention to Merleau-Ponty's characterization of what is required if our envisioning closeness to the dead is to be respectful. Merleau-Ponty says, "The only memory which respects them is the one which maintains the actual use they have made of themselves and of their world, the accent of their freedom and the incompleteness of their lives." Maurice Merleau-Ponty, "In Praise of Philosophy," in *In Praise of Philosophy and Other Essays*, trans. John Wild, James M. Edie, and John O'Neill (Evanston, IL: Northwestern University Press, 1988), 65. Stokes is concerned with the form of remembering the dead that does not include this.

47 This problem is a central theme of *Solaris*, as we have seen.

48 Joel Krueger and Lucy Osler maintain that chatbots do not pose the threat that Stokes suggests, arguing that users recognize the fictional character of the surrogate and the fact that the chatbot does not have a full world, as a human being does. They think that chatbots can help grieving people to maintain connections with the dead and that the practice of using them can actually help us to restore habits of intimacy. See their "Communing with the Dead Online: Chatbots, Grief, and Continuing Bonds," *Journal of Consciousness Studies* 29, nos. 9–10 (2022): 222–52.

49 C. Jason Throop, "Singular Particulars: Some Reflections on the Excessiveness of Death, Mourning, and Loss," presented at "The Phenomenology of Grief and Loss: A Symposium," University of Vienna, April 16, 2018.

50 Nehamas, *On Friendship*, 45–46, 119.

51 Keefer, "Speaking Well of the Dead," 310.

52 Ratcliffe, *Grief Worlds*, 121, 175.

53 My thanks to Garret Sokoloff, who first suggested to me the basic difficulty with this kind of thinking: you feel guilty because you cannot do enough on behalf of the deceased loved one, yet you will never feel that you have done enough in the case of someone you love.

54 Arlie Russell Hochschild, *The Managed Heart: Commercialization of Human Feeling* (Berkeley: University of California Press, 1983), 65, 68.

55 My thanks to Betty Sue Flowers for suggesting that one of the emotionally distressing aspects of bereavement is the sense that you can't do much for the deceased person anymore.

56 Stokes, *Digital Souls*, 110.

57 Mozi takes it as obvious that funerals of some sort are essential, and he uses the argument that adopting a policy of having the same kind of funeral for everyone would ensure that everyone's own parents would receive a proper burial.

58 Hsün Tzu, *Basic Writings*, trans. Burton Watson (New York: Columbia University Press, 1963), 109.

59 Cf. Lear, who says, "Mourning typically involves attempting to join a cultural ritual that puts itself forward as an adequate manner of response to the death of the loved one." Lear, *Imagining the End*, 33. He notes, however, that such rituals do not necessarily succeed, for some people are alienated from them to a greater or lesser degree.

CONCLUSION

1 Lear, *Imagining the End*, 17.

2 Lear, 39–40.

3 Werner Stegmaier, *What Is Orientation? A Philosophical Investigation*, trans. Reinhard G. Mueller (Berlin: Walter de Gruyter, 2019).

4 Cf. Ratcliffe, *Grief Worlds*, 216–24.

5 Higgins, "Kitsch in Relation to Loss."

6 Herbert Fingarette sees this view as basic to Confucius's emphasis on ritual. See his *Confucius: The Secular as Sacred* (New York: Harper & Row, 1972). I thank Roger Ames, David Hall, and Henry Rosemont for drawing my attention further to the extent to which Confucian thought's extolling of ritual depends on the idea that it brings together the kind of balance between lived experience and established form that I have been emphasizing.

7 Cf. Fingarette.

8 My thanks to Janet McCracken for pointing this out to me decades ago.

9 Yuriko Saito, *Aesthetics of Care: Practice in Everyday Life* (London: Bloomsbury, 2022).

Bibliography

BOOKS

Allen, William Rodney. *Understanding Kurt Vonnegut.* New York: Columbia University Press, 1991.

American Foundation for Suicide Prevention. "Digital Memory Quilt." 2020. https://afsp.org/quilt/.

American Psychiatric Association. "Highlights of Changes from DSM-IV-TR to DSM-5," 2013. https://www.psychiatry.org/File%20Library/Psychiatrists/Practice/DSM/APA_DSM_Changes_from_DSM-IV-TR_-to_DSM-5.pdf.

American Psychiatric Association. "Prolonged Grief Disorder." 2022. https://www.psychiatry.org/File%20Library/Psychiatrists/Practice/DSM/DSM-5-TR/APA-DSM5TR-ProlongedGriefDisorder.pdf.

Ames, Roger T., and Henry Rosemont Jr., trans. and eds. *The Analects of Confucius.* New York: Ballantine, 1998.

AngelAire. "An Elegant and Memorable Approach to the Intimate Ceremony of Ash Scattering," 2020. https://angelaire.com.

Anti-Defamation League. "Hate Symbol: Thor's Hammer," May 3, 2022. https://www.adl.org/education/references/hate-symbols/thors-hammer.

Appelbaum, Paul. "Prolonged Grief Disorder." American Psychiatric Association, May 2022. https://psychiatry.org/patients-families/prolonged-grief-disorder.

Aristotle. *De Poetica* (*Poetics*). Translated by Ingram Bywater. In *The Basic Works of Aristotle.* Edited by Richard McKeon, 1455–487. New York: Random House, 1941.

Armstrong, Joey. "Grief as a Dream: Andrei Tarkovsky's *Solaris.*" *The Stake,* October 24, 2016. http://thestake.org/2016/10/24/grief-as-a-dream-andrei-tarkovskys-solaris/.

Árnason, Arnar. "Biography, Bereavement, Story." *Mortality* 5, no. 2 (2000): 189–204.

Arnold, Magda B. *Emotion and Personality*. 2 vols. New York: Columbia University Press, 1960.

Arnold, Michael, Tamara Kohn, Martin Gibbs, James Meese, and Bjorn Nansen. *Death and Digital Media*. London: Routledge, 2018.

Attig, Thomas. *How We Grieve: Relearning the World*. Rev. ed. Oxford: Oxford University Press, 2011.

Attig, Thomas. "Meanings of Death Seen through the Lens of Grieving." *Death Studies* 28, no. 4 (2004): 341–60.

Audi, Robert. *The Good and the Right: A Theory of Intuition and Intrinsic Value*. Princeton, NJ: Princeton University Press, 2009.

Augustine. *Confessions*. Translated by Frank Sheed. Indianapolis: Hackett, 1993.

Averill, James R. "Grief: Its Nature and Significance." *Psychological Bulletin* 70, no. 6, pt. 1 (1968): 721–48.

Barnes, Julian. *Levels of Life*. New York: Alfred A. Knopf, 2013.

Barsanti, Chris. "Love Is a Ghost in 'Solaris.'" *Eyes Wide Open*, July 3, 2017. https://medium.com/eyes-wide-open/love-is-a-ghost-in-solaris-4d0f77632367.

Barthes, Roland. *Camera Lucida: Reflections on Photography*. Translated by Richard Howard. New York: Hill & Wang, 1981.

Bauer-Lechner, Natalie. *Recollections of Gustav Mahler*. Edited by Peter Franklin. Translated by Dika Newlin. Cambridge: Cambridge University Press, 1980.

Baxter, Donald L. M. "Altruism, Grief, and Identity." *Philosophy and Phenomenological Research* 70, no. 2 (2005): 371–83.

Bayer, Andrea. "Connections: Grief." *The Met*. http://www.metmuseum.org/connections/grief#/Feature/.

Bednar, Robert M. 2011. "Materialising Memory: The Public Lives of Roadside Crash Shrines." *Memory Connection* 1, no. 1 (2011): 18–33. http://www.memoryconnection.org/article/materialising-memory-the-public-lives-of-roadside-crash-shrines-2/.

Bednar, Robert Matej. *Road Scars: Place, Automobility, and Road Trauma*. Lanham, MD: Rowman & Littlefield, 2020.

Beischel, Julie, Chad Mosher, and Mark Boccuzzi. "The Potential Therapeutic Efficacy of Assisted After-Death Communication." In *Continuing Bonds in Bereavement: New Directions in Research and Practice*, edited by Dennis Klass and Edith Maria Steffen, 176–87. New York: Routledge, 2018.

Bell, Bethan. "Taken from Life: The Unsettling Art of Death Photography." *BBC News*. June 5, 2016. https://www.bbc.com/news/uk-england-36389581.

Benedikt, Michael. "One, Two, Three, . . . Louis, I., Kahn." In *Louis Kahn: The*

Importance of a Drawing, edited by Michael Merrill, 327–52. Baden: Lars Müller, 2021.

Berleant, Arnold. *Art as Engagement*. Philadelphia: Temple University Press, 1991.

Berleant, Riva. "Paleolithic Flints: Is an Aesthetics of Stone Tools Possible?" *Contemporary Aesthetics* 5 (2007). http://www.contempaesthetics.org/newvolume/pages/article.php?articleID=488.

Bicknell, Jeanette, Jennifer Judkins, and Caroline Korsmeyer, eds. *Philosophical Perspectives on Ruins, Monuments, and Memorials*. New York: Routledge, 2020.

Bicknell, Jeanette. "Architectural Ghosts." In "Symposium: The Aesthetics of Ruin and Absence." Special issue, *Journal of Aesthetics and Art Criticism* 72, no. 4 (2014): 435–41.

Bilimoria, Purushottama. "Of Grief and Mourning: Thinking a Feeling, Back to Robert Solomon." In *Passion, Death, and Spirituality: The Philosophy of Robert C. Solomon*, edited by Kathleen Higgins and David Sherman, 149–74. Dordrecht: Springer, 2012.

Boelen, Paul A., Maarten C. Elsma, Geert E. Smid, and Lonneke I. M. Lenferink. "Prolonged Grief Disorder in Section II of DSM-5: A Commentary," *European Journal of Psychotraumatology* 11, no. 1 (2020), https://doi.org/10.1080/20008198.2020.1771008.

Boerner, Kathrin, and Jutta Heckhausen. "To Have and Have Not: Adaptive Bereavement by Transforming Mental Ties to the Deceased." *Death Studies* 27, no. 3 (2003): 199–226.

Böhme, Gernot. "Atmosphere as the Fundamental Concept of a New Aesthetics." Translated by David Roberts. *Thesis Eleven* 36, no. 1 (1993): 113–26.

Bonanno, George A., *The Other Side of Sadness: What the New Science of Bereavement Tells Us about Life after Loss*. New York: Basic Books, 2009.

Bourdieu, Pierre. *Distinction: A Social Critique of the Judgement of Taste*. Translated by Richard Nice. Cambridge, MA: Harvard University Press, 1984.

Bowlby, John. *Attachment and Loss*. Vol. 3, *Loss: Sadness and Depression*. London: Pimlico, 1980.

Bowlby, John. "Processes of Mourning." *International Journal of Psychoanalysis* 42 (1961): 317–40.

Bowlby, John, and Colin Murray Parkes. "Separation and Loss within the Family." In *The Child in His Family*, edited by Elwyn James Anthony, 197–216. New York: Wiley, 1970.

Brady, Emily, and Arto Haapala. "Melancholy as an Aesthetic Emotion." *Contemporary Aesthetics* 1 (2003). https://www.contempaesthetics.org/newvolume/pages/article.php?articleID=214&searchstr=melancholy.

Bruner, Jerome. *Acts of Meaning*. Cambridge, MA: Harvard University Press, 1990.

Bullamore, Tim. "The Postmodern Obituary: Why Honesty Matters." In *Emotion, Identity, and Death: Mortality across Disciplines,* edited by Douglas J. Davies and Chang-Won Park, 2–13. Surrey: Ashgate, 2012.

Burke, Sarah. "The Surreal, Awkward Parts of Grief That No One Talks About." *Vice*, January 23, 2018. https://www.vice.com/en/article/vbykpj/we-need-to-talk-about-death-modern-loss.

Butler, Judith. *Frames of War: When Is Life Grievable*? London: Verso, 2016.

Butler, Judith. "Violence, Mourning, Politics." In *Precarious Life: The Powers of Mourning and Violence*, 19–49. New York: Verso, 2004.

Carovillano, Brian. "Diocese Says 'Danny Boy' Not Appropriate at Mass." Providence, RI (AP). *Standing Stones*, October 24, 2001. http://www.standingstones.com/danny3.html#mass.

Carr, Deborah, Randolph M. Neese, and Camille B. Wortman, eds. *Spousal Bereavement in Late Life*. New York: Springer, 2005.

Carroll, Noël. "Art and Recollection." In *Art in Three Dimensions,* 163–74. New York: Oxford University Press, 2010.

Carroll, Noël. *The Philosophy of Horror; or, Paradoxes of the Heart*. London: Routledge, 1990.

Carroll, Noël. "Sympathy for the Devil." In *"The Sopranos" and Philosophy: I Kill Therefore I Am,* edited by Richard Greene and Peter Vernezze, 121–36. New York: Open Court, 2004.

Castle, Terry. *The Female Thermometer: Eighteenth-Century Culture and the Invention of the Uncanny*. New York: Oxford University Press, 1995.

Charon, Rita. *Narrative Medicine: Honoring the Stories of Illness*. New York: Oxford University Press, 2006.

Choi, Amy S. "Entrepreneurs Reinvent the Funeral Industry." *Bloomberg Businessweek Magazine*, June 19, 2008. http://www.businessweek.com/stories/2008-06-19/entrepreneurs-reinvent-the-funeral-industry.

Cholbi, Michael. "Finding the Good in Grief: What Augustine Knew That Meursault Could Not." *Journal of the American Philosophical Association* 3, no. 1 (2017): 91–105.

Cholbi, Michael. *Grief: A Philosophical Guide*. Princeton, NJ: Princeton University Press, 2021.

Cholbi, Michael. "Grief's Rationality, Backward and Forward." *Philosophy and Phenomenological Research* 94, no. 2 (2017): 255–72.

Colombetti, Giovanna. "From Affect Programs to Dynamical Discrete Emotions." *Philosophical Psychology* 22, no. 4 (2009): 407–25.

Colvin, Howard. *Architecture and the After-Life*. New Haven, CT: Yale University Press, 1991.

Coplan, Amy. "Understanding Empathy: Its Features and Effects." In *Empathy: Philosophical and Psychological Perspectives*, edited by Amy Coplan and Peter Goldie, 3–18. Oxford: Oxford University Press, 2011.

Cornish, Audie, with Martha Mullen. "The Search Is Over: Boston Bombing Suspect Has Been Buried," National Public Radio, May 10, 2013. https://www.npr.org/templates/story/story.php?storyId=182938654.

Cremation Solutions. "Scattering Release Urn Purchase," 1998–2022. https://www.cremationsolutions.com/scattering-release-urn-purchase.

Cromer, Michelle. *Exit Strategy: Thinking Outside the Box.* New York: Jeremy P. Tarcher/Penguin, 2006.

Cullen, Lisa T. *Remember Me: A Lively Tour of the New American Way of Death.* New York: Collins, 2006.

Cumming, Laura. *The Vanishing Velázquez: A Nineteenth-Century Bookseller's Obsession with a Lost Masterpiece.* New York: Scribner, 2016.

Cvetkovich, Ann. *Depression: A Public Feeling.* Durham, NC: Duke University Press, 2012.

Dannenbaum, Sandra M., and Richard T. Kinnier. "Imaginal Relations with the Dead." *Journal of Humanistic Psychology* 49, no. 1 (2009): 100–113.

Danto, Arthur C. *The Abuse of Beauty: Aesthetics and the Concept of Art.* Chicago: Open Court, 2003.

Danto, Arthur C. *The Transfiguration of the Commonplace: A Philosophy of Art.* Cambridge, MA: Harvard University Press, 1981.

Darwall, Steven. "Empathy, Sympathy, Care." *Philosophical Studies* 89, nos. 2–3 (1998): 261–82.

Davey, Nicholas. "Baumgarten, Alexander G(ottlieb)." In *A Companion to Aesthetics*, edited by Stephen Davies et al., 162–63. 2nd ed. Oxford: Wiley-Blackwell, 2009.

Davies, Stephen. *Adornment: What Self-Decoration Tells Us about Who We Are.* London: Bloomsbury, 2020.

Davies, Stephen. *The Artful Species.* Oxford: Oxford University Press, 2012.

Davies, Stephen, Kathleen Higgins, Robert Hopkins, Robert Stecker, and David Cooper, eds. *Companion to Aesthetics.* 2nd ed. Oxford: Wiley-Blackwell, 2009.

Deigh, John, ed. *On Emotions: Philosophical Essays.* New York: Oxford University Press, 2013.

Deraniyagala, Sonali. *Wave.* New York: Random House, 2013.

Derrida, Jacques. *The Work of Mourning.* Edited by Pascale-Anne Brault and Michael Nass. Chicago: University of Chicago Press, 2001.

De Sousa, Ronald. *The Rationality of Emotion.* Cambridge, MA: MIT Press, 1987.

Dewey, John. *Art as Experience.* New York: Perigee, 1934.

Dissanayake, Ellen. *Homo Aestheticus: Where Art Comes from and Why?* Seattle: University of Washington, 1995.

Dobrin, Arthur. "Grief Feels Like You're Going Crazy." *Psychology Today* blog, July 26, 2011. https://www.psychologytoday.com/us/blog/am-i-right/201107/grief-feels-youre-going-crazy.

Doka, Kenneth. "Complicated Grief Is Complicated: Grief in the DSM-5," *Psychology Today* blog, January 3, 2017. https://www.psychologytoday.com/blog/good-mourning/201701/complicated-grief-is-complicated.

Dr. Natural. "Pencils Made from Cremated Humans." April 1, 2007, Next Nature Network. https://nextnature.net/2007/04/pencils-made-from-cremated-humans.

Dunn, James. "Painter Creates Portraits of Dead People Using Their Own Remains Embedded in Wax." *Daily Mail*, February 28, 2017. https://www.dailymail.co.uk/news/article-4267418/Painter-creates-portraits-dead-people-using-ashes.html.

Ebert, Heidi. "Profiles of the Dead: Mourning and Memorial on Facebook." In *Digital Death: Mortality and Beyond in an Online Age*, edited by Christopher M. Moreman and A. David Lewis, 23–42. Santa Barbara, CA: Praeger, 2014.

Eisenberg, Nancy, and Janet Strayer. "Critical Issues in the Study of Empathy." in *Empathy and Its Development*, edited by Nancy Eisenberg and Janet Strayer, 3–13. Cambridge: Cambridge University Press, 1987.

Ekman, Paul. "Biological and Cultural Contributions to Bodily and Facial Movements in the Expression of Emotions." In *Explaining Emotions*, edited by Amelie O. Rorty, 73–101. Berkeley: University of California Press, 1980.

Ekman, Paul. *Emotions in the Human Face*. New York: Pergamon Press, 1972.

Ekman, Paul. *Emotions Revealed: Recognizing Faces and Feelings to Improve Communication and Emotional Life*. New York: Henry Holt, 2003.

Eliade, Mircea. *Myth and Reality*. 1963. Translated by Willard R. Trask. New York: Harper & Row, 1981.

Eliot, Thomas D. "Identification in Bereavement." *Midwest Sociologist* 16, no. 2 (1954): 7–11.

Farrell, James. *Inventing the American Way of Death, 1830–1912*. Philadelphia: Temple University Press, 1980.

Feagin, Susan, and Carolyn Korsmeyer. "More than Bare Bones: The Artistry and Ethics of Ossuaries." In *Philosophical Perspectives on Ruins, Monuments, and Memorials*, edited by Jeanette Bicknell, Jennifer Judkins, and Caroline Korsmeyer, 67–79. New York: Routledge, 2020.

Federal Trade Commission. "The FTC Funeral Rule," July 2012. https://www.consumer.ftc.gov/articles/0300-ftc-funeral-rule.

Feld, Steven. *Jazz Cosmopolitanism in Accra: Five Musical Years in Ghana*. Durham, NC: Duke University Press, 2012.

Feld, Steven. "Wept Thoughts: The Voicing of Kaluli Memories." *Oral Tradition* 5, nos. 2–3 (1990): 241–66.

Ferrero, Luca, ed. *Routledge Handbook for the Philosophy of Agency*. Abingdon, Oxon: Routledge, 2022.

Field, Nigel P. "Unresolved Grief and Continuing Bonds: An Attachment Perspective." *Death Studies* 30, no. 8 (2006): 739–56.

Field, Nigel P. "Whether to Relinquish or Maintain a Bond with the Deceased." In *Handbook of Bereavement Research and Practice*, edited by Margaret S. Stroebe, Robert O. Hansson, Henk Schut, and Wolfgang Stroebe, 113–32. Washington, DC: American Psychological Association, 2008.

Fingarette, Herbert. *Confucius: The Secular as Sacred*. New York: Harper & Row, 1972.

Foltyn, Jacque Lynn. "Sojourn, Transformative: Emotion, Identity in the Dying, Death, and Disposal of an Ex-Spouse." In *Emotion, Identity, and Death: Mortality across Disciplines*, edited by Douglas J. Davies and Chang-Won Park, 85–98. Surrey: Ashgate, 2012.

Frank, Arthur W. "*Philoctetes* and the Good Companion Story." *Enthymema* 16 (2016): 119–27.

Frank, Arthur W. *The Wounded Storyteller: Body, Illness, and Ethics*. 2nd ed. Chicago: University of Chicago Press, 2013.

Freud, Sigmund. "Mourning and Melancholia." 1917. In *General Psychological Theory: Papers on Metapsychology*, 164–79. New York: Macmillan, 1963.

Freud, Sigmund. *The Psychopathology of Everyday Life*. Translated by Anthea Bell. London: Penguin, 2002.

Frijda, Nico H. "Emotions Are Functional, Most of the Time." In *The Nature of Emotion: Fundamental Questions*, edited by Paul Ekman and Richard J. Davidson, 112–22. Oxford: Oxford University Press, 1994.

Frijda, Nico H. *The Laws of Emotion*. Mahwah, NJ: Lawrence Erlbaum, 2006.

Frijda, Nico H., and Louise Sundararajan. "Emotion Refinement: A Theory Inspired by Chinese Poetics." *Perspectives on Psychological Science* 2, no. 3 (2007): 227–41.

Fuchs, Thomas. "Presence in Absence: The Ambiguous Phenomenology of Grief." *Phenomenology and the Cognitive Sciences* 17, no. 1 (2018): 43–63.

Fuchs, Thomas. "Temporality and Psychopathology." *Phenomenology and the Cognitive Sciences* 12, no. 1 (2013): 75–104.

Funeral Guide. "How to Plan a Star Wars Funeral." *Funeral Guide* (blog), August 17, 2016. https://www.funeralguide.co.uk/blog/how-plan-star-wars-funeral.

Gadamer, Hans Georg. *Reason in the Age of Science*. Translated by Frederick G. Lawrence. Cambridge, MA: MIT Press, 1981.

Garces-Foley, Kathleen, ed. *Death and Religion in a Changing World*. Abingdon: Routledge, 2006.

Gaut, Berys Nigel. *Art, Emotion and Ethics*. Oxford: Oxford University Press, 2007.

Gershman, Nancy, and Barbara E. Thompson. *Prescriptive Memories in Grief and Loss: The Art of Dreamscaping*. New York: Routledge, 2019.

Gibson, Margaret. *Objects of the Dead*. Melbourne: Melbourne University Press, 2008.

Goffman, Erving. *Frame Analysis: An Essay on the Organization of Experience*. New York: Harper & Row, 1974.

Goldie, Peter. "Grief: A Narrative Account." *Ratio* 24, no. 2 (2011): 119–37.

Goldie, Peter. *The Mess Inside: Narrative, Emotion, and the Mind*. Oxford: Oxford University Press, 2012.

Goldman, Alan. "Aesthetic Qualities and Aesthetic Value." *Journal of Philosophy* 87, no. 1 (1990): 23–37.

Gorodeisky, Keren. "Aesthetic Agency." In *Routledge Handbook for the Philosophy of Agency*, edited by Luca Ferrero, 456–66. Abingdon, Oxon: Routledge, 2022.

Goswamy, B. N. *Essence of Indian Art*. San Francisco: Asian Art Museum of San Francisco, 1986.

Gould, Melissa. "Life after Death: A Surreal Reality." *HuffPost* blog, updated April 19, 2015. https://www.huffpost.com/entry/life-after-death-a-surreal-reality_b_6685418.

Griffiths, Paul E. *What Emotions Really Are: The Problem of Psychological Categories*. Chicago: University of Chicago Press, 1997.

Gustafson, Donald. "Grief." *Noûs* 23, no. 4 (1989): 457–79.

Haapala, Arto. "On the Aesthetics of the Everyday: Familiarity, Strangeness and the Meaning of Place." In *The Aesthetics of Everyday Life*, edited by Andrew Light and Jonathan Smith, 39–55. New York: Columbia University Press, 2005.

Harries, Karsten. *The Ethical Significance of Architecture*. Cambridge, MA: MIT Press, 1997.

Hatten, Robert. *A Theory of Virtual Agency for Western Art Music*. Bloomington: University of Indiana Press, 2018.

Hedtke, Lorraine, and John Winslade, *The Crafting of Grief: Constructing Aesthetic Responses to Loss*. New York: Routledge, 2017.

Hegel, G. W. F. *Introductory Lectures on Aesthetics*. Translated by Bernard Bosanquet. Edited by Michael Inwood. Harmondsworth: Penguin, 1993.

Hegel, G. W. F. *Phenomenology of Spirit*. Translated by A. V. Miller. New York: Oxford University Press, 1977.

Heidegger, Martin. *Being and Time*. Translated by John Macquarrie and Edward Robinson. New York: Harper & Row, 1962.

Henrich, Joseph, Steven Heine, and Ara Norenzayan. "The Weirdest People in the World?" *Behavioral and Brain Sciences* 33, nos. 2–3 (2010): 61–83.

Hermans, Hubert J. M., and Giancarlo Dimaggio. "The Dialogical Self in Psychotherapy: Introduction." In *The Dialogical Self: Meaning as Movement*, 1–10. San Diego: CA: Academic Press, 1993.

Hermans, Hubert J. M., and Harry J. G. Kempen, eds. *The Dialogical Self: Meaning as Movement.* San Diego: CA: Academic Press, 1993.

Hershock, Peter D. *Liberating Intimacy: Enlightenment and Social Virtuosity in Ch'an Buddhism.* Albany: State University of New York Press, 1996.

Hertz, Robert. "Contribution à une Étude sur la Représentation Collective de la Mort." *Année Sociologiques* 10 (1907): 48–137; English translation as "A Contribution to the Study of the Collective Representation of Death." In *Death and the Right Hand.* Translated by Rodney Needham and Claudia Needham, 197–212. New York: Free Press, 1960.

Higgins, Kathleen. "Beauty and the Sense of Life." In *Artistic Visions and the Promise of Beauty: Cross-Cultural Perspectives*, edited by Kathleen Higgins, Shakti Maira, and Sonia Sikka, 151–65. Dordrecht: Springer, 2017.

Higgins, Kathleen. "Collective Memorials in the Face of Loss: The Multiple Roles of the Aesthetic." In *Aesthetics in Dialogue: Applying Philosophy of Art in a Global World*, edited by Zoltán Somhegyi and Max Ryynänen, 15–28. Berlin: Peter Lang, 2020.

Higgins, Kathleen. "Death and the Skeleton." In *Death and Philosophy*, edited by J. E. Malpas and Robert C. Solomon, 39–49. London: Routledge, 1998.

Higgins, Kathleen. "Kitsch in Relation to Loss." In *The Changing Meaning of Kitsch: From Rejection to Acceptance*, edited by Max Ryynänen and Paco Barragán, 119–41. London: Palgrave Macmillan, 2023.

Higgins, Kathleen. "Love and Death." In *On Emotions: Philosophical Essays*, edited by John Deigh, 159–78. New York: Oxford University Press, 2013.

Higgins, Kathleen. *The Music between Us: Is Music a Universal Language?* Chicago: University of Chicago Press, 2012.

Higgins, Kathleen. *The Music of Our Lives.* 2nd ed. Lanham, MD: Lexington, 2011.

Higgins, Kathleen. "Music's Role in Relation to Phenomenological Aspects of Grief." In "Understanding Grief: Intentionality, Regulation, and Interpretation." Special issue, *Journal of Consciousness Studies* 29, nos. 9–10 (2022): 128–49.

Higgins, Kathleen. "Putting the Dead in Their Place." In *Philosophies of Place: An Intercultural Dialogue*, edited by Peter D. Hershock and Roger T. Ames, 318–27. Honolulu: University of Hawai'i Press, 2019.

Hochschild, Arlie Russell. *The Managed Heart: Commercialization of Human Feeling.* Berkeley: University of California Press, 1983.

Hoffman, Jordan. "The Best Movies about Grief You Probably Haven't Seen." *Slashfilm*, May 25, 2012. http://www.slashfilm.com/movies-grief/.

Höttges, Bärbel. “Blogging the Pain: Grief in the Time of the Internet.” *Gender Forum* 29, no. 4 (2009): 1–10.

Hsün Tzu. *Basic Writings.* Translated by Burton Watson. New York: Columbia University Press, 1963.

HuffPost Entertainment. “‘Best Funeral Ever’: Singer of Chili’s ‘Baby back Ribs’ Jingle Gets Barbecue Themed Funeral Service (Video).” *Huffington Post,* January 7, 2013. https://www.huffpost.com/entry/best-funeral-ever-singer-bbq-theme-video_n_2422725.

HuffPost Entertainment. “TLC’s ‘The Best Funeral Ever’: Golden Gate Funeral Home Hosts Christmas-Themed Ceremony.” *Huffington Post,* January 3, 2013, updated January 23, 2014. https://www.huffingtonpost.com/2013/01/03/tlc-best-funeral-ever-christmas_n_2405019.html.

Humphreys, Helen. *True Story: The Life and Death of My Brother.* London: Serpent’s Tail, 2013.

Hunter, Jack. “Ontological Flooding and Continuing Bonds.” In *Continuing Bonds in Bereavement: New Directions in Research and Practice,* edited by Dennis Klass and Edith Maria Steffen, 191–200. New York: Routledge, 2018.

Inge, Denise. *A Tour of Bones: Facing Fear and Looking for Life.* London: Bloomsbury, 2014.

Ingerslev, Line Ryberg. “Ongoing: On Grief’s Open-Ended Rehearsal.” *Continental Philosophy Review* 51, no. 3 (2018): 343–60.

Iwasaka, Michiko, and Barre Tolken. *Ghosts and the Japanese: Cultural Experience in Japanese Death Legends.* Logan: Utah State University Press, 1994. https://www.jstor.org/stable/j.ctt46nrwv.6.

Jacobson, Kirsten. “The Temporality of Intimacy: Promise, World, and Death.” *Emotion, Space, and Society* 13 (2014): 103–10.

Jakoby, Nina R. “Grief as a Social Emotion: Theoretical Perspectives.” *Death Studies* 36 (2012): 679–711.

Joyce, James. *Dubliners.* New York: Random House, 1967.

Joyce, James. *A Portrait of the Artist as a Young Man.* New York: Viking, 1964.

Kant, Immanuel. *Critique of Judgment.* Translated by Werner S. Pluhar. Indianapolis: Hackett, 1987.

Kasket, Elaine. “Continuing Bonds in the Age of Social Networking: Facebook as a Modern-Day Medium.” *Bereavement Care* 31, no. 2 (2012): 62–69.

Keefer, Donald. “Speaking Well of the Dead: On the Aesthetics of Eulogies.” *Sophia* 50, no. 2 (2011): 303–11.

Kelly, Michael R. “Grief: Putting the Past Before Us.” *Quaestiones Disputatae* 7, no. 1 (2016): 156–77.

Kinkaraco Green Funeral Products. “The Kinkara-Kart Processional.” https://kinkaraco.com/products/kinkara-kart.

Kinkaraco Green Funeral Products. "Press Page." https://kinkaraco.com/pages/press?_pos=1&_sid=97bca1def&_ss=r.

Kinkaraco Green Funeral Products. "Shrouds for Green Burial." https://kinkaraco.com/collections/shrouds-for-green-burial.

Klass, Dennis. "Prologue: A Personal History." In *Continuing Bonds in Bereavement: New Directions in Research and Practice*, edited by Dennis Klass and Edith Maria Steffen, xiii–xix. New York: Routledge, 2018.

Klass, Dennis, and Edith Maria Steffen, eds. *Continuing Bonds in Bereavement: New Directions in Research and Practice*. New York: Routledge, 2018.

Klass, Dennis, and Edith Maria Steffen. "Introduction." In *Continuing Bonds in Bereavement: New Directions in Research and Practice*, edited by Dennis Klass and Edith Maria Steffen, 1–16. New York: Routledge, 2018.

Klass, Dennis, Phyllis R. Silverman, and Steven L. Nickman, eds. *Continuing Bonds: New Understandings of Grief*. Washington, DC: Taylor & Francis, 1996.

Kominsky, Phyllis S. "Working with Continuing Bonds from an Attachment Theoretical Perspective." In *Continuing Bonds in Bereavement: New Directions in Research and Practice*, edited by Dennis Klass and Edith Maria Steffen, 112–28. New York: Routledge, 2018.

Koopmann-Holm, Birgit, and Jeanne L. Tsai. "Focusing on the Negative: Cultural Differences in Expressions of Sympathy." *Journal of Personality and Social Psychology* 107, no. 6 (2014): 1092–1115.

Korsmeyer, Carolyn. "The Triumph of Time: Romanticism Redux." In "Symposium: The Aesthetics of Ruin and Absence." Special issue, *Journal of Aesthetics and Art Criticism* 72, no. 4 (2014): 429–35.

Korsmeyer, Carolyn. *Savoring Disgust*. New York: Oxford University Press, 2011.

Korsmeyer, Carolyn. *Things: In Touch with the Past*. New York: Oxford University Press, 2019.

Køster, Allan. "Bereavement and the Meaning of Profound Feelings of Emptiness." In *Time and Body: Phenomenological and Psychopathological Approaches*, edited by Christian Tewes and Giovanni Stanghellini, 125–43. Cambridge: Cambridge University Press, 2020.

Køster, Allan. "The Felt Sense of the Other: Contours of a Sensorium." *Phenomenology and the Cognitive Sciences* 20, no. 1 (2021): 57–73.

Køster, Allan. "Longing for Concreteness: How Body Memory Matters to Continuing Bonds." *Mortality* 25, no. 4 (2020): 389–401.

Koudounaris, Paul. *The Empire of Death: A Cultural History of Ossuaries and Charnel Houses*. New York: Thames & Hudson, 2011.

Krell, David Farrell, and Donald L. Bates. *The Good European: Nietzsche's Work Sites in Word and Image*. Chicago: University of Chicago Press, 1997.

Krueger, Joel, and Lucy Osler. "Communing with the Dead Online: Chatbots, Grief, and Continuing Bonds." *Journal of Consciousness Studies* 29, nos. 9–10 (2022): 222–52.

Kübler-Ross, Elisabeth, and David Kessler. *On Grief and Grieving: Finding the Meaning of Grief through the Five Stages*. New York: Scribner, 2005.

Kundera, Milan. *Immortality*. Translated by Peter Kussi. New York: Grove Weidenfeld, 1991.

Lamm, Maurice. *The Jewish Way in Death and Mourning*. Rev. ed. New York: Jonathan David, 2000.

Laqueur, Thomas. "Bodies, Death, and Pauper Funerals." *Representations* 1 (1983): 109–31.

Laqueur, Thomas W. "The Deep Time of the Dead." *Social Research: An International Quarterly* 78 (2011): 799–820.

Laqueur, Thomas. "Form in Ashes." *Representations* 104, no. 1 (2008): 50–72.

Laqueur, Thomas W. *The Work of the Dead: A Cultural History of Mortal Remains*. Princeton, NJ: Princeton University Press, 2015.

Larson-Miller, Lizette. "Roman Catholic, Anglican, and Eastern Orthodox Approaches to Death." In *Death and Religion in a Changing World*, edited by Kathleen Garces-Foley, 93–121. Abingdon: Routledge, 2006.

Lear, Jonathan. *Imagining the End: Mourning and Ethical Life*. Cambridge, MA: Harvard University Press, 2022.

Le Carré, John. *The Constant Gardener*. New York: Pocket Books, 2001.

Leddy, Thomas. "Everyday Surface Aesthetic Qualities: 'Neat,' 'Messy,' 'Clean,' 'Dirty.'" *Journal of Aesthetics and Art Criticism* 53, no. 3 (1995): 259–68.

Leddy, Thomas. *The Extraordinary in the Ordinary: The Aesthetics of Everyday Life*. Peterborough, ON: Broadview Press, 2012.

Leddy, Thomas. "Sparkle and Shine." *British Journal of Aesthetics* 37, no. 3 (1997): 259–73.

Levine, Stephen K. "Poesis, Praise and Lament: Celebration, Mourning and the 'Architecture' of Expressive Arts Therapy." In *Grief and the Expressive Arts: Practices for Creating Meaning*, edited by Barbara E. Thompson and Robert A. Neimeyer, 14–18. New York: Routledge, 2014.

Lewis, C. S. *A Grief Observed*. New York: HarperCollins, 1961.

Li, Yu-Chan, and Cypress Chang. "The Grief Healing Garden." In *Grief and the Expressive Arts: Practices for Creating Meaning*, edited by Barbara E. Thompson and Robert A. Neimeyer, 241–53. New York: Routledge, 2014.

Lindemann, Erich. "Symptomatology and Management of Acute Grief." *American Journal of Psychiatry* 101, no. 2 (1944): 141–48.

Lopate, Phillip. "*Solaris*: Inner Space." *The Criterion Collection*, 2002; reposted May 24, 2011. https://www.criterion.com/current/posts/239-solaris-inner-space.

Lopes, Dominic McIver. *Being for Beauty: Aesthetic Agency and Value.* New York: Oxford University Press, 2018.

Luzzi, Joseph. *Through a Dark Wood: A Memoir*. New York: HarperCollins, 2015.

Lyons, William. *Emotion.* Cambridge: Cambridge University Press, 1985.

Machemer, Theresa. "You Can Now Explore All 48,000 Panels of the AIDS Memorial Quilt Online." *Smithsonian Magazine*, July 21, 2020. https://www.smithsonianmag.com/smart-news/aids-memorial-quilt-now-online-180975370/.

Maciejewski, Paul K., Baohui Zhang, Susan D. Block, and Holly G. Prigerson. "An Empirical Examination of the Stage Theory of Grief." *Journal of the American Medical Association* 297, no. 7 (February 21, 2007): 716–23.

Maclaren, Kym. "Emotional Clichés and Authentic Passions: A Phenomenological Revision of a Cognitive Theory of Emotion." *Phenomenology and the Cognitive Sciences* 10, no. 1 (2011): 45–65.

Mandoki, Katya. *Everyday Aesthetics: Prosaics, the Play of Culture and Social Identities.* Aldershot, Hampshire: Ashgate, 2007.

Mandoki, Katya. *Prosaica: Introducción a La Estética de lo Cotidiano*. Ciudad de México: Grijalbo, 1994.

Martin, Rachel. "'Love, Me' Is a Community Poem Crowdsourced from Hundreds of Letters." *Morning Edition*, National Public Radio, July 28, 2022.

Marušić, Berislav. "Do Reasons Expire? An Essay on Grief." *Philosophers' Imprint* 18, no. 25 (2018): 1–25.

Marvin, Thomas F. *Kurt Vonnegut: A Critical Companion.* Westport, CT: Greenwood, 2002.

Mattingly, Cheryl. *The Paradox of Hope: Journeys through a Clinical Borderland.* Berkeley: University of California Press, 2010.

McCarter, Robert. *Aldo van Eyck*. New Haven, CT: Yale University Press, 2015.

McCracken, Janet. "Falsely, Sanely, Shallowly: Reflections on the Special Character of Grief." *International Journal of Applied Philosophy* 19, no. 1 (2005): 139–56.

McCracken, Janet. "Grief and the Mnemonics of Place: A Thank You Note." In *Passion, Death, and Spirituality: The Philosophy of Robert C. Solomon*, edited by Kathleen Higgins and David Sherman, 139–47. Dordrecht: Springer, 2012.

McCracken, Janet. *Taste and the Household: The Domestic Aesthetic and Moral Reasoning.* Albany: State University of New York, 2001.

McFee, Graham. "Empathy: Interpersonal vs. Artistic?" in *Empathy: Philosophical and Psychological Perspectives*, edited by Amy Coplan and Peter Goldie, 185–208. Oxford: Oxford University Press, 2011.

Meek, Miki. "Really Long Distance." *This American Life*, 597: "One Last Thing Before I Go." Aired September 23, 2016. https://www.thisamericanlife.org/597/one-last-thing-before-i-go.

Meier, Allison, "The 65 Symbols on US Military Tombstones." *Hyperallergic*, May 29, 2017. https://hyperallergic.com/381933/the-65-symbols-on-us-military-tombstones/.

Mencius. Translated by D. C. Lao. Harmondsworth: Penguin, 1970.

Merleau-Ponty, Maurice. "In Praise of Philosophy." In *In Praise of Philosophy and Other Essays.* Translated by John Wild, James M. Edie, and John O'Neill, 3–67. Evanston, IL: Northwestern University Press, 1988.

Merleau-Ponty, Maurice. *Phenomenology of Perception.* Translated by Colin Smith. London: Routledge, 1962.

Merleau-Ponty, Maurice. *The Prose of the World.* Edited by Claude Lefort. Translated by John O'Neill. Evanston, IL: Northwestern University Press, 1973.

Millar, Becky, Matthew Ratcliffe, Louise Richardson, and Emily Hughes. *Experiences of Grief: A Phenomenological Survey.* Colchester, Essex: UK Data Service, 2020. DOI: 10.5255/UKDA-SN-856067.

Moller, Dan. "Love and the Rationality of Grief." In *The Oxford Handbook of Philosophy of Love*, edited by Christopher Grau and Aaron Smuts. Oxford: Oxford University Press, 2017.

Morley, John. *Death, Heaven, and the Victorians.* Pittsburgh: University of Pittsburgh Press, 1971.

Morley, Nicole. "Artist Creates Portraits of Dead People Using Their Own Remains." *Metro*, March 1, 2017. https://metro.co.uk/2017/03/01/artist-creates-portraits-of-dead-people-using-their-own-remains-6480545/.

Mo Tzu. In *Basic Writings of Mo Tzu, Hsün Tzu, and Han Fei Tzu.* Translated by Burton Watson. New York: Columbia University Press, 1964.

Nadel, Siegfried. "The Origins of Music." *Music Quarterly* 16 (1930): 531–46.

Neese, Randolph M. "An Evolutionary Framework for Understanding Grief." In *Spousal Bereavement in Late Life*, edited by Deborah Carr, Randolph M. Neese, and Camille B. Wortman, 195–226. New York: Springer, 2005.

Nehamas, Alexander. *On Friendship.* New York: Basic Books, 2016.

Nettl, Bruno. *The Study of Ethnomusicology: Twenty-Nine Issues.* Urbana: University of Illinois Press, 1983.

Neu, Jerome. "A Tear Is an Intellectual Thing." In *A Tear Is an Intellectual Thing*, 14–40. New York: Oxford University Press, 1999.

Newland, Guy. *A Buddhist Grief Observed.* Somerville, MA: Wisdom Publications, 2016.

Nguyen, C. Thi. *Games: Agency as Art.* New York: Oxford University Press, 2020.

Nietzsche, Friedrich. *Beyond Good and Evil: Prelude to the Philosophy of the Future.* Translated by Walter Kaufmann. New York: Random House, 1967.

Nietzsche, Friedrich. *The Gay Science.* Translated by Walter Kaufmann. New York: Random House, 1974.

Nietzsche, Friedrich. *Thus Spoke Zarathustra.* Translated by Walter Kaufmann. New York: Penguin, 1966.

Nussbaum, Charles. *The Musical Representation: Meaning, Ontology, and Emotion.* Cambridge, MA: MIT Press, 2007

Nussbaum, Martha C. *Upheavals of Thought: The Intelligence of Emotions.* Cambridge: Cambridge University Press, 2001.

Oates, Joyce Carol. *A Widow's Story: A Memoir.* New York: HarperCollins, 2011.

Ochieng, Akinyi. "The Fantasy Coffins of Ghana." *Roads & Kingdoms.* January 22, 2016. http://roadsandkingdoms.com/2016/the-fantasy-coffins-of-ghana/.

Parkes, Colin Murray. *Bereavement: Studies of Grief in Adult Life.* 3rd ed. London: Routledge, 1996.

Parkes, Colin Murray, and Holly G. Prigerson. *Bereavement: Studies of Grief in Adult Life.* 4th ed. London: Routledge, 2010.

Paz, Octavio. "Use and Contemplation." In *In Praise of Hands: Contemporary Crafts of the World*, translated by Helen R. Lane, 17–24. New York: World Crafts Council, 1974.

Pennebaker, James W., and Robin C. O'Heeron. "Confiding in Others and Illness Rate among Spouses of Suicide and Accidental-Death Victims." *Journal of Abnormal Psychology* 93, no. 4 (1984): 473–76.

Pennebaker, James W., and J. D. Seagal. "Forming a Story: The Health Benefits of Narrative." *Journal of Clinical Psychology* 55, no. 10 (1999): 1243–54.

Poole, Ross. "Two Ghosts and an Angel: Memory and Forgetting in *Hamlet, Beloved*, and *The Book of Laughter and Forgetting*." *Constellations* 16, no. 1 (2009): 125–49.

Potash, Jordan S., and Rainbow T. H. Ho. "Expressive Therapies for Bereavement: The State of the Arts." In *Grief and the Expressive Arts: Practices for Creating Meaning*, edited by Barbara E. Thompson and Robert A. Neimeyer, 28–32. New York, Routledge, 2014.

Preston, S. D., and F. B. de Waal. "Empathy: Its Ultimate and Proximate Bases." *Behavioral and Brain Sciences* 25, no. 1 (February 2002): 1–20.

Price, Carolyn. "The Rationality of Grief." *Inquiry* 53, no. 1 (2010): 20–40.

Proust, Marcel. *The Sweet Cheat Gone.* Translated by C. K. Scott Moncrieff. In *Remembrance of Things Past.* 2 vols., 2: 670–868. New York: Random House, 1932.

Ratcliffe, Matthew. *Grief Worlds: A Study of Emotional Experience.* Cambridge, MA: MIT Press, 2022.

Ratcliffe, Matthew. "Phenomenological Reflections on Grief during the COVID-19 Pandemic." *Phenomenology and the Cognitive Sciences* (2022). https://doi.org/10.1007/s11097-022-09840-8.

Ratcliffe, Matthew. "Relating to the Dead: Social Cognition and the Phenomenology of Grief." In *Phenomenology of Sociality: Discovering the 'We,'"* edited by Thomas Szanto and Dermot Moran, 202–15. London: Routledge, 2016.

Ratcliffe, Matthew. "Sensed Presence without Sensory Qualities: A Phenomenological Study of Bereavement Hallucinations." *Phenomenology and the Cognitive Sciences* 20 (2020): 601–16. https://doi.org/10.1007/s11097-020-09666-2.

Ribeiro, Anna Christina. "Heavenly Hurt." In *Suffering Art Gladly: The Paradox of Negative Emotion in Art,* edited by Jerrold Levinson, 186–201. New York: Palgrave Macmillan, 2014.

Richardson, Jan. "What to Say When There Are No Words: Supporting the Bereaved with Respect and Sensitivity." *Wild Grief,* June 3, 2019. https://wildgrief.org/blog/what-to-say-when-there-are-no-words.

Richardson, Louise. "Absence Experience in Grief." *European Journal of Philosophy* (2022): 1–16. https://doi.org/10.1111.ejpo.12778.

Richardson, Louise, Matthew Ratcliffe, Becky Millar, and Ellie Byrne. "The COVID-19 Pandemic and the Bounds of Grief." *Think* 20, no. 57 (2021): 89–101.

Ricoeur, Paul. *Time and Narrative.* Translated by Kathleen McLaughlin and David Pellauer. 3 vols. Chicago: University of Chicago Press, 1984.

Riley, Denise. *Time Lived, Without Its Flow.* London: Picador, 2019.

Rimé, Bernard. "Emotion Elicits the Social Sharing of Emotion." *Emotion Review* 1, no. 1 (2009): 60–85.

Rimé, Bernard, Catrin Finkenauer, Olivier Luminet, Emmanuelle Zech, and Pierre Philippot. "Social Sharing of Emotion: New Evidence and New Questions." *European Review of Social Psychology* 9, no. 1 (1992): 145–89.

Rinofner-Kreidl, Sonja. "Grief: Loss and Self-Loss," In *Emotional Experiences: Ethical and Social Significance,* edited by John Drummond, 91–120. London: Rowman & Littlefield, 2018.

Roiphe, Anne. *Epilogue: A Memoir.* New York: HarperCollins, 2009.

Rosaldo, Renato. "Introduction: Grief and a Headhunter's Rage." In *Culture and Truth: The Remaking of Social Analysis,* 1–21. Boston: Beacon Press, 1993.

Rosenblatt, Paul C. "Grief across Cultures: A Review and Research Agenda." In *Handbook of Bereavement Research and Practice: Advances in Theory and Intervention,* edited by Margaret S. Stroebe, Robert O. Hansson, Henk Schut, and Wolfgang Stroebe, 207–22. Washington, DC: American Psychological Association, 2008.

Rosenblatt, Paul C. "Grief That Will Not End." In *Continuing Bonds: New Understandings of Grief,* edited by Dennis Klass, Phyllis R. Silverman, and Steven L. Nickman, 45–58. Washington, DC: Taylor & Francis, 1996.

Rosenfeld, Juliet. *The State of Disbelief: A Story of Death, Love and Forgetting.* London: Short Books, 2020. Kindle ed.

Rosenstein, Leon. "The Aesthetic of the Antique." *Journal of Aesthetics and Art Criticism* 45, no. 4 (1987): 393–402.

Rowling, J. K. *The Casual Vacancy*. London: Little, Brown, 2012.

Rubin, Simon Shimshon. "The Wounded Family: Bereaved Parents and the Impact of Adult Child Loss." In *Continuing Bonds: New Understandings of Grief*, edited by Dennis Klass, Phyllis R. Silverman, and Steven L. Nickman, 217–34. Washington, DC: Taylor & Francis, 1996.

Rubin, Simon Shimshon, Ruth Malkinson, and Eliezer Witztum. "The Two-Track Model of Bereavement and Continuing Bonds." In *Continuing Bonds in Bereavement: New Directions in Research and Practice*, edited by Dennis Klass and Edith Maria Steffen, 17–30. New York: Routledge, 2018.

Saito, Yuriko. *Aesthetics of Care: Practice in Everyday Life*. London: Bloomsbury, 2022.

Saito, Yuriko, "Aesthetics of the Everyday." In *The Stanford Encyclopedia of Philosophy* (Spring 2021 ed.), edited by Edward N. Zalta. https://plato.stanford.edu/archives/spr2021/entries/aesthetics-of-everyday/.

Saito, Yuriko. *Aesthetics of the Familiar: Everyday Life and World Making*. New York: Oxford University Press, 2017.

Saito, Yuriko. *Everyday Aesthetics*. New York: Oxford University Press, 2007.

Saito, Yuriko. "Letting Objects Speak: Beauty in the Japanese Artistic Tradition." In *Artistic Visions and the Promise of Beauty: Cross-Cultural Perspectives*, edited by Kathleen M. Higgins, Shakti Maira, and Sonia Sikka, 195–207. Dordrecht: Springer, 2017.

Sanders, George. "Themed Death: Novelty in the Funeral Industry." *Consumers, Commodities, and Consumption* 10, no. 1 (2008). http://csrn.camden.rutgers.edu/newsletters/10-1/sander.htm.

Sanders, Jasmine. "Memorial T-Shirts Create a Little Justice, a Tiny Peace." *New York Times*, November 14, 2017. https://www.nytimes.com/2017/11/14/style/memorial-t-shirts.html.

Sands, Diana C. "Restoring Hope Following Suicide." In *Grief and the Expressive Arts: Practices for Creating Meaning*, edited by Barbara E. Thompson and Robert A. Neimeyer, 215–21. New York: Routledge, 2014.

Santino, Jack. "'Not an Unimportant Failure': Rituals of Death and Politics in Northern Ireland." In *Displayed in a Mortal Light*, ed. Michael McCaughan. Antrim: Antrim Arts Council, 1992.

Santino, Jack. "Performative Commemoratives, the Personal and the Public: Spontaneous Shrines, Emergent Ritual, and the Field of Folklore." *Journal of American Folklore* 117, no. 446 (2004): 363–72.

Sartre, Jean-Paul. *Being and Nothingness: An Essay on Phenomenological Ontology*. Translated by Hazel Barnes. New York: Simon and Schuster, 1956.

Savage, Kirk. *Monument Wars: Washington, D.C., the National Mall, and the*

Transformation of the Memorial Landscape. Los Angeles: University of California Press, 2009.

Schapiro, Meyer. "The Still Life as a Personal Object—A Note on Heidegger and Van Gogh." In *The Art of Art History: A Critical Anthology*, edited by Donald Preziosi, 296–300. New York: Oxford University Press, 2009.

Scheler, Max. *The Nature of Sympathy*. Translated by Peter Heath. London: Routledge Kegan Paul, 1954.

Schopenhauer, Arthur. *The World as Will and Representation*. Translated by E. F. J. Payne. 2 vols. New York: Dover, 1969.

Schumann, Scott C. "The Presence of Absence in Stravinsky's *Élégie*." Unpublished manuscript presented at West Coast Conference of Music Theory and Analysis, 2011.

Scott, A. O. "Review: 'A Ghost Story' Has a Sensitive Specter with Time on His Hands." *New York Times*, July 5, 2017. https://www.nytimes.com/2017/07/05/movies/review-a-ghost-story.html.

Shelley, James. "The Concept of the Aesthetic." *The Stanford Encyclopedia of Philosophy* (Spring 2022 ed.), edited by Edward N. Zalta. https://plato.stanford.edu/archives/spr2022/entries/aesthetic-concept/.

Shriver, Lionel. *We Need to Talk about Kevin*. New York: Counterpoint, 2003.

Shweder, Richard A. "The Cultural Psychology of the Emotions." In *Handbook of Emotions*, edited by Michael Lewis and Jeannette M. Haviland, 417–31. New York: Guilford Press, 1993.

Sibley, Frank. "Aesthetic Concepts." *Philosophical Review* 68, no. 4 (1959): 421–50.

Simpson, Judith M. "Materials for Mourning: Bereavement Literature and the Afterlife of Clothes." *Critical Studies in Fashion and Beauty* 5, no. 2 (2014): 253–70.

Sköld, Alfred Bordado. "Relationality and Finitude: A Social Ontology of Grief." PhD diss., Aalborg University, 2021.

Smith, Adam. *The Theory of Moral Sentiments*. 1790. Edited by K. Haakonssen. Cambridge: Cambridge University Press, 2002.

Smith, Anna Deavere. *Twilight: Los Angeles, 1992: On the Road: A Search for American Character*. New York: Anchor Books, 1994.

Smith, Murray. "Empathy, Expansionism, and the Extended Mind." In *Empathy: Philosophical and Psychological Perspectives*, edited by Amy Coplan and Peter Goldie, 99–117. Oxford: Oxford University Press, 2011.

Sofka, Carla J. "Social Support 'Internetworks,' Caskets for Sale, and More: Thanatology and the Information Superhighway." *Death Studies* 21, no. 6 (1997): 553–74.

Solomon, Robert C. *In Defense of Sentimentality*. New York: Oxford University Press, 2004.

Solomon, Robert C. *The Passions: Emotions and the Meaning of Life*. Rev. ed. Indianapolis: Hackett, 1993.

Solomon, Robert C. *Spirituality for the Skeptic*. New York: Oxford University Press, 2002.

Solomon, Robert C. *True to Our Feelings*. New York: Oxford University Press, 2007.

Sontag, Susan. *On Photography*. New York: Dell, 1973.

Southward, Brandon. "Robotics Firm Inspired to Connect Mourners." *Statesman Journal*, June 5, 2015. https://www.statesmanjournal.com/story/money/business/2015/06/05/robotics-firm-works-connect-mourning-loss-loved-one/28557803/.

Spitzer, Michael. *A History of Emotion in Western Music: A Thousand Years from Chant to Pop*. Oxford: Oxford University Press, 2020.

Stecker, Robert. *Intersections of Value: Art, Nature, and the Everyday*. Oxford: Oxford University Press, 2019.

Stegmaier, Werner. *What Is Orientation? A Philosophical Investigation*. Translated by Reinhard G. Mueller. Berlin: Walter de Gruyter, 2019.

Stepakoff, Shanee. "Graphopoetic Process." In *Grief and the Expressive Arts: Practices for Creating Meaning*, edited by Barbara E. Thompson and Robert A. Neimeyer, 66–70. New York, Routledge, 2014.

Stokes, Patrick. *Digital Souls: A Philosophy of Online Death*. London: Bloomsbury, 2021.

Strawson, Galen. "Against Narrativity." *Ratio* 17, no. 4 (2004): 428–52.

Stroebe, Margaret S., Robert O. Hansson, Henk Schut, and Wolfgang Stroebe. "Bereavement Research: Contemporary Perspectives." In *Handbook of Bereavement Research and Practice: Advances in Theory and Intervention*, edited by Margaret S. Stroebe, Robert O. Hansson, Henk Schut, and Wolfgang Stroebe, 3–25. Washington, DC: American Psychological Association, 2008.

Stroebe, Margaret S., Robert O. Hansson, Henk Schut, and Wolfgang Stroebe, eds. *Handbook of Bereavement Research and Practice: Advances in Theory and Intervention*. Washington, DC: American Psychological Association, 2008.

Stroebe, Margaret S., and Henk Schut. "The Dual Process Model of Coping with Bereavement: Overview and Update." *Death Studies* 23, no. 3 (1999): 197–224.

Stroebe, Margaret, Henk Schut, and Kathrin Boerner. "Continuing Bonds in Adaptation to Bereavement: Toward Theoretical Integration." *Clinical Psychology Review* 30 (2010): 259–68.

Stroebe, Wolfgang, Henk Schut, and Margaret S. Stroebe. "Grief Work, Disclosure and Counseling: Do They Help the Bereaved?" *Clinical Psychology Review* 25, no. 4 (2005): 395–414.

Stroebe, Margaret S., Henk Schut, and Wolfgang Stroebe. "Who Benefits from

Disclosure? Exploration of Attachment Style Differences in the Effects of Expressing Emotions." *Clinical Psychology Review* 26, no. 4 (2005): 66–85.

Sunflower Cosmos. "My Dad Died and It's Been Shocking and Surreal." *Grief in Common*, May 15, 2021. https://222.griefincommon.com/connect/threads/my-dad-died-and-its-been-shocking-and-surreal.2642/.

Survivors of Suicide Loss. "Create a Virtual Quilt Square to Honor a Loved One Lost to Suicide." https://www.soslsd.org/memorial-quilt-donate/.

Szuhany, Kristin L., Matteo Malgaroli, Carly D. Miron, and Naomi M. Simon. "Prolonged Grief Disorder: Course, Diagnosis, Assessment, and Treatment." *Focus* 19, no. 2 (2021): 161–72.

Tan, Amy. *The Hundred Secret Senses*. New York: G. P. Putnam's Sons, 1995.

Tateo, Luca. "The Cultures of Grief: The Practice of Post-Mortem Photography and Iconic Internalized Voices." *Human Affairs* 28 (2018): 471–82.

Tetrault, Sam. "17 Star Wars Themed Funeral and Memorial Ideas." *Cake* (blog). https://www.joincake.com/blog/star-wars-funeral/.

Thom, Paul. *For an Audience: A Philosophy of the Performing Arts*. Philadelphia: Temple University Press, 1993.

Thompson, Barbara E., and Robert A. Neimeyer, eds. *Grief and the Expressive Arts: Practices for Creating Meaning*. New York, Routledge, 2014.

Throop, C. Jason. "Singular-Particulars: Some Reflections on the Excessiveness of Death, Mourning, and Loss." Unpublished paper, presented at "The Phenomenology of Grief and Loss: A Symposium," University of Vienna, March 16, 2018.

Tisdale, Sallie. "How a Common Death Ritual Made It Harder to Mourn the Loss of My Mother." *Time*, March 4, 2019. https://time.com/5542117/death-embalming-preservation-cremation-mourning/.

Troyer, John. *Technologies of the Human Corpse*. Cambridge, MA: MIT Press, 2020.

TVTropes. "Our Ghosts Are Different." https://tvtropes.org/pmwiki/pmwiki.php/Main/OurGhostsAreDifferent.

UK News, "Themed Funerals Becoming a Celebration of Life," *UK News*, May 8, 2017. https://www.expressandstar.com/news/uk-news/2017/05/08/themed-funerals-becoming-a-celebration-of-life/.

Urban, Greg. "Ritual Wailing in Amerindian Brazil." *American Anthropologist* 90 (1988): 385–400.

U.S. Department of Veterans Affairs. "National Cemetery Administration: Emblems of Belief." Updated February 23, 2023. https://www.cem.va.gov/hmm/emblems.asp.

Vanderhoek, Jonathan. "The Indispensability of Empathy: The Role of Empathy in Making Moral Judgments." PhD diss. University of Texas at Austin, 2016.

Vatomsky, Sonya. "Thinking about Having a 'Green' Funeral? Here's What to

Know." *New York Times*, March 22, 2018. https://www.nytimes.com/2018/03/22/smarter-living/green-funeral-burial-environment.html?emc=edit_nn_20180323&nl=morning-briefing&nlid=6087934620180323&te=1.

Vittachi, Nury. "You Are What You Burn." *New York Times*, April 27, 2015. https://www.nytimes.com/2015/04/28/opinion/hong-kong-you-are-what-you-burn.html.

Vonnegut, Kurt. *Slapstick; or, Lonesome No More*. New York: Random House, 2004.

Vonnegut, Kurt. *Slaughterhouse-Five; or, The Children's Crusade*. New York: Delacorte Press, 1969.

Vonnegut, Kurt, David Hayman, David Michaelis, George Plimpton, and Richard Rhodes. "Kurt Vonnegut, The Art of Fiction, No. 64." *Paris Review* 69 (1977): 55–103.

Walter, Tony. "Communication Media and the Dead: From the Stone Age to Facebook." *Mortality* 20, no. 3 (2015): 215–32.

Walter, Tony. "How People Who Are Dying or Mourning Engage with the Arts." *Music and Arts in Action* 4, no. 1 (2012): 73–98.

Walter, Tony. "A New Model of Grief: Bereavement and Biography," *Mortality* 1, no. 1 (1996): 7–25.

Walton, Kendall L. "Categories of Art." *Philosophical Review* 79 no. 3 (1970): 334–67.

Walton, Kendall L. *Mimesis as Make-Believe: On the Foundations of the Representational Arts*. Cambridge, MA: Harvard University Press, 1990.

Walton, Kendall L. "*Thoughtwriting*—in Poetry and Music." *New Literary History* 42, no. 3 (2011): 455–76.

Walton, Kendall L. "Transparent Pictures: On the Nature of Photographic Realism." *Critical Inquiry* 11, no. 2 (1984): 246–77.

Webster, Robert. *Does This Mean You'll See Me Naked?: A Funeral Director Reflects on Thirty Years of Serving the Living and the Deceased*. Bloomington, IN: Rooftop Publishing, 2007.

Wilkinson, Stephen. "Is 'Normal Grief' a Mental Disorder?" *Philosophical Quarterly* 50, no. 200 (2000): 289–304.

Wilson, Catherine. "Grief and the Poet." *British Journal of Aesthetics* 53, no. 1 (2013): 77–91.

Winnicott, Donald Woods. "Transitional Objects and Transitional Phenomena." In *Playing and Reality*, 1–25. New York: Routledge, 2002.

Wittgenstein, Ludwig. *Philosophical Investigations*. Translated by G. E. M. Anscombe. Oxford: Blackwell, 1953.

Wolfelt, Alan D. "You're Not Going Crazy—You're Grieving." Center for Loss & Life Transition, December 14, 2016. https://www.centerforloss.com/2016/12/youre-not-going-crazy-youre-grieving/.

Women of Green. "Eileen Fisher Award Goes to a Woman of Green." Women of Green, 2015. https://womenofgreen.com/2011/04/26/eileen-fisher-award-goes-to-woman-of-green/.

Wordsworth, William. "Preface to the Lyrical Ballads." In *Lyrical Ballads, with Other Poems, 1800*. Vol. 1. 2nd ed. Project Gutenberg. http://www.gutenberg.org/cache/epub/8905/pg8905-images.html.

Wortman, Camille B., and Roxane Cohen Silver. "The Myths of Coping with Loss." *Journal of Consulting and Clinical Psychology* 57, no. 3 (1989): 349–57.

Xie, Qin. "Laptops, Mansions and Helicopters: The Weirdest Paper Offerings Chinese People Burn for the Deceased to Ensure Them a Happy Afterlife." *Daily Mail Online*, April 1, 2016. http://www.dailymail.co.uk/news/peoplesdaily/article-3515806/Laptops-mansions-helicopters-weirdest-paper-offerings-Chinese-people-burn-deceased-ensure-happy-afterlife.html.

Yates, Clinton. "'Best Funeral Ever': Most Frightening Reality TV Show to Date?" *Washington Post*, January 7, 2013. https://www.washingtonpost.com/blogs/therootdc/post/best-funeral-ever-most-frightening-reality-tv-show-to-date/2013/01/07/8106d82a-58ed-11e2-9fa9-5fbdc9530eb9_blog.html.

Young, D. G., and S. E. Caplan. "Online Dating and Conjugal Bereavement." *Death Studies* 34, no. 7 (2010): 575–605.

Zeami, Izutsu. In *Masterworks of the Nō Theater*. Translated and edited by Kenneth Yasuda, 186–226. Bloomington: Indiana University Press, 1989.

Zech, Emmanuelle, Bernard Rimé and James W. Pennebaker. "The Effects of Emotional Disclosure during Bereavement." In *The Scope of Social Psychology: Theory and Applications (A Festschrift for Wolfgang Stroebe)*, edited by Miles Hewstone, Henk A. W. Schut, John B. F. de Wit, Kees Van Den Bos, and Margaret S. Stroebe, 277–92. London: Psychology Press, 2007.

FILMS

Bertolucci, Bernardo, dir. *Last Tango in Paris*. United Artists, 1972.

Costner, Kevin, dir. *Open Range*. Buena Vista Pictures, 2003.

Delaporte, Chris, and Pascal Pinon, dirs. *Kaena: The Prophecy*. Xilam, 2003.

Doillon, Jacques, dir. *Ponette*. BAC Films, 1996.

Eastwood, Clint, dir. *High Plains Drifter*. Universal Pictures, 1973.

Egoyan, Atom, dir. *The Sweet Hereafter*. Alliance Communications, 1997.

Feld, Steven, dir. and prod. *A Por-Por Funeral for Ashirife*, assoc. dir. Nii Yemo Nunu. Jazz Cosmopolitanism in Accra Series. Montage Video Productions, 2009.

Gould, Vanessa, dir. *Obit*. Green Fuse Films, 2017. https://www.kanopy.com/product/obit.

Katz, Ross, dir. *Taking Chance*. HBO Films, 2009.

Kleslowski, Krzysztof, dir. *Tres Couleurs: Bleu*. MK2 Diffusion/Rialto Film, 1993.

Kubrick, Stanley, dir. *2001: A Space Odyssey*. Stanley Kubrick Productions, 1968.

Lawrence, Ray, dir. *Lantana*. Palace Films, 2001.

Linklater, Richard, dir. *Waking Life*. Thousand Words, 2001.

Malick, Terrence, dir. *Tree of Life*. Fox Searchlight Pictures, 2011.

Mazursky, Paul, dir. *Enemies: A Love Story*. 20th Century Fox, 1989.

Meirelles, Fernando, dir. *The Constant Gardener*. Universal Studios, 2005.

Minghella, Anthony, dir. *Truly, Madly, Deeply*. Samuel Goldwyn, 1991.

Scott, Ridley, dir. *Black Hawk Down*. Sony Pictures, 2001.

Shyamalan, M. Night, dir. *The Sixth Sense*. Buena Vista Pictures, 1999.

Takita, Yōjirō, dir. *Departures*. Shochiku, 2008.

Tarkovsky, Andrei, dir. *Solaris*. Mosfilm, 1972.

Urabe, Ryo, and Tomohiko Yokoyama, dirs. *The Phone of the Wind: Whispers to Lost Families*. NHK, 2016. https://www.youtube.com/watch?v=ke-H5EEqvRs.

Zemeckis, Robert, dir. *Back to the Future*. Universal Pictures, 1985.

MUSIC

Feld, Steven. *Bosavi: Rainforest Music from Papua New Guinea*. Smithsonian Folkways Recordings Center for Folklife and Cultural Heritage, in collaboration with the Institute of Papua New Guinea Studies, 2001. SFW CD 40487.

TELEVISION SHOWS

Six Feet Under. Season 1, episode 1, "Six Feet Under." Directed by Alan Ball. Aired June 3, 2001, on HBO. https://www.hbo.com/six-feet-under/season-1/1-pilot.

Six Feet Under. Season 5, episode 10, "All Alone." Directed by Adam Davidson. Aired August 7, 2005, on HBO. https://www.hbo.com/six-feet-under/season-05/10-all-alone.

The Sopranos. 6 seasons. David Chase, creator. Aired January 10, 1999–June 10, 2007, on HBO. https://www.hbo.com/the-sopranos.

Index